Photoshop® Elements 4 Solutions

Photoshop® Elements 4 Solutions

Solutions

The Art of Digital Photography

Mikkel Aaland

Wiley Publishing, Inc.

Acquisitions and Development Editor: Peter Gaughan

Author's Assistant: Ed Schwartz

Technical Editor: Doug Nelson

Production Editor: Daria Meoli

Copy Editor: Sarah Lemaire

Production Manager: Tim Tate

Vice President and Executive Group Publisher: Richard Swadley

Vice President and Executive Publisher: Joseph B. Wikert

Vice President and Publisher: Dan Brodnitz

Book Designer: Lori Barra, Tonbo Design

Compositor: Franz Baumhackl

Proofreader: Nancy Riddiough

Indexer: Ted Laux

Cover Design: John Nedwidek

Cover production: Ryan Sneed

Cover photography: Mikkel Aaland

To my daughters

Ana Mikaela and Miranda Kristina

Acknowledgments

For the fourth edition of this book, I take off my hat to Ed Schwartz. He assisted me on previous editions, but for this edition, Ed pulled out all the stops and took over much of the research and updating. Thanks, Ed! You are the best.

Many people have made this book, in all its editions, possible. I'll start with Sybex's Bonnie Bills, Dan Brodnitz, and Pete Gaughan, with whom I have shared many successful years of creative collaboration and friendship. Studio B's Neil J. Salkind and David Rogelberg stood solidly behind me. Technical editor Doug Nelson was superb.

I'd especially like thank my good friend Tom Mogensen, who contributed his wisdom, images, and techniques to the book. Other special friends who were there when I needed them are Rudy Burger, Michael Rogers, Scott Highton, Maggie Hallahan, Monica Suder, Michelle Vignes, Laena Wilder, Paul Persons, Monica Lee, Luis Delgado, Mark Ulriksen, Marcia Briggs, Julie Christensen, Sebastian DeWitt, Jacques Gauchey, and, as always, Sean Parker and Valerie Robbins. I'd also like to thank Michael Angelo, Laura Laverdiere, Maurice Martell, David Miodzik, Brett Newsom, and William Rutledge.

Thank you to Rodney Koeneke, Chuck Snyder, Barbara Smyth, Dennis Fitzgerald, Micha X. Peled, Tracy and Chris Cantello, David Robertson, Cindy Adams, Peter Banks, and Jeanne Zimmermann. Thanks to production editor Daria Meoli and copyeditor Sarah Lemaire.

It's been an absolute thrill working with several people at Adobe: Mark Dahm, the product manager for Photoshop Elements, was always responsive and helpful. Others at Adobe include Richard Coencas, Chad Rolf, Kevin Connor, Susan Doering, John Peterson, Jeff Chien, Marc Pawliger, Karen Gauthier, Christie Evans, Gregg Wilensky, Scott Wellwood, and Gary Cohen.

Thanks to Hal Leith, a loyal reader, who contacted me and asked revealing questions and gracefully made useful suggestions that I incorporated in earlier editions. Thanks also to Richard Hirschman, another reader who sent e-mails full of helpful corrections and suggestions. And thanks to the many other readers of the earlier versions, many of them loyal viewers of my *Call for Help* and *Screensavers* appearances, for their support and contributions. I'd also like to acknowledge the input from the community of Photoshop Elements 4 beta testers. The final version of the program, and this book, benefit enormously from such an active and generous support group.

Finally, thanks to my wife Rebecca, who makes it all worthwhile.

—MIKKEL AALAND, SAN FRANCISCO, 2005

Contents

"No longer will you look at an image simply for what it is. From now on you'll see what it can become."

Introduction

The full potential of your digital images will never be fully realized without the help of editing and processing software. Nowadays, there are many such software packages to choose from, but there is only one that combines professional-level quality with consumer ease-of-use and cost—and that's Photoshop Elements.

With Photoshop Elements—and information presented in this book—you'll quickly get up to speed and organize your digital images so they are readily accessible. You'll be able to fix digital images that are over- or underexposed; sharpen images that are out of focus; get rid of annoying red eye; and reduce digital-camera-produced electronic noise. With a little more expertise, you'll be able to remove unwanted objects from outdoor shots, remove and replace distracting backgrounds, add type, create stunning panoramas by stitching together adjacent shots, and much more.

In short, Photoshop Elements and *Photoshop Elements 4 Solutions* are for anyone familiar with a computer who wants to both organize and create great-looking images. No longer will you look at an image simply for what it is. From now on you'll see what it can become.

What's New in 4?

Photoshop Elements 3 was—and is—a great program. Believe it or not, with version 4, it got even better. First of all, a lot of engineering time went into optimizing code; Elements 4 is significantly faster to load and more responsive than its predecessor. The application—which really is two applications, the Editor and the Organizer—also includes several new features and improvements to an already over-the-top list:

- More compelling slide show creations, with pan and zoom capabilities
- A new Magic Extractor that makes it easier than ever to separate foregrounds from backgrounds

- A new command—Adjust Color for Skin Tone—that makes people look more natural, even in difficult lighting conditions or when harsh electronic strobes are used
- Several new Creation templates that make sharing of your digital photos more compelling and easier than ever
- A new Straighten tool that automatically corrects a horizon line
- Better integration with Adobe Premiere Elements
- A new Defringe command that makes seamless copying and pasting possible
- Crop tool enhancements
- More control over color management
- Support for Adobe DNG, a new RAW file format
- Easier downloading of images from a digital camera
  And, as you'll see in the book, much more.

 Note: Photoshop Elements 4, and this book, are Windows specific. (Adobe claims that a Mac version is expected "in the near future.")

What You Need to Know

I've written this book with the assumption that the reader has basic computer skills, such as using the mouse and saving and storing digital files. However, if this is the first time you've worked with a graphics or image-editing program, you may find Photoshop Elements a bit challenging. After all, this is a powerful, feature-rich program. It's unrealistic to think that you can jump right in and get exactly what you want without some trial and error. But the Elements interface is extremely intuitive and will enable you to quickly get up to speed. The Adobe online help is the best I've ever seen. Also, just waving your cursor over a tool brings up the tool's name and a link to Adobe Help.

The Wiley website devoted to this book contains files for almost all of the "before" images shown in this book (the starting images for procedures)—you can visit this site and download the files at **www.wiley.com/go/elementssolutions**. Using those files, you can follow along with the procedures to create the "after" images. If you have any specific questions about the material in this book, or the program, feel free to e-mail me at **mikkel@cyberbohemia.com**. You can also find additional support, information, and files at my personal website, **www.shooting-digital.com**.

The Future Is Now

Fifteen years ago I wrote a book titled *Digital Photography* (Random House, 1992). The book was dedicated in part to the great photographer Ansel Adams, who introduced me to digital photography in 1980. In that book, I wrote that the future of digital photography is now. I wrote "the new technology would enable people to make photographic expressions for their own amusement, for the enjoyment of others, or for professional gain." Well, I was a little ahead of myself. Adobe had just introduced Photoshop 1, and the first consumer digital cameras and scanners were on the market. I thought it would be just a matter of months or, at the most, a few years, and the digital photography revolution would be in full swing.

We all had to grow a little. Photoshop had to evolve and so did digital cameras and scanners. Now, with the introduction of Photoshop Elements 4 and increasingly affordable digital cameras and scanners, that time I anticipated so many years ago is here. I really enjoyed writing this book and then updating it for version 4, especially since I can truly say, "The future is now."

—MIKKEL AALAND, SAN FRANCISCO, 2005

Photoshop®
Elements 4
Solutions

Tools
and Terminology

The following chapters of this book focus on giving you straightforward solutions to common challenges associated with acquiring, organizing, and processing digital images. This first chapter, however, is more reference-oriented, zooming in on the details of some of Photoshop Elements' preferences, tools, and features. This is by no means a definitive guide. For that, it's best to refer to Photoshop Elements 4's excellent Help database, located in the toolbar under the word Help, where you'll find a massive hyperlinked and searchable document with tons of information.

1

Chapter Contents

Setting Preferences

Adobe ships Photoshop Elements with preferences set in a way that may or may not suit your particular needs. Through these settings, you can change how Photoshop Elements handles a whole range of tasks, from color management to memory allocation to saving files. Let's look at some of the more important choices you can make, and see what you can do to customize the program so that it works better for you. (These preferences refer to the Photoshop Elements Editor workspace, not the Organizer. I'll cover many of the Organizer preferences in Chapter 2.)

Color Settings

Every scanner, every computer system, and every printer handles color differently. In order to maintain some control over the way your digital images look in this chaotic world, you need to know how Photoshop Elements handles color.

Photoshop Elements 4 can assign an International Color Consortium (ICC) color profile to your image file, depending on your choice of color setting, as described in this section. It can also preserve an already embedded ICC color profile. A *color profile* is a universally accepted point of reference developed by the ICC. In theory, this means that when you open the file with another computer and monitor, the image will be displayed exactly as it was on your monitor. Also, in theory, if you have an ICC-compliant printer, you'll get a printout that closely matches the image on your monitor. This is fine in theory, but in reality it doesn't always work. All the devices need to understand your color profile, and if they don't, you may have unexpected results.

Elements 4 preserves *existing* color profiles in images that you open—with one exception. If you use the No Color Management setting, existing profiles in images that you open are discarded. For this reason alone I do not recommend this setting unless all other attempts to have your monitor and printer reflect true colors fail.

On the Edit menu at the top of the Photoshop Elements Editor window, you'll see an option for Color Settings. When you choose this, you are faced with four options:
- No Color Management
- Always Optimize Colors for Computer Screens
- Always Optimize for Printing
- Allow Me to Choose

These settings are described in this section. The default setting is Always Optimize Colors for Computer Screens.

The two color profiles supported by Elements are sRGB and Adobe RGB. Adobe RGB has a wider color gamut, the ability to handle a wider range of colors. The sRGB profile is primarily used for images destined for the Web and for many inkjet printers. Adobe RGB is primarily used for images destined for printers that can handle the wider color gamut. A large number of monitors work well with sRGB and may not benefit from the larger color space of Adobe RGB.

No Color Management This option discards any assigned profiles when opening images and does not assign profiles by default to newly created or saved images. If you use Save As, however, an option exists for saving your default monitor profile with the image, which is commonly sRGB. If you have created a custom monitor profile using Adobe Gamma or a third-party product, this profile will be listed as the ICC Profile in the Save As dialog. Images are displayed and edited in the color space of your monitor. Figure 1.1 is an example of the Save As dialog when a monitor profile has been created. In this case, a colorimeter from Monaco Systems was used to create the custom profile. This normally lists sRGB as the ICC profile if you have not created a custom profile. (☞ "Calibrate Your Display" in Chapter 3.)

Figure 1.1: Your monitor profile is listed as the ICC Profile.

Always Optimize for Computer Screens (Default) With this setting—which is the default— you will find yourself working in the sRGB color space. This setting preserves any existing color profiles in images that you open. All newly created documents are assigned an sRGB profile. When you open an image without an existing color profile, it is assigned the sRGB profile. You can elect to use Save As and turn off the profile assignment—just remove the check from the ICC profile box.

Always Optimize for Printing If you choose this setting, you'll work in the Adobe RGB color space. This setting preserves any existing color profiles in images that you open. All newly created documents are assigned an Adobe RGB profile. When you open an image without an existing color profile, it is assigned the Adobe RGB profile. In this case, you can still elect to use Save As and turn off the profile assignment—just remove the check from the ICC profile box.

Allow Me to Choose This color setting allows you to assign a profile when you open an image with no existing profile. When you open such an image, the dialog shown in Figure 1.2 appears. Your choices are to leave the image as is or to attach one of the two profiles shown in the dialog.

Figure 1.2: Choosing a color profile.

If you place a check in the "Always take this action, and don't show me again" box, when you subsequently open images without a profile, the choice you made is always applied without bothering you. For example, if you always want to work in the sRGB space and you make that choice here, all subsequent images that are opened without a profile are assigned the sRGB profile. If you wish to reinstate this dialog, open the Color Settings and select Allow Me to Choose.

Identifying the Image's Profile

You can always tell which color profile is attached to your image (if any) by looking at the status bar, provided you have enabled this feature. Just click the black arrow and check Document Profile. You can also use the Info palette (Window ➤ Info). In the Info palette, click the More button, select Palette Options, and place a check in Document Profile.

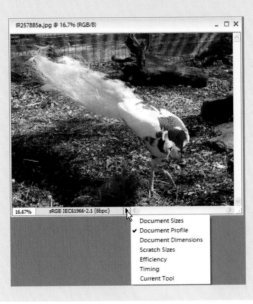

Color Management Commands

Elements 4 added a couple of new features related to color management. However, it's possible in a majority of situations to edit and print images and obtain excellent results without ever using these features. Since there may be an instance when these features might be useful, a description of them follows.

The new menu items related to color management that have been added are accessed in the Image menu (Image ➤ Convert Color Profile). Notice three choices in the submenu: Remove Profile, Apply sRGB Profile, and Apply Adobe RGB Profile. The active choices depend on the existing profile, if any, in the selected image. For example, if your image is already assigned the sRGB profile, the choice to apply that profile is grayed out.

Applying a profile can either Assign a Profile or Convert to Profile. The default is Convert to Profile but that can be temporarily changed to Assign Profile by holding the Control key while using the Apply command.

Using these new commands, assigning and converting to profiles, is not something to do casually. Without some knowledge of color management, you might irreversibly alter the color data in an image beyond what you had intended. Therefore, always work with copies of your images and keep the originals in a safe place.

Assigning a profile tells Elements how to interpret the color information in an image. An example of using this command is when you know the color profile of an image but it has no profile assigned to it. When you open such an image without a profile attached, Elements assigns a profile automatically if you have set your Color Settings preferences to either Optimize for Computer Screens or Optimize for Printing. If your setting is Allow Me to Choose, a window opens allowing you to make a choice.

Apply sRGB Profile or Apply RGB Profile, which defaults to Convert to Profile, is generally used when you know what type of color an output device expects. For example, if you have an image with an Adobe RGB profile attached and you know your printer prefers sRGB data, or if the image is destined for the Web, use the default Apply sRGB command to convert the image to sRGB.

Even though Elements only allows you to assign/convert with just two profiles, it recognizes other profiles that are attached to images. For example, if you have an image that has a scanner profile attached, Elements displays the colors correctly on your monitor. After opening the image, you can convert the profile to sRGB or Adobe RGB. Don't use Assign, or the colors may not look correct.

Preset Manager

When you use a brush, gradient, pattern, or swatch, you are presented with a default set of corresponding brushes, gradients, patterns, or colors. Except for the swatches, these options appear in the options bar at the top of the Photoshop Elements window. The swatches are found in the Color Swatches palette. For most people, the default sets provide enough options, but you can add or customize sets by using the Preset Manager, which is found on the Edit menu. Select the Preset Type to see the default options. To load a set of *custom libraries,* as the custom sets are called, you can click Load and select a saved library to open, or click the More icon at the top of the Preset Manager dialog box. A pop-up menu appears with a list of choices, including the choice to reset back to the default set. You can also create your own set by Ctrl+clicking various brushes and clicking Save Set.

Undo History States

Most of the time, when you work on the pixels of a digital image, Photoshop Elements records each step of the process in the Undo History palette. You can go back to a previous step at any point, but only as long as that step remains in the Undo History palette. Photoshop Elements records 50 steps by default, but if you have enough RAM, you can boost that number to as many as 1000. To change the default, choose Edit ➢ Preferences ➢ General and then simply type in a new number.

Saving Files

There are three options for saving files; your choice will depend on your workflow. The selection is made using the On First Save option. The default setting is Ask If Original, and in most cases, you'll find this setting works just fine (see Figure 1.3).

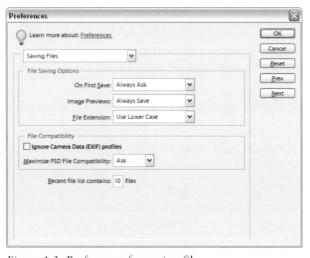

Figure 1.3: Preferences for saving files.

Taking the options in the On First Save box in order, here is how they behave:

Always Ask This setting opens the File Save As dialog on the initial save of any image, whether it is part of a version set or not. (A *version set* is when Elements saves a copy of an image and leaves the original unchanged. For more on version sets, ➢ "Using Version Sets" in Chapter 2.) For example, if you open an image, edit it, and choose File ➢ Save, the Save As dialog opens instead. You can obviously overwrite the original if you choose.

Should you close the image and reopen it, the same behavior occurs on the initial save. This setting is to provide protection against unintentionally overwriting images.

Ask If Original (Default) This option brings up the Save As dialog for all original images. These are images that are not part of a version set. The advantage of this setting is that it asks you if you want to specify a version set the first time, but not if it is already a version. If you're happy with one original and one version set image, and don't care to create multiple versions, you can use the Save command and be assured that you will not add additional versions to your file. You can always use Save As to create an additional version.

Save Over Current File This option just saves over the original file. An exception would be if you added a layer to a JPEG file, you would get the Save As dialog with PSD as the suggested file format. Of course, you can always use Save As to avoid overwriting the original.

With any option you choose, you can always accidentally or purposely overwrite an original image. For that reason alone, always keep a backup set of your images in a safe place.

Here are the rest of file-saving options:

Image Preview When you save a file, Photoshop Elements can create an image preview thumbnail. Many applications, including Microsoft Office 2003 and the Windows XP operating system, create their own thumbnails, allowing you to turn this option off.

File Extension This should be set to Use Lower Case for maximum compatibility with other applications.

Ignore Camera Data (EXIF) Profiles This option really pertains to opening images, not saving them. If this option is enabled (checked), Elements ignores the EXIF color data in camera images. This is best illustrated by an example.

Let's assume that your camera creates an image in the sRGB color space, but you want to edit your images in the Adobe RGB color space. Here's what you do:

1. In your Editor Preferences (Edit ➤ Preferences ➤ Saving Files), place a check next to Ignore Camera Data (EXIF) Profiles.
2. In your Color Settings (Edit ➤ Color Settings), select Always Optimize for Printing.
3. Transfer images from your camera to your computer.
4. Your images are now in the Adobe RGB color space.

If you want to have a choice of profiles, change the color settings to Allow Me to Choose.

Maximize PSD File Compatibility In the Saving Files Preferences dialog box, you also have the choice of whether to Always Maximize Compatibility for Photoshop (PSD) Files. To save up to a third of your file size, I suggest you turn this option off. You need this option only if you are planning to use Photoshop version 2.5 or earlier, which is unlikely. Keep in mind that turning off backward compatibility affects only PSD files, not GIFs or JPEGs.

Recent File List By default, the recent file list (found under File ➤ Open Recently Edited File) includes 10 recent files. In the Saving Files Preferences dialog box, you can change this to any value from 0 to 30.

Units and Rulers

Photoshop Elements displays dimensions in inches by default (in the U.S.). You can change that setting to centimeters, millimeters, or pixels in the Units & Rulers dialog box (Edit ➢ Preferences ➢ Units & Rulers). You can also change these preferences in the Info palette. When I am working on images destined for the Web, I always use pixels; otherwise, I leave my setting at inches. (Picas, points, and percent are useful for only a select few users.)

Plug-Ins

When Photoshop Elements is launched, it automatically searches for a folder called Plug-Ins in the application folder. Plug-ins are mini software programs developed by Adobe or third-party vendors to add various functionalities to Photoshop Elements. You may also be using another program that uses compatible Photoshop plug-ins. You can tell Photoshop Elements where to find and open those plug-ins by going to Edit ➢ Preferences ➢ Plug-Ins & Scratch Disks.

Memory

If you don't have enough RAM, Photoshop automatically creates and uses a portion of your startup hard drive as a scratch disk. It's never as fast or as optimal as having enough RAM, but if you have a large hard disk, you'll avoid the dreaded "out-of-memory" warning. If you have more hard drives, you can assign scratch disks to them by choosing Edit ➢ Preferences ➢ Plug-Ins & Scratch Disks. Choose the drive that is the fastest and has the most contiguous free space to use as your primary scratch disk. You can create up to 200GB of scratch disk space.

The Memory and Image Cache preferences allow you to specify how much memory you want to use for Photoshop Elements. The cache levels affect the speed of zooming and drawing, and the Use Cache for Histograms setting affects how quickly histograms display. These settings are best left at the default levels for most projects.

Note: Sometimes cameras and other devices that mount themselves on the desktop as drives show up as valid options in the Memory Preferences dialog box. It is important that you do not choose them. They are usually small in size and slow. Choose only devices that are real hard disks, and not removables.

Customizing and Organizing the Work Area

Look at anyone's desk and you'll see variations in the way people like to work. It's the same with the Photoshop Elements Editor work area. One person might prefer a desktop tiled with palettes, whereas someone else might find this cluttered look distracting. With Photoshop Elements, palettes can be stacked and tiled and moved wherever you want. Look at Figure 1.4; it shows the entire editing work area of Photoshop Elements.

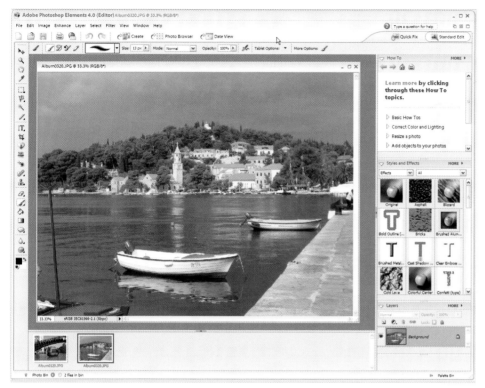

Figure 1.4: The Photoshop Elements Editor work area.

At the top is the *menu bar*, which contains drop-down menus for performing tasks. On the Enhance menu, for example, you'll find ways to modify the contrast and color of your digital image. Unlike most of the other components of the work area, the menu bar can't be moved or altered in any way. There is a search field for using keywords to access the Help database in the upper-right corner. Additionally, there are two icons at the upper right that allow you to either cascade or tile open images. A third icon there maximizes the active image. As in any Windows program, clicking the Maximize button causes it to be replaced by both a Minimize and Restore button. This Restore button, which restores a maximized window, shouldn't be confused with the buttons directly above, which operate on the Elements application.

Below the menu bar is the *shortcuts bar*. Position the pointer over any icon in the shortcuts bar, and its name appears. Here you'll find buttons for common commands such as Open, Print, Save, and Undo. You'll also find buttons that jump you to the Organizer, actually labeled Photo Browser (denoted by a sweeping arrow, or swoosh). There are also icons on the right that allow you to switch between the Quick Fix and Standard Edit workspace modes.

Below the shortcuts bar and palette well is the *options bar*, which contains various options for using a selected tool. As you select a tool from the toolbox, different options appear in the options bar. Some settings are common to several tools, and others are specific to one tool.

To the left of the work area is the *toolbox*. The icons in the toolbox give you access to various tools for creating and editing images. When you position the pointer over an icon in the toolbox, the name of the tool appears. An icon with a small arrow in its lower-right corner indicates a group of tools. When you select one of these icons, the tools it provides appear on the options bar. You can also click and hold the mouse on one of these icons to display a pop-up menu of the tools it provides. By default, the toolbox is docked, but it can be torn off into a floating palette by grabbing on to its gripper and dragging.

To the right of the work area is the *palette bin*. Palettes help you modify and monitor images. You open a palette by clicking its "twist down" arrow. A palette will remain open until you click its arrow again. The palette bin is closed easily by clicking the Close button (a right-facing arrow) at the bottom of the bin—you can actually click the words Palette Bin. You can also drag a palette's tab to move the palette from the bin to any place you want on the screen (☞ "Docking, Stacking, and Resizing Tool Palettes," next).

At the bottom of the work area is the *photo bin*. This container displays the currently opened files. For every open image you see a live thumbnail representation. You can switch between files by clicking the thumbnails. You can also close, minimize, duplicate, or rotate images via the photo bin by right-clicking a thumbnail.

Docking, Stacking, and Resizing Tool Palettes

When you open Photoshop Elements for the first time, the How To, Styles and Effects, and Layers palettes are in the palette bin. You can move a palette to and from the palette bin and the work area by dragging the palette's tab in or out of the bin. You can change the order of palettes in the bin by dragging the title bar above or below other palettes found in the bin. You can resize a palette found in the palette bin by grabbing the gripper at the bottom of the palette. You can also dock palettes together on the work area by dragging one palette's tab onto the body of the other palette (see Figure 1.5).

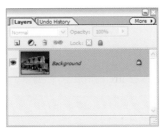

Figure 1.5: For easy access, dock palettes together on the work area.

Personally, because I use them so much, I make both the Layers and Undo History palettes visible in the palette bin.

 Note: Choosing Window ➢ Reset Palette Locations places all palettes back in their default locations.

The Welcome Screen

When you open Photoshop Elements, you are greeted with a Welcome screen (Figure 1.6), where you have seven options:
- See a brief overview of the Photoshop Elements product.
- Open the Organizer (View and Organize Photos).
- Open the Editor's Quick Fix mode (Quickly Fix Photos).

- Open the Editor's Standard Edit mode (Edit and Enhance Photos).
- Open directly into the Organizer's Creation Setup dialog (Make Photo Creations).
- Create a new file (Start From Scratch).
- Access Adobe's online tutorials.

Figure 1.6: The Welcome screen.

The Welcome screen disappears when you select an option, but you can get it back at any time by choosing Window ➢ Welcome from either the Editor or the Organizer.

Histograms

A *histogram* shows the distribution of an image's pixel value in a bar chart representation. The left side (level 0) shows the values of an image's darker areas, and the right side (level 255) shows the image's highlight values. For a properly exposed photo, you want the entire spectrum to be covered, with the base high in the center.

You can view the current histogram of your frontmost document by choosing Window ➢ Histogram from the main menu. You can change which channel you view along with the source from the Histogram palette (see Figure 1.7).

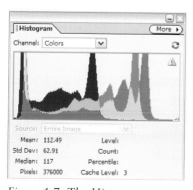

Figure 1.7: The Histogram.

From the Channel pop-up menu you can select RGB, Red, Green, Blue, Luminosity, or Colors. RGB displays a composite of individual color channels. Red, Green, and Blue display the histogram for the individual color channel. Luminosity displays the luminance (or intensity) values of the composite channel. Colors displays

- Red, Green, and Blue colors represented as individual channels
- Cyan, Magenta, and Yellow colors represented as an overlap of channels
- Gray represented as an overlap of all three channels

From the Source pop-up menu you can select Entire Image, Selected Layer, or Adjustment Composite. Entire Image does just that—it looks at the whole image to get its values (including all layers). Selected Layer uses only the selected layer to base the histogram on. Adjustment Composite displays the histogram for all layers below the selected adjustment layer in the Layers palette.

All about Layers

Following most of the examples in this book requires an understanding of layers and the Layers palette. Layers are one of the most powerful features in Photoshop Elements, and once you get used to using them, you will never understand how you managed without them. Some people use layers as a filing cabinet where they keep various versions of their work, as well as commonly used templates. One such template is a screen shot of a web browser window that is used for previewing web graphics and type. Many users make changes on a duplicate layer while always keeping an original version of their work handy on a separate layer, for comparison.

When you first open a digital image, Photoshop Elements places the image on a layer that is by default called the **Background** layer. Many Elements users may never need to go beyond this point. Later in the book, you will learn to resize, crop, or apply simple color and tonal corrections to a digital image, without going beyond one layer (Chapter 3). However, even if you never consciously create a new layer, layers will creep into your document. For example, a new layer is added automatically when you cut and paste a selection or if you add text to an image.

The minute you have more than one layer, the relationship between different layers is controlled by the Mode and Opacity settings in the Layers palette. For example, if the Mode is set to Normal and the Opacity is set to 100 percent, pixels in the top layer replace pixels in the layer underneath. This relationship changes when you select another Mode, or you lower the Opacity. Several ways of using different Mode settings for effects will be shown throughout this book.

Figure 1.8 shows the Layers palette. Note the various states of the layers. Some layers have their visibility turned on, as indicated by the eye icon in the leftmost side; other layers are turned off, as indicated by the absence of the eye. Only a single layer can be selected at a time, as indicated by the gray shading. One of the most common mistakes people make is not selecting the layer they want to work on. The result is that a command, such as a blur filter, doesn't affect the desired image at all, but in fact affects the content of another layer instead.

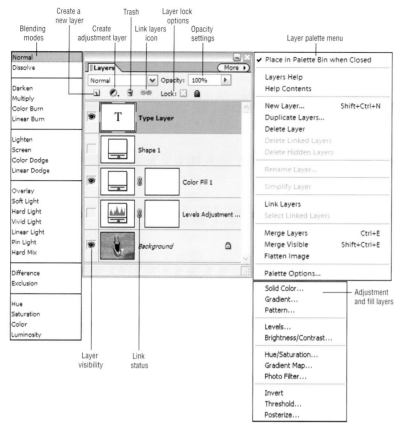

Figure 1.8: The Layers palette revealed.

Most of the time, when you add a layer, you increase the file size of your image—how much depends on the contents of the layer. Adjustment and fill layers, which are discussed later in this section, don't add any appreciable file size. Also remember that you'll need to save your work in the PSD or advanced TIFF file formats in order to keep layers intact. The JPEG file format, for example, doesn't allow you to save layers, and if you save your file as an animated GIF, layers are retained, but not in the same state as they were saved.

Here are some of the other things you need to know to create and otherwise work with and manage multiple layers. Photoshop Elements offers many ways to accomplish the same tasks:

Turn the visibility of layers on and off by toggling the eye icon in the leftmost side of the Layers palette.

Select a layer by clicking its thumbnail or name in the Layers palette. Highlighting indicates the layer is active. Choosing the Move tool (⊹) from the toolbar and clicking an image in the image window selects the layer containing that image (as long as Auto Select Layer is selected in the Move tool options bar). With the Move tool selected, right-clicking the image opens a pop-up menu listing the names of the various layers that are under the cursor. To select a layer, click its name in the pop-up menu.

Link layers by first selecting the layers you wish to link; multiple layers can be selected by Shift+clicking or Ctrl+clicking. After selecting the layers, click the Link

Layers button at the top of the Layers palette. In Figure 1.9, the **Background** and **Layer 2** layers have been linked. The small linked icon appears on the right side of the layer. To unlink these layers, select them again and click the Link Layers button.

Figure 1.9: The Link Layers icon.

Group layers by holding down the Alt key and positioning the pointer over the line dividing two layers in the Layers palette. Click when the pointer changes to two overlapping circles ( ). When layers are grouped together, the bottommost layer, called the *base layer*, becomes dominant and defines the subsequent layers. Imagine a base layer consisting of type grouped with another layer containing texture. The type would define the shape of the texture. You can also choose Layer ➤ Group with Previous (Ctrl+G) after selecting a layer. To ungroup layers, choose Layer ➤ Ungroup, or hold down the Alt key, position the pointer over the line dividing the layers, and click.

Lock the properties of a layer by selecting it and clicking the Lock All button ( ). Note the appearance of a solid black lock icon to the right of the layer name, indicating that the layer is protected from any changes.

Lock a layer's transparency by selecting it and clicking the Lock checkered square button. Note the hollow lock icon in the layer bar, which indicates that changes will be made in this layer only on existing pixels. This is useful for modifying an image while maintaining its exact shape and size.

Move a layer by selecting it and then dragging and dropping it into a new position in the Layers palette. A background layer cannot be moved from its background position without first changing its name. You can also reorder layers by choosing Layer ➤ Arrange.

Add a layer by clicking the More button and choosing New Layer from the palette menu, or by clicking the Create a New Layer icon ( ) at the top and far left. Some actions, such as cut and paste, automatically create a new layer. You can also choose Layer ➤ New ➤ Layer or press Ctrl+Shift+N.

Duplicate a layer by clicking the More button and choosing Duplicate Layer from the palette menu. Or in the Layers palette, select the layer you wish to duplicate and drag it to the Create a New Layer icon ( ) at the top of the Layers palette. Or choose Layer ➤ Duplicate Layer.

Delete a layer by dragging a selected layer to the trash icon ( ) at the top of the Layers palette, or select a layer and click the trash icon. You can also choose Layer ➤ Delete Layer, or choose Delete Layer from the More palette menu.

Rename a layer in the Layers palette by double-clicking the layer name, or clicking the More button and choosing Rename Layer from the palette menu. Or choose Layer ➢ Rename Layer.

Flatten linked layers into one layer by clicking the More button and choosing Merge Linked from the palette menu. Or choose Layer ➢ Merge Linked (Ctrl+E).

Flatten visible layers by clicking the More button and choosing Merge Visible from the palette menu. Or choose Layer ➢ Merge Visible, or press Ctrl+Shift+E.

Flatten all layers by clicking the More button and choosing Flatten Image from the palette menu. All layers will become one. All layer information is lost after the image is flattened. You can also choose Layer ➢ Flatten Image.

> **Note:** Many of the commands described in this section are available by right-clicking a layer in the Layers palette.

Adjustment and Fill Layers

When Adobe first added layers to Photoshop many years ago, I was thrilled. When they came up with adjustment and fill layers, I was amazed. As you'll see throughout this book, adjustment layers enable you to affect a single layer or group of layers while making it possible to remove the effect any time later without changing the rest of the image or greatly increasing your file size. Adjustment and fill layers retain the same opacity, blending, and grouping properties.

You access adjustment and fill layers by clicking the black-and-white circle at the top of the Layers palette ( ) or by choosing Layer ➢ New Adjustment Layer or Layer ➢ New Fill Layer.

You can choose from the following kinds of adjustment layers: Levels, Brightness/Contrast, Hue/Saturation, Photo Filter, Gradient Map, Invert, Threshold, Solid Color, Gradient, Pattern, and Posterize. In the chapters that follow, I'll mostly refer to the first four types. However, I encourage you to try the others. *Gradient Map*, for example, is a great way to create special color effects by mapping the equivalent grayscale range of your image to a colorful gradient fill. *Invert* makes your image look like a negative. Threshold converts images into high-contrast, black-and-white images that look like lithographs. *Posterize* gives you control over the number of tonal levels; choosing lower numbers radically changes the look and feel of your image.

Fill layers include fills based on a solid color, a gradient, or a pattern. I'll use fill layers throughout this book, especially when manipulating product shots (☞ Chapter 7).

To change an adjustment or fill layer, double-click the thumbnail in the Layers palette or choose Layer ➢ Layer Content Options. To delete an adjustment or fill layer, drag it to the trash icon at the bottom of the Layers palette, or with the adjustment layer selected, choose Layer ➢ Delete Layer.

Layer Styles

Another amazing feature is layer styles. You most likely have no idea how long it used to take to create a simple drop shadow before Photoshop introduced layer styles. Now you can do it with a click of the mouse.

Layer styles provide a way to apply a predetermined look and feel to a layer itself. These are removable and nondestructive, just like adjustment and fill layers. You can choose the way layer styles are displayed—list or thumbnails—via the More button at the top of the Styles and Effects palette. Thumbnails are the most useful in previewing a style's effect. Figure 1.10 shows a few layer styles.

Figure 1.10: Here are a few of the many layer styles.

To apply a layer style, be sure the Layer Styles option is selected in the first popup of the Styles and Effects palette and then drag and drop a style from the palette onto an image. You can also double-click a style to apply it to the active layer. Be careful: clicking more than one style will apply all your choices additively. This is great if this is what you want, but if not, make liberal use of the Undo History palette or the Undo command.

The Styles and Effects palette offers 14 categories of styles as starting points. However, with the power to customize style settings, the possibilities are endless. You can manipulate layer styles in the following ways:

Customize a layer style by double-clicking the f symbol in the Layers palette, which brings up a dialog box where you can specify the exact thickness, angles, and other characteristics of the style you desire. Or choose Layer ➢ Layer Style ➢ Style Settings from the menu.

Repeat a custom layer style on other layers by simply copying and pasting styles from one layer to another. Choose Layer ➢ Layer Style ➢ Copy Layer Style and then choose Layer ➢ Layer Style ➢ Paste Layer Style.

Clear a layer style by choosing Layer ➢ Layer Style ➢ Clear Layer Style or by right-clicking the layer in the Layers palette and choosing Clear Layer Style.

Effects

Effects are like automatic cameras. They make you look good even if you don't know what you are doing. Built into most effects are a complex series of filters, layer styles, and/or program functions. Figure 1.11 shows all the effects in the Styles and Effects palette window.

Figure 1.11: Thumbnails provide a useful preview of an effect.

To apply an effect, first select Effects from the first pop-up in the Styles and Effects palette. Then you select an effect and drag it from that palette onto an image, or simply double-click the effect. Remember that you don't have to apply an effect to an entire image. If you make a selection before applying an effect, some effects will apply only to that selection. (Each effect has its own policy for honoring selections.)

It may seem that effects are similar to layer styles, but there are some huge differences: Effects are not changeable in the same way that layer styles are, and they often require you to simplify a type layer before you apply an effect to it. Some effects flatten the image, some replace content, and some make entirely new layers (or combine with other layers). Blending modes may or may not be relevant.

Selection Tools

Much of the power of Photoshop Elements lies in its capability to manipulate both entire images and discrete portions of images. Selection tools enable you to target which pixels to operate upon. As you'll see throughout this book, knowing which selection tool to use when makes a big difference. Some selection tools, such as the Rectangular Marquee, are straightforward to use; others, such as the Magic Wand and the Magnetic Lasso, are more complex and require a little more skill to use. Most users will find that the Selection Brush tool falls somewhere in between. Each selection tool has multiple options for its use, which are accessed via the options bar found below the shortcuts bar.

Marquee Tools

The Marquee tools include the Rectangular (⬚) and Elliptical (◯) selection tools. They share the same spot on the toolbar. When you click the Marquee tool, buttons for both tools appear on the options bar. Switch between the two by clicking one of the buttons, or by clicking and holding the Marquee tool and then selecting Rectangular or Elliptical from the flyout.

Press M at any time (except when you are in text edit mode) to select the Marquee tool. Pressing M repeatedly toggles back and forth between the Rectangular and Elliptical tools.

These tools are most appropriate for making selections in the general area of what you want. Holding down the Shift key forces a Marquee tool into a circle or square shape. You can also use either Marquee tool as a rectangular cropping tool. Just make your selection and then choose Image ➢ Crop. If you are using the Elliptical Marquee tool, the crop will go to the outermost points of the ellipse but still be rectangular.

Lasso Tools

Lasso tools include the Lasso, Magnetic Lasso, and Polygonal Lasso. All three tools are at the same spot on the toolbar. When you click the Lasso tool, buttons for all three tools appear on the options bar. Switch between the tools by clicking one of the buttons, or by clicking and holding the Lasso tool and then selecting Lasso, Magnetic Lasso, or Polygonal Lasso from the pop-up menu.

Press L at any time (except when you are in text edit mode) to select the Lasso tool. To toggle among the three Lasso tools, press the L key repeatedly. While using the Magnetic Lasso, pressing the Alt key switches it to the Lasso; release the Alt key to revert to the Magnetic Lasso.

The Lasso tool (⬚) is great for tracing areas with jagged edges. Hold down the mouse button and freehand trace the desired selection shape. When you release the mouse, Photoshop Elements closes the shape if you haven't already done so. For maximum accuracy, magnify the image to see the border details.

The Magnetic Lasso tool (⬚) is an enhanced version of the Lasso tool that snaps to pixels of similar colors. Width, edge-contrast, and frequency parameters let you specify the range of pixel similarity to which the lasso is attracted. Double-click to finish making your selection. Again, Photoshop Elements closes the shape if you haven't already done so. I explain the Magnetic Lasso in great detail elsewhere in this book (⌇ "Separating a Product from Its Background" and "Adding Motion Blur" in Chapter 7).

The Polygonal Lasso tool (⬚) lets you specify the points of a multi-sided shape you wish to select. This is useful for selections with straight edges.

While using either the Magnetic Lasso or Polygonal Lasso selection tools, you can start over by pressing the Esc key.

Magic Wand

The Magic Wand tool (⬚), located in its own spot in the toolbar, magically chooses pixels of the same color within the specified tolerance limits throughout your image. Use this tool for irregularly shaped areas of the same color. I explain the Magic Wand in great detail elsewhere in this book (⌇ "Separating a Product from Its Background" in Chapter 6).

Selection Brush

The Selection Brush tool (![icon]), which shares a spot with the Magic Selection Brush tool in the toolbar, selects an area by painting over it. To add to a selection, simply paint over the area you wish to add. To subtract from a selection, hold the Alt key, and the areas you paint will be deselected. At any time you can start over by choosing Select ➢ Deselect from the menu bar or by using the keyboard command Ctrl+D. Holding the Shift key while dragging this tool will approximately constrain it to straight lines or connect two clicked points. In the Selection Brush options bar, you can control the brush size and hardness. Increasing the Hardness setting is much like using the feather command found in the other selection tool options. 0 percent produces a soft selection edge, while 100 percent makes the edge of the selection more sharply defined. (Keep in mind that this is only a slight feathering. For radical feathering, you need to use Select ➢ Feather and choose higher pixel values.)

In the Selection Brush options bar, you can choose between working in Selection mode or Mask mode. The default, Selection mode, produces the familiar pulsing, dotted "marching ants" lines that define and protect the area contained within the dots. If you select Mask, the areas you paint over will be colored. The default is a red overlay at a 50 percent opacity, but you can change both the color and the opacity in the options bar.

Keep in mind that Selection and Mask modes are essentially opposite selection methods. When you use Mask mode, areas that are colored by the Selection Brush are "protected" as opposed to being "selected." It's really important to understand the difference. When something is selected, either by using the Selection Brush in Selection mode or one of the other selection tools, you can apply Enhance commands, filters, or effects only to the selected areas. But when you use the Selection Brush in Mask mode, the colored areas are the areas that won't be affected by such commands. In other words, they are protected (remember this by thinking of the Mask mode as a way to put virtual "masking" tape over parts of an image to protect it). Now this gets really confusing if you go from Mask mode back to Selection mode. The color overlay you created with the Selection Brush is replaced by the familiar pulsing dotted line; however, don't be fooled. The area within the parameter of the dotted line is still protected, not selected. If you look carefully, you'll see more dotted lines that show the boundaries of the actual selection.

You can selectively deselect masked areas by holding down the Alt key while painting with the Selection Brush in Mask mode.

Magic Selection Brush

The Magic Selection Brush tool can do amazing things—sometimes. There are images that are meant for this tool, and there are some that are not. The Magic Selection Brush selects an object by having you just scribble or draw a line on it. Items that are easily selected with this tool include flowers, fruit, and Halloween pumpkins of all things. The best way to explain this tool is with an example.

Here's what I did to quickly select the pumpkin in an image:

1. Using the pumpkin image, I chose the Magic Selection Brush tool, which shares a palette location with the Selection Brush tool (press the F key).

2. I changed the color for the selection markup to yellow to make it stand out; I also changed the brush size to 7 pixels. If your selection is more than you expected, try a smaller brush.

3. I drew a line from the top of the stem to the bottom of the pumpkin, as shown in Figure 1.12 on the left. If I had started below the stem, just the pumpkin would have been selected. Since the tool always switches to the option with the plus sign (+), it adds to the selection when next used. This can be easily forgotten, so keep an eye on it.

Figure 1.12: Left, during selection. Right, after selection.

4. After releasing the mouse, the marquee appeared around the pumpkin, as seen in the right-hand image of Figure 1.12. It may be necessary in some cases to touch up the selection with the Selection Brush.

Magic Extractor

The Magic Extractor tool is not a selection tool per se, but it can be used to extract an object from its background, and like the Magic Selection Brush, it performs better with some images than others. An example of this tool in action is presented in Chapter 7. In that chapter, I mention that this tool is not the only way to extract an object, but just one more option to call upon when the need arises. Sometimes it's necessary to use a combination of tools to extract an object from its background, depending on the level of difficulty. Examples of techniques for doing this are also explained in Chapter 7.

Selection Tool Options

Generally, options for the selection tools other than the Selection Brush include the following:

Adding, subtracting, or merging selection shapes. You can add to (Shift), subtract from (Alt), or intersect with selections (Shift+Alt) by holding down these additional keys while making selections. You can also click the respective icons in the options bar. If you use the options bar, the setting remains until you change it. Using the keyboard has its advantages.

Moving, copying, or pasting selections and layers. After you make a selection shape, you can move the outline of the defined area by dragging it with your mouse, provided a selection tool is still selected, or you can more precisely position it with the arrow keys. However, the New Selection option must be selected on the options bar. You can move a selection this way with either the Marquee, Lasso, or Magic Wand selected, regardless of which tool made the selection. For example, you can make a selection with the selection brush and move it by selecting a marquee tool and dragging it with your mouse.

Softening edges of a selection. You can blur the edges of selections by typing a specific number of pixels in the Feather field, or by choosing Select ➢ Feather (Ctrl+Alt+D).

Anti-aliasing a selection. This controls the smoothness of a selection's edges by including transition pixels. By default, the anti-aliasing option is selected.

Controlling Selections

There are several ways to control the shape and size of a selection:

- You can specify the exact dimensions or proportions of a Marquee selection in the options bar Mode pop-up menu.
- You can reverse or invert any selection and choose unselected pixels by choosing Select ➢ Inverse or by pressing Ctrl+Shift+I.

There are several ways you can modify a selection:

Select ➢ Modify ➢ Border selects a border of pixels the specified number of pixels inside and outside the current selection.

Select ➢ Modify ➢ Smooth excludes pixels outside the specified range from the current selection. This is especially useful when you use the Magic Wand and get small selections all over the image. The Smooth option unifies the many selections into one.

Select ➢ Modify ➢ Expand makes the current selection larger by the specified number of pixels.

Select ➢ Modify ➢ Contract makes the current selection smaller by the specified number of pixels.

Select ➢ Grow incorporates, into the current selection, pixels that are similar and in a contiguous area.

Select ➢ Similar incorporates, into the current selection, pixels that are similar anywhere within the image.

Select ➢ Save Selection allows you to save a selection and load it for later use.

Except for the options that apply specifically to the Marquee selection tool, all of these commands apply to a selection created by the Selection Brush.

At any time, you can remove a selection by using the Esc key or by pressing Ctrl+D. If you change your mind, you can get the selection back using the trusty Undo command (Ctrl+Z) or by choosing Select ➢ Reselect.

You can turn a selection into a colored outline by using the Stroke command. Make a selection with any of the selection tools and choose Edit ➢ Stroke. In the Stroke dialog box, specify a line width and color, as well as the location of where the pixels fall in relationship to the selection outline: inside, center, or outside. You can also select a blending mode and opacity.

Cookie Cutter Tool

The Cookie Cutter tool ( ) crops an image into a shape you can choose. An example of this is shown in Figure 1.13. First, choose the shape you want to constrict your image to by selecting it in the Cookie Cutter's options bar. Then click and drag over your image to see the shape appear. You can move or resize the shape by moving the cursor over the edge of the bounding regions. Once you are happy with the placement, commit the selection by choosing the Commit button in the options bar. There are a few options you can select for your Cookie Cutter tool: the shape's options, the amount to feather the selection, and whether to crop the image.

Figure 1.13: The Cookie Cutter tool automatically turns an image into a shape.

Under the shape's options you can choose Unconstrained, Defined Proportions, Defined Size, Fixed Size, and From Center. Choosing Unconstrained enables you to draw the shape to any size you like. Defined Proportions keeps the height and width of the shape in proportion. Use Defined Size to crop the image to a defined size (as determined by clicking and dragging the bounding boxes), and use Fixed Size to enter the exact size you want for the completed shape. Select From Center to draw the shape from the center of your first click.

Viewing and Navigation Tools

For precise work, it is essential to be able to zoom in and out of an image, and to navigate around the window if the image is large. Several tools and commands are available to help you.

Zoom Tool

To select the Zoom tool ( ), click it on the toolbar or press Z. The Zoom In tool ( ) enlarges image detail, and the Zoom Out tool ( ) achieves the opposite effect. You can switch between Zoom In and Zoom Out by clicking their buttons on the toolbar. Hold down the Alt key to temporarily change the currently selected Zoom tool to the opposite tool; when you release the Alt key, the tool changes back to its original state. Double-clicking the Zoom tool icon in the toolbox returns the image to 100 percent.

The percent magnification appears in the lower-left corner of the work area. You can type a desired percent magnification in this box. You can also choose View ➢ Zoom In or View ➢ Zoom Out.

With the Zoom In tool selected, you can fill the screen with a particular area of an image by clicking and dragging the mouse to define a bounding box surrounding the area of interest. Let go of the mouse, and zoom!

In the Zoom tool options bar, if Resize Windows to Fit is selected, the Photoshop Elements window is resized as necessary to display the image. When the option is deselected, the window remains the same size regardless of magnification.

If you have more than one image open, you can have the Zoom tool zoom in on all the images at the same time by selecting the Zoom All Windows check box in the options bar. To temporarily set this behavior, you can hold down the Shift key while clicking the Zoom tool. You can also Shift+double-click the Zoom tool to display all open images at 100 percent.

View Commands

Several view commands are found in the main menu bar. These include the following:

View ➢ New Window for ‹*Filename*› creates multiple views of the same image. Any changes made are applied to all views. You can close any but the last view before you are prompted to save the file.

View ➢ Fit on Screen fills the entire window with the entire image. This is equivalent to double-clicking the Hand tool.

View ➢ Actual Pixels displays an image at 100 percent while taking into account the height and width of the image, as well as the resolution of the monitor. Two images can have the same height and width and different resolutions, and yet appear the same size on the monitor.

View ➢ Print Size displays an image at 100 percent if the resolution is 72ppi. This view takes into account the resolution of the image, as well as the resolution of the monitor. Two images can have the same height and width in pixels, but if the resolution is different, they will appear as different sizes on the monitor.

Navigator Palette

The Navigator palette is hidden by default. (You can find it by choosing Window ➢ Navigator from the main menu bar.) The colored view box in this palette helps orient your current position in the image. This is useful when an image gets too large to display on-screen. The slider at the top of this palette offers yet another option to increase or decrease the percent magnification of the image. Change the color of the view box by selecting Palette Options from the More pop-up menu.

Hand Tool

The Hand tool ( ), located in the toolbar, is used to move the image around in the work area when the image is magnified outside the boundaries of the work area. The Navigator palette provides a thumbnail view to orient your position relative to the entire image. Use the hand in the Navigator palette to move the view box to target areas within the image. Areas outside the view box remain intact but are simply off-screen.

You can access the Hand tool temporarily at any time by holding down the spacebar, or you can switch to it by pressing H. Double-click the Hand tool to reveal the entire image in the image window. You can optionally select the Scroll All Windows check box in the options bar. This enables you to scroll all windows at the same time, which is useful when you have similar images side by side. To temporarily set this behavior, hold down the Shift key while dragging the Hand tool. You can also Shift+double-click the Hand tool to apply the Fit on Screen option to all open images.

Scrubbers

Scrubbers originate in Adobe's After Effects and provide a whole new way to control items in numeric entry fields. To use this feature, place your cursor over the numeric field you want to change. Then move your cursor to the left, over its textual label. You should see the cursor change to a double-ended arrow, as shown in Figure 1.14. If you click and drag to the left, the numeric entry decreases; if you click and drag to the right, it increases. A common scrubber you may use can be found on the Options bar when using a brush. Just scrub the word Size or Opacity to change the numeric field.

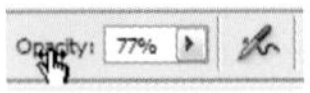

Figure 1.14: Move your cursor over a label, and it turns into a scrubber, which gives you mouse control over numeric entry fields.

Brushes

Many Photoshop Elements tools use brushes to apply different effects. These brushes can be customized far beyond their size and shape. Elements makes it especially easy to customize a brush and control the look and feel of a particular brush stroke.

When you select the Brush (B) tool from the toolbar, options for controlling the brush size, shape, and characteristics appear in the options bar. For the other tools that use brushes—Blur, Sharpen, Sponge, Smudge, Dodge, Burn, Clone Stamp, Pattern Stamp, Pencil (N), Color Replacement Tool (B), Selection Brush (A), Impressionist Brush (B), Spot Healing Brush (J), Healing Brush (J), Magic Selection Brush (F), and eraser tools—you have more limited options.

Available to all tools that use brushes are several brush presets, including the default set shown on the left in Figure 1.15. There are several other presets as well, including Calligraphic Brushes, Drop Shadow Brushes, and Web Media Brushes. You can control the size of the preset brushes in the options bar.

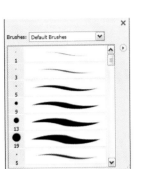

Figure 1.15: The default brush presets (left). More presets are found in the drop-down menu. The More Options menu (right) provides additional ways to customize the Brush tool.

When you select the Brush tool, you can use the options on the More Options drop-down menu (shown on the right in Figure 1.15) to control the Spacing, Fade, Hue Jitter, Hardness, Scatter, and other characteristics of the brush, as well as the precise shape of the tip through Angle and Roundness controls.

If you are feeling really ambitious, you can even create a brush from an image. Make a selection from your image and then choose Edit ➢ Define Brush. Name your brush and select OK. A grayscale brush based on your selection is now available, along with the other preset options.

Impressionist Brush

I don't use the Impressionist Brush in this book. It's a complex tool, and you can spend countless hours just trying to figure out what it does and then realize that you've only scratched the surface. Through different texture and color settings, you can simulate various painting styles—think Van Gogh and Cezanne. Play with different Styles, Fidelity, Area, and Spacing settings. Then when you've figured those out, change the Mode and Opacity settings and see what else you can come up with. The possibilities are limitless. Enjoy!

Healing Brushes

Two great brushes take the pain out of cleaning up and removing unwanted blemishes and artifacts.

If the problem area is small, the Spot Healing Brush (✏️) is ideal at fixing it. In most cases you can choose a brush size that is slightly larger than the area you want to fix, center the brush over the area, and click. You can set two options for the Spot Healing Brush: Proximity Match and Create Texture. The Proximity Match option tries to use the pixels around the edge of the selection as a patch. Create Texture uses all the pixels in the selected area to create a texture to place over the selected area.

If, however, the regions are more complex, you can use the more powerful Healing Brush (✏️). In fact, the Healing Brush not only covers up unwanted areas, but it also removes objects entirely from view. There are four options available to control the brush: Mode, Source, Aligned, and Sample All Layers. The Mode option controls how the source blends with the existing pixels. Source allows you to choose where to get the repairing pixels: Sampled uses pixels from the current image, whereas Pattern uses pixels from a pattern. Aligned moves the sampling point relative to where you are stroking. If you want to always use the original sampling point, deselect this option. Sample All Layers samples data from all visible layers. If you want to use only the currently selected layer, deselect this option.

Filters

Photoshop Elements includes a large number of filters, which can be applied through the Filter menu entry or via the Filters palette. Like effects, filters can be applied to a selection. Figure 1.16 shows all of the filters at a glance.

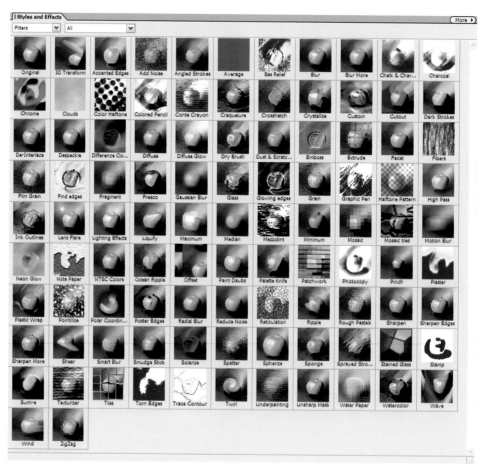

Figure 1.16: All the filters revealed.

Liquify Filter

It seems inappropriate to refer to the Liquify filter as a mere filter in the same way that the Unsharp Mask is a filter. The Liquify filter is more of an experience. When you select the Liquify filter (Filter ➤ Distort ➤ Liquify), you enter a world where the image becomes totally fluid, as if it were molten pixels that you can move and shove around, much like finger paint. In many ways, it's like an application within an application. Figure 1.17 shows the Liquify filter work area and tools.

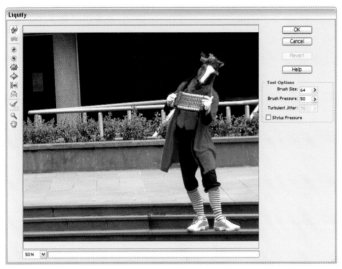

Figure 1.17: The Liquify filter work area and tools.

In this book, I use the Liquify filter for several purposes—for example, straightening a crooked nose, fixing a broken tooth, and altering type. But I encourage you to play around with all the Liquify filter's tools and options. You'll find yourself spending hours and hours getting to know this filter and exploring its creative capabilities.

Some points to keep in mind when using the Liquify filter:

- To revert an image to its original form, click Revert in the Liquify work area.
- To reset the Liquify filter tools to their previous settings *and* to revert an image, hold the Alt key and, when the Cancel button changes to Reset, click it.
- Use the Reconstruct tool to restore specific areas of your image. Just brush over the areas you want to reconstruct.
- If you are working on a particularly large image, make a selection of the area that you wish to work on first before opening the filter. This greatly speeds up the time it takes for certain Liquify tools (such as the Turbulence tool) to operate.

Note: ☞ "Viewing and Navigation Tools" earlier in this chapter for shortcuts and tips on using the Liquify filter navigation and viewing tools.

Importing
and Managing
Digital Images

This chapter shows you various options for bringing your digital images directly into Photoshop Elements from a digital camera, card reader, scanner, file, or folder. It also describes how to organize and manage imported images so you can find the image you want, when you want it. Subsequent chapters focus on the editing and processing capabilities of Photoshop Elements.

2

Chapter Contents

Importing Digital Images into Photoshop Elements

There are several ways to get your digital images into Photoshop Elements. The way you choose depends on the source of the digital images—folder, digital camera, card reader, scanner, and so forth.

Photoshop Elements has two main work areas: the Editor and the Organizer. The Organizer launches separately from the Editor, but they operate in conjunction. Digital files can be passed relatively easily between the two workspaces. Users can import digital files into the Organizer, where they can be organized, managed, and shared—or transferred to the Editor for extensive editing. Alternatively, users can import digital files directly into the Editor and bypass the Organizer entirely.

Let's start by learning how to import images into the Organizer. After that, I'll show you how to import images directly into the Editor.

Importing Images into the Organizer

You can bring images into the Organizer from at least three basic sources:
- An existing folder or offline media such as a CD or DVD
- A digital camera or card reader
- A scanner

The easiest and most foolproof method is to bring digital files in from an existing folder, so let's start there.

Importing from an Existing Folder or Offline Media

I'll assume you are starting from the Welcome screen that appears when you first launch the application from your desktop (see Figure 2.1).

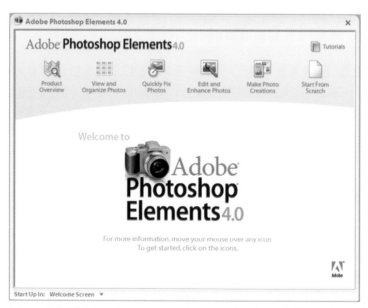

Figure 2.1: This is what you see when you first launch Photoshop Elements.

Take the following steps to import your files:

1. In the Welcome screen, click View and Organize Photos. This opens the Organizer.
2. Choose File ➢ Get Photos from the main menu bar. Alternatively, you can click the camera icon found in the shortcuts menu bar (see Figure 2.2).

Figure 2.2: Get image files by clicking the Get Photos icon located in the shortcuts menu bar.

3. Now select From Files and Folders. A window like the one shown in Figure 2.3 should appear.

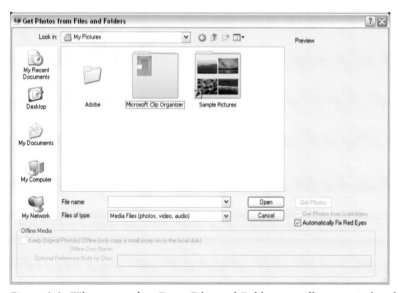

Figure 2.3: When you select From Files and Folders, you'll see a window like this one.

4. Navigate to the files or folders you wish to import.

5. Select the file or folder by clicking the thumbnail; then click the Get Photos button.

Note: You can also drag and drop files and folders from your desktop directly into the Organizer.

The Organizer is not copying the image file itself. It creates a thumbnail version of the file and a link between your actual image files and the Organizer. Your original image file remains in its original location. (If you move the original file, you'll need to "reconnect" the link. ↪ "Reconnecting Photos" later in this chapter.)

If you are importing images from an offline source (for example, from a CD), you have two choices: either copy the entire file or files onto your hard disk, or import only a small proxy (that is, a thumbnail and basic file info) of the file (or files). You can set the size of the proxy thumbnail, from 320×240 pixels to 1280×960 pixels, in the Organizer preferences: Edit ➢ Preferences ➢ Files.

To bring in only a thumbnail version, select the Keep Original Photo(s) Offline check box at the bottom of the Get Photos from Files and Folders window. At first, it may seem practical to copy only a small proxy and not the full image. Obviously, you'll save space on your hard disk. However, if you try to edit the small proxy, a message appears asking you to insert the offline media (CD or DVD, for example) so a full-resolution version of the image can be accessed. This can take time, especially if you haven't located your offline media quickly. (Personally, I'm shying away from storing images on CD and DVDs. I'm using huge, multi-gigabyte hard disks, which are cheap, yet fast and reliable. When I run out of storage space, I just buy another hard disk and daisy-chain it to my computer so all my images are quickly available.)

Note: Some file formats are not supported by the Organizer. For example, if you try to import files from a Kodak Photo CD, an error message tells you that the format cannot be included in the Organizer. You can, however, import most image files directly into the Editor, save them in a common format such as TIFF, JPEG, or PSD, and then bring the files into the Organizer. (↪ "Opening Images in the Editor" later in this chapter.)

Importing from a Digital Camera or Card Reader

Photoshop Elements uses Adobe Photo Downloader to transfer images from a digital camera or card reader. Photo Downloader is installed automatically when you install Elements, and it's managed primarily from a camera icon (📷) in the System Tray (located in the lower right of your Windows Desktop). Right-click the icon to enable, disable, or exit the Photo Downloader; this icon has a green arrow when Photo Downloader is enabled and a red one when it's disabled. You can also launch Photo Downloader by right-clicking the icon and selecting Launch.

With the Organizer open, you can import from either a camera or card reader by choosing File ➢ Get Photos ➢ From Camera or Card Reader or by clicking the

Camera icon on the shortcuts bar. Whether or not the Organizer is open, the insertion of a card into a card reader or hooking up a camera to your PC opens Photo Downloader. The main difference is that when you use the Organizer to import, you must select a device in step 1 on the right-hand side of the Photo Downloader window.

Any thumbnails that represent videos have an icon like the one shown in Figure 2.4. Photo Downloader has two buttons at the top left that control the importing of stills and videos. Select the button on the left if you want to import only stills, the button on the right to import only videos, or both buttons to import everything. Both icons are selected by default, assuming that the device you inserted contains both types of media.

Figure 2.4: Thumbnail with icon indicating a video.

Note: Holding down the Shift key while inserting the memory card prevents the Microsoft wizard from starting, but allows Photo Downloader to start.

Where do the images go when you download them? As I said earlier, the Organizer doesn't bring in the actual file but creates a link to the file. When you import from a camera or a card reader, however, a copy of the file is transferred to your hard disk. You can specify where these files reside in the Organizer preferences (shown in Figure 2.5). By default, they go in your **My Documents\My Pictures\Adobe** folder. However, the Organizer still creates a link to those files, and if you move the files from their original location, you will need to reconnect them by choosing the File ➤ Reconnect menu item.

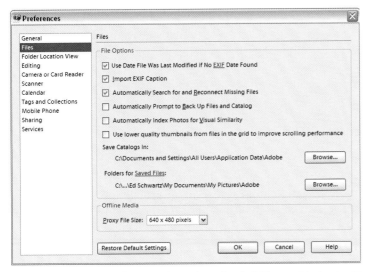

Figure 2.5: You can change where downloaded files reside in the Organizer preferences.

Note: If you install software that came with your digital camera, it may launch an application offering to transfer images from your camera to your PC. This may only add confusion, since there are already two applications attempting to do this—Elements and Windows. For this reason, I recommend not installing any camera software, especially if you plan to use Elements. Use Adobe Photo Downloader, which is usually superior to the software that is bundled with a camera.

Importing from a Scanner

To import from a scanner in the Organizer, from the main menu choose File ➤ Get Photos ➤ From Scanner. This provides more consistent results than using the icon on the shortcuts bar. The Get Photos from Scanner dialog box is shown in Figure 2.6. After you select your scanner from the list, you have a choice of saving your files as JPEG, TIFF, or PNG. You can use the Browse button to select the destination for the scans; otherwise, the default location is used.

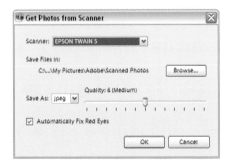

Figure 2.6: The Get Photos from Scanner dialog box.

If you are going to import from your scanner, make sure that the scanner is turned on before you launch the Organizer or the scanner will not be recognized. Frankly, you may find it better to do all your scanning from within the Editor (File ➤ Import), not the Organizer. If you scan from within the Editor, you have many more choices of file formats for saving files. You also have direct access to the Divide Scanned Photos feature (Image ➤ Divide Scanned Photos). With this feature, you can scan several images at once, and Photoshop Elements automatically straightens, crops, and places each image into a separate file.

Note: You can have the Organizer automatically search for new image files by choosing File ➤ Watch Folders from the main menu bar. If you enable this feature, the Organizer either notifies you when new files are added to folders you specify or automatically adds the files to the Organizer.

Opening Images in the Editor

Here are your choices for opening images from within the Editor:

File ➤ Open opens all compatible file formats. This brings up an Open dialog box with controls for locating and previewing files.

File ➢ Open Recently Edited File opens up to 30 of the most recently viewed files. (The default is 10, but you can increase that number in Saving Files preferences.)

File ➢ Import gives you access to any Import plug-in module compatible with Photoshop Elements. You may need to install the specific plug-in yourself. See the documentation for your scanner or digital camera for more instructions. You can also use Import to bring scans or digital camera images directly into Photoshop Elements. Frame from Video is a quick and easy way to bring in individual frames from MPEG movies, or just about any video footage that Media Player supports.

File ➢ New ➢ Image from Clipboard enables you to create a new file from a selection. Make a selection in an image by using any of the marquee selection tools and then copy that selection (Ctrl+C); you can then create a new file containing that selection by choosing File ➢ New from Clipboard. You can also create a new file when other programs send data to the clipboard. For example, use your Ptr Scr (Print Screen) key to capture your screen to the clipboard and then select File ➢ New ➢ Image from Clipboard.

Clicking the Photo Browser icon in the shortcuts bar opens the Organizer, from which you can select and import photos into the Editor. (Why did Adobe name the icon Photo Browser and not Organizer? Because clicking it opens the Organizer in Photo Browser mode. I know, it's confusing, but you'll get used to it.)

> **Note:** Photoshop Elements (Editor) opens most image file formats, even images saved at 16 bits per color and high-end prepress formats. (If an image is saved in the CMYK color mode, Photoshop Elements asks whether it is OK to convert to RGB before opening.) Open digital images saved in the Photoshop Elements file format directly from the desktop by double-clicking the image icon or filename. However, you may need to open other file formats from within the Photoshop Elements application. (You can re-associate file types by choosing Edit ➢ File Association from the Editor menu bar.)

You can also open files by clicking the Open folder icon (📁) in the shortcuts bar or create a new file by clicking the New icon (🗋) in the shortcuts bar.

Finally, you can open files by double-clicking the dark-gray, empty window area, which is called the *work area*. The Windows Open dialog box appears, where you can choose a file or files to open.

Managing Files with the Organizer

After you have imported your digital files into the Organizer, you can do many things. Not only can you choose the way the images are displayed—single image, multiple images, and so forth—you can also use different criteria to sort and organize the images. With only a little effort you can organize your images according to date, folder location, filename, media type, and more. You can also apply custom or generic *tags* based on the content of the image, and sort and organize the images that way.

Of course, the Organizer is also a gateway to the Editor, where you can use Photoshop Elements' powerful editing and processing capabilities. Furthermore, within the Organizer you can process and print multiple images, labels, and contact sheets, as well as create slide shows, VCDs, photo album pages, greeting cards, postcards, wall calendars, photo books, and a web photo gallery. As I mentioned earlier, the editing capabilities of Photoshop Elements are discussed in detail in subsequent chapters. I'll get into the printing and sharing capabilities of the Organizer in Chapter 11.

Let's get up to speed with the organizing and managing capabilities within the Organizer.

Viewing Files

The Organizer is extremely flexible, especially when it comes to the ways it displays your images. You can choose to display images in a variety of ways, ranging from tiny thumbnails to large, side-by-side views. Let's look at some of your options.

Viewing Photos in the Photo Well

Look at Figure 2.7. The images are displayed in the Photo Well as small thumbnails and organized by the date they were created, with the oldest displayed first in the upper-left corner. Because most of these shots were created with a digital camera, the Organizer used the date and time information contained in the EXIF data generated by the camera. For other types of digital media, the Organizer uses file-creation information.

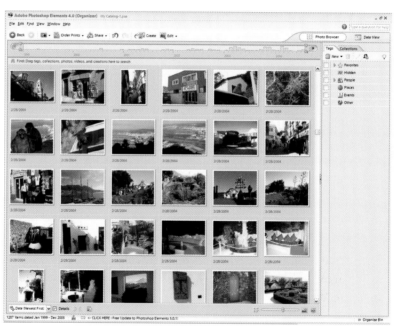

Figure 2.7: Images are displayed as small thumbnails and sorted by date.

Note: You can always change the date and time associated with an image file. Select the thumbnail of the image, right-click, and choose Adjust Date and Time from the pop-up menu. You can also do this by choosing Edit ➢ Adjust Date and Time from the main menu bar. In addition, you can select multiple thumbnails and adjust them simultaneously.

Now look at Figure 2.8. I didn't do a thing to the images. I changed only two Organizer settings and created a very different view of the same catalog of images.

Figure 2.8: Images are now displayed as larger thumbnails, and they are sorted by folder location.

> **Note:** When you import images into the Organizer, it creates a catalog, named My Catalog by default. A catalog can contain an unlimited number of photos, so it is likely you'll need only one catalog. You can create new catalogs if you wish, but only one can be open at a time. To create a new catalog, choose File ➤ Catalog and follow the prompts. To rename your existing catalog, choose File ➤ Catalog ➤ Save As and change the filename in the dialog box.

To create this new view, I selected Folder Location from the pop-up menu that appears at the bottom left of the Organizer (see Figure 2.9). Alternatively, you can use the main menu bar: View ➤ Arrangement ➤ Folder Location. I also increased the size of the thumbnails with the slider found at the bottom right of the Organizer (again, see Figure 2.9). Move the slider to the left, and the thumbs are shrunk; move the slider to the right, and they are enlarged. Obviously, the larger that the thumbnails become, the fewer that fit into the Photo Well.

Figure 2.9: View your images with different criteria (left). Change the size of the thumbnails by moving the slider to the left or right (right).

Folder Location View

The Folder view, shown in Figure 2.8, can be both perplexing and extremely useful. The tips that follow should help you to avoid the landmines that lurk ahead while you enjoy the advantages of this view. The term "manage" in these tips is used to indicate that the files or folders have been added to the Organizer.

- The Folder view can show all folders, or just those that have been managed. Right-click any folder to choose a view.
- When viewing only the folders that have been managed, some folders may not have the indication that they are being managed ( ). Just drill down using the plus sign (+) to the left of the folder to see any subfolders' images that have been managed.
- To manage a folder, make sure you are viewing all folders. Right-click any folder and choose View All Folders. Next, right-click the folder you want to manage and choose Add Unmanaged Files to Catalog.
- After selecting View All Folders, the Folder view may only contain the icons representing your drives. Keep expanding the icon that contains the subfolders or folders you're looking for.
- After adding a folder to the Organizer, you most likely will not see any images in the Photo Well. Click the Back to All Photos button at the top and then select the folder you just imported.
- After exiting a full screen review or a slideshow creation, you may not have any images in the Photo Well. Just reselect a folder on the left to place its contents in the Photo Well.
- When you leave the Folder view and then return to it, you will only see the folder icons representing your drives (actually the root folder of each drive).
- When not in the Folder view, you can still find out the location or path of an image. It is shown at the bottom of the General section of the Properties palette, along with the filename.

Timeline Bar

You can use the timeline bar to further refine your viewing. The timeline bar is located near the top of the Photo Well (see the indicator back in Figure 2.8). If you choose to view by date, the timeline bar displays the year and 12 marks that represent 12 months. Blocks represent collections of images based on their creation date. The larger the block, the larger the collection. Click and hold and then drag the bottom of the blue frame that hangs on the timeline to the desired month. As you move the frame, thumbnails in the Photo Well change accordingly. If you chose to view by folder, you can use the blue frame to scroll between folders. If you select Import Batch, the timeline changes to reflect the relevant criteria.

Note: Remove the timeline bar by choosing View ➤ Timeline from the main menu bar. Bring it back by choosing View ➤ Timeline again. Ctrl+L toggles it on and off also.

Date View

Figure 2.10 shows yet another viewing option: Date view. Date view doesn't create a calendar (you can do that in the Create menu); it enables you to select a year, month, or day as criteria for viewing your images. You access the Date view by selecting the calendar icon followed by the words *Date View* at the far right of the options bar.

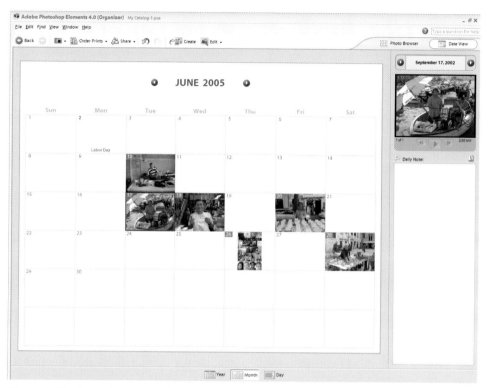

Figure 2.10: Date view is another viewing option.

When you first open this view, you may not see any images, just a calendar with empty boxes. You need to select a viewing range that covers the creation dates of your images. You can do this in two ways: Either click the Year, Month, or Day icons on the bottom of the Date View window and scroll by using the arrows at the top of the window to the correct date(s), or set a range by clicking the date found in the upper right of the Date View window. This brings up the Set Date dialog box. Type in the parameters you know will include the dates your images were created. Or easier still, select a time in the timeline bar before switching to the Date view.

You can customize the Date view in the Organizer preferences to display different holidays or events. Choose Edit ➢ Preferences ➢ Calendar from the main menu bar.

If there is more than one image on a single date in the Month view, switch to the Day view by using the icons at the bottom of the Date view. There you'll see a filmstrip along the right-hand side. Right-click any image to make it the top photo in the calendar for that day. To view the various images while in the Month view, use the viewer located at the top right to sequence through them. Double-clicking an image in the Month view opens a window where you can scroll through the various images.

Full Screen View and Side by Side View

As if all the preceding options weren't enough, the Organizer also provides yet another way to view your photos: Full Screen view and Side by Side view. Figure 2.11 shows the Full Screen view and Side by Side view windows.

Figure 2.11: Full Screen view window (left). The Side by Side view window (right).

You access these views via the main menu bar: View ≻View Photos in Full Screen (or F11 key), or View ≻ Compare Photos Side by Side (or F12 key). You can also access Full Screen view by right-clicking a thumbnail in the Photo Well and choosing it from the pop-up menu or by clicking the Full Screen view icon located at the bottom right of the Photo Well window (▤). Full Screen view and Side by Side view both create an interactive on-screen slideshow, sequencing one image after another at a pace you determine in the opening Review dialog box, shown in Figure 2.12. (Here you can also choose to add music if you like.) If you don't get this dialog, right-click your image and select Full Screen View Options. Here, you can choose whether to always show this dialog or not.

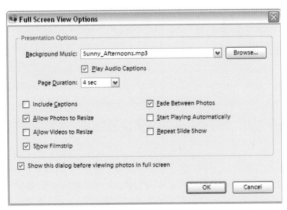

Figure 2.12: Options for Full Screen and Side by Side views.

Don't confuse these views with the Slide Show Maker found in the Create menu, which is much more versatile and provides a myriad of transition and pacing controls. These two views are meant to help the editing process. You can stop the slideshow at any time, rotate an image, trash it, Auto Fix it, or attach a tag (more on that later). When you are finished with one image, you can move on to the next image by using familiar VCR-like Play and Stop controls. If the controls are not visible, just move your mouse and they will appear. Use the Play button to cycle automatically and the Pause button to stop the show. To end the slideshow and return to the Organizer, click the X button on the control bar or the Esc key on the keyboard. To see a filmstrip along the right-hand side, right-click an image and select Show Filmstrip. (Crtl+F toggles this on and off also.)

The Side by Side view adds the option of selecting a "master" image that remains static, which the other images cycle past. You can use the master image to compare or contrast with the other images. Either window can be the master and can be selected as follows: If you click the image on the left, the right side becomes the static or master image, and vice versa. You can also switch the roles of the two windows by pressing the Tab key. You cannot hit the Play button in this mode, but the Next Photo and Previous Photo buttons on the control bar do function. You can also cycle through the images with the up-arrow and down-arrow keys, or you can click any image in the filmstrip along the right-hand side to replace the slide in the non-static window.

To change from one view to the other without returning to the Organizer, just click the appropriate icon on the control bar. There is an icon for Full Screen view and for Side by Side view, as shown in Figure 2.13. If you click the black arrow to the right of these icons, you can switch the Side by Side view to an Above and Below view.

Figure 2.13: Changing views.

Avoid switching to these views with no images selected in the Photo Well. It will still work, but the images that are displayed may not be what you expect. An exception is when in the Folder view. Switching to these views in this case adds the folder contents to the view (unless you select a subset of the images first).

After you are finished reviewing your images in the Full Screen or Side by Side views, hit the Esc key to return to the main Organizer window or select Exit (X) on the control bar.

Reconnecting Photos

As I said, the Organizer doesn't import image files into the catalog; it creates a link to the image file. If you move a folder or file from your hard disk to another location, you break this link. You know a link is broken when you see a thumbnail like the ones in Figure 2.14. To reconnect your image file, choose File ➢ Reconnect from the menu bar. The Organizer tries to find the missing file, or prompts you to browse to the missing file yourself. In the Reconnect Missing Files dialog box (shown in Figure 2.15), navigate to the original file and click Reconnect. To bring up this dialog, double-click an image that requires reconnecting; when Elements starts to search for it, click the Browse button and navigate to the folder containing the image. If it no longer exists, delete it from the catalog. Use the Delete key or right-click the image to do this. When you are finished, click Close.

Figure 2.14: When a link is broken, you get an icon that looks like either of the ones shown here.

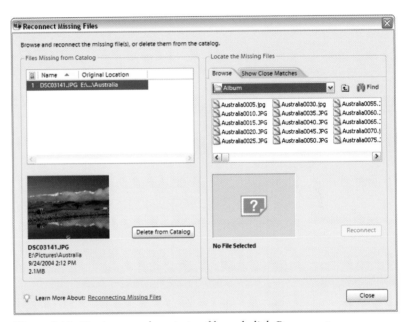

Figure 2.15: Navigate to the missing file and click Reconnect.

Managing Properties

Most image files contain additional information besides the pixels that make up the image. This information includes EXIF data generated by a digital camera, file information created by an application, filenames and file locations, file size, custom tags, and more.

    This information is referred to as *properties*, and you can view it by choosing Window ➢ Properties from the Organizer menu bar or by clicking the Properties icon at the bottom of the Organizer window (⊞). Figure 2.16 shows the Properties dialog box, where you can change or add such properties as captions and date and time.

    Additionally, you can add captions via the menu bar (Edit ➢ Add Caption) or, if the Details button at the bottom of the Photo Well is selected, by double-clicking a thumbnail in the Photo Well and typing the caption you want in the caption field at the bottom of the image window. Click the "Click here to add caption" box to reveal the caption field. Select an image or a group of images and press Ctrl+Shift+T to bring up a caption window. Captions can be added to multiple images and used for locating them later (Find ➢ By Caption or Note). You can also add audio notes to a photo by clicking the Audio icon (◀») located next to the caption field. (Your computer must be appropriately configured to use the Audio feature.)

Figure 2.16: The Properties dialog box

Adding and Deleting Tags

The more unique the information that is associated with an image file, the easier it is to find the image later when it is buried in a stack of thousands of other image files. I already mentioned how easy it is to sort and organize a catalog of images by date, filename, or folder location. By adding customized tags, it's even easier.

Figure 2.17 shows the Tags tab found in the Organize Bin. What you see are the standard preloaded tags that are included by default. You can create your own tags or Tags categories at any time by clicking the New icon at the top of the tab. (You can delete tags or Tags categories by clicking the Trash icon (), or edit tags by clicking the Pencil icon (✏).

Figure 2.17: The Tags tab with categories and subcategories. You can create your own categories as well.

Adding tags to image files is super easy. Simply click and drag the tag from the Organize Bin on top of the image you wish to tag. A tag icon appears and remains associated with the thumbnail. To apply a tag to multiple images, Shift+click to select the images, and then click and drag the tag from the Organize Bin on top of any of them. You can also add a tag by right-clicking a thumbnail and choosing Attach Tag (or Attach Tag to Selected Items if multiple thumbnails are selected).

You can assign as many tags as you wish to a single image. To remove a tag from an image file, select the file in the Photo Well, right-click the thumbnail, and choose Remove Tag from Select Items from the pop-up menu. Do not use the Delete key unless you want to remove the image file from the catalog or delete the file from your hard disk.

If you see a tag with a question mark () on it, it means that the tag has not been assigned to any images.

Here's an example of how flexible the Organizer is. I just imported several images from my camera card. I then created a new tag for them but in my haste, I clicked the Back to All Photos button before applying the tag. I then switched to the Import Batch view and quickly located the images. I could tell which batch it was, since the batches are arranged by the date on which they were imported. How convenient for me in my current dilemma! I selected them all and dragged and dropped the new tag on one of the images.

Note: If you have several tags selected and want to switch to another tag by itself, just double-click the one you want to select.

Using Face Tags

This feature lets you search through a selection of images for faces. It's best to make a modest selection of images rather than let the Organizer search through a very large number of them. Here's the process:

1. Select a number of images in the Photo Well.
2. Select the Tags tab on the right and click the Find Faces for Tagging icon (🐾).
3. When the Face Tagging window appears, select those images that you are interested in by Ctrl+clicking or Shift+clicking.
4. Drag a tag from the Tag palette and drop it on any of the selected images to tag them. At this point, the window may go blank. If it does, click the Show Already Tagged Faces check box. The images will reappear.
5. Click the Done button at the lower right.
6. Select the tag you used in step 4 to see the recently tagged "face" images.

The face tagging is not extremely accurate, and the program can seem to grind to a halt occasionally. When this happens, click the Done button and try again with another or smaller selection.

Searching for Tags and Other Properties

You can search for specific images in many ways. In the Find menu, you can search by Date, Caption, Filename, History, Media Type, or even items with audio attachments (select the By Media Type choice). The easiest way to search is via the Find bar at the top of the Photo Well (see Figure 2.18) or, if you have applied tags, via the Tags tab.

🔍 Find: Drag tags, collections, photos, videos, and creations here to search

Figure 2.18: Search criteria can be dragged and dropped into the Find bar.

To use the Find bar, simply drag a thumbnail of an image containing the criteria you are looking for (for example, color) to the Find bar. You can also drag tags from the Tags tab into the Find bar and search that way. To search by tags, simply double-click the tag you want to search or click the check box next to the tag. A binocular icon appears, signifying your selection, as shown in Figure 2.19. You can also search for multiple tags by selecting more than one check box. Matching items will appear in the Photo Well.

Figure 2.19: When you select the check box next to a tag, a binocular icon appears signifying your selection. You can select multiple tags.

Using Collections and Stacks

Collections and stacks provide another way to customize your image collection.

To stack a series of related images, first select more than one image by Shift+clicking the image icon. Choose Edit ➤ Stack ➤ Stack Selected Photos from the menu bar. All your selected images are combined into one icon, designated by the icon you see in Figure 2.20. To reveal the contents of the stack, right-click the image icon and choose Stack ➤ Reveal Photos in Stack from the pop-up menu. If you select Unstack Photos, all the images in the stack revert to individual thumbnails that appear in the Photo Well. If you select Flatten Stack, all the photos except the top photo in the stack are deleted from the catalog.

Figure 2.20: The icon in the upper right of the thumbnail designates this a stack of grouped images.

To create an image collection, click the Collections tab in the Organize Bin (see Figure 2.21) and select New. Collections are especially handy when you use the Organizer's Create options. For example, if you want to create a slideshow from a selection of images, place all the appropriate images into a collection. Next, place a check mark on the newly created Collection box, and then choose Slide Show after clicking the Create button. Just the images from your collection are added to the slideshow. To add additional media to the slideshow, use the Add Media button.

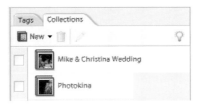

Figure 2.21: Creating a collection is another way to customize your images.

Collections differ from tags in that only one collection can be selected at a time. You can combine collections, however. With the Collections tab showing, choose a collection that you want to combine with another collection. Then select all of the thumbnails in the first collection and drag and drop the icon from the second collection and drop it on any of the selected images.

Working on and Fixing Photos

The Organizer provides some rudimentary editing tools accessible from the Edit menu. For example, you can rotate images or apply an Auto Smart Fix command.

As you will see in Chapter 3, I suggest you do most of your editing in the Editor, not the Organizer. To bring an image into the Editor, simply select it and choose either Edit ➢ Go to Quick Fix or Edit ➢ Go to Standard Edit. Either command takes you out of the Organizer and into the Editor. (You can also use the Edit button in the shortcuts bar.)

Using Version Sets

When you rotate or otherwise edit an image in the Organizer, Photoshop Elements creates a new version of your original image. You can tell that an image has been placed in a version set by the presence of a small icon in the upper-right corner (🖳). This signifies a version set. If you right-click the image and choose Version Set ➤ Reveal Photos in Version Set from the pop-up menu (shown in Figure 2.22), you can view all the versions of a particular image (see Figure 2.23). The original image is left untouched unless you right-click the image and choose Version Set ➤ Flatten Version Set. From this pop-up menu, you can also revert to the original and delete all the subsequent versions.

Figure 2.22: When you right-click an edited image, you get this pop-up menu and choices.

Figure 2.23: When you select Reveal Photos in Version Set, you can view all the versions of a particular image.

When you bring an image from the Organizer into the Editor and work on it there, versions work slightly differently. As soon as an image is brought in and worked on in the Editor, a padlock appears on the icon of the image in the Organizer (see

Figure 2.24), signifying an edit in progress. When you are finished editing an image in the Editor, save it (File ➢ Save from the Editor menu bar). This brings up the dialog box. Notice under Save Options the option to Save in Version Set with Original. If you select this check box, Photoshop Elements automatically saves both the original and the edited version. Now when you look at the thumbnail of your image in the Organizer, you'll see the familiar version icon.

Figure 2.24: When you work on an image in the Editor, this icon appears on the thumbnail of the image in the Organizer.

By the way, the Organizer saves copies of your work in predetermined locations. You can change the location in the Preferences (Edit ➢ Preferences ➢ Files).

See Figure 2.25 for a reference to the various icons that the Organizer places on images. Starting at the top left and moving clockwise is the icon for a stack, a version set, a tag, and a collection. The bottom center of the image shows the Disconnected icon. For the Tag and Collection icons to be visible, you must click Details at the bottom of the Organizer.

Figure 2.25: Icons used by the Organizer.

Backing Up and Archiving

You can use the Organizer to create backups of your image files either offline on a CD or DVD or onto another hard disk. Choose File ➢ Burn or File ➢ Backup from the Organizer menu bar. Either command brings up the dialog box.

Where Do You Go for Help?

Within Photoshop Elements, there are several ways to get help on specific subjects without ever taking your eyes off the screen. Adobe has provided some of the best screen help I've encountered, and because Photoshop Elements is such a powerful program with so many features, I encourage you to use the help whenever you have a question about a particular tool or feature.

The How To palette, located in the Editor's palette bin, is full of useful step-by-step instructions, including "how tos" that help you enhance text, correct color and brightness, design web graphics, and retouch photos.

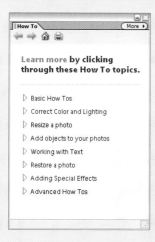

On the Help menu, you'll find Help and Photoshop Elements Tutorials, both of which are useful HTML-based systems. Help is a hyperlinked version of the printed manual, with a powerful index and search engine so you can quickly get the answer to just about any Photoshop Elements question. The tutorials walk you step-by-step through various tasks by using images that come on the program disk.

If you position your mouse over a tool or palette and hold it there, a tiny pop-up box appears, telling you the name of the tool and what keyboard shortcut (if any) to use.

You can view a comprehensive list of tips and shortcuts from the companion web site.

Your Images:
Global Solutions

It doesn't matter whether an image is taken with a low-resolution camera phone or a high-end digital camera. The truth is, most digital images benefit from software tweaking. This chapter focuses on using Photoshop Elements' Editor— and to a much lesser degree, Organizer—to make improvements that affect your entire image, including cropping; optimizing color and tonal range; removing unwanted dust, scratches, and camera noise; sharpening; and resizing. (Other, subsequent chapters concentrate on more localized problems that require you to work on a specific area or part of an image.)

3

Chapter Contents

Quick Fix or Standard Edit: Choosing an Editing Workspace

Photoshop Elements' Editor 4 offers two primary modes, or workspaces, in which to fix your image: Quick Fix and Standard Edit. Standard Edit is the default workspace that appears when you first open the Editor.

You can tell you are in Standard Edit when you see the extensive toolbar on the left of the screen and the palette bin on the right. You can access Quick Fix by clicking the Quick Fix icon found to the far right of the shortcuts bar, in the grayed-out area that looks like a folder tab. The icon is located next to the Standard Edit icon, which takes you back to that mode from Quick Fix. You can also access these two choices directly from the Organizer. The Edit icon is located in the middle of the shortcuts bar, and the pop-up menu gives you a choice of edit workspaces.

Figure 3.1 shows the Quick Fix workspace; Figure 3.2 shows the Standard Edit workspace. A new feature in version 4 is the status bar just under the image in Standard Edit. By clicking the black arrow, you can display any one of a number of items, including the document dimensions. To the left is the new zoom box where you can type a number followed by the Enter key to quickly zoom to that magnification. The zoom box is always visible, but you may have to widen your image window to see the status bar.

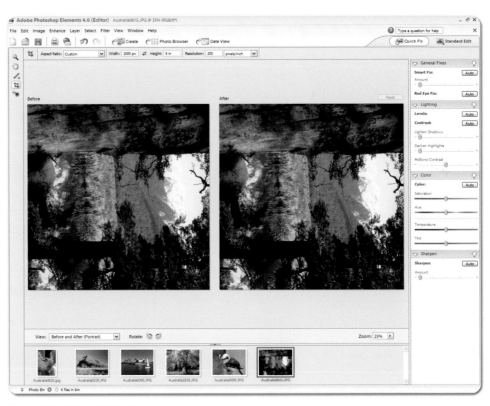

Figure 3.1: The Quick Fix workspace.

Figure 3.2: The Standard Edit workspace.

As you can see, Quick Fix is a streamlined version of the Standard Edit, with an abbreviated toolbar on the left and a Control Center on the right instead of the palette bin. Once you are in Quick Fix, many of the menu commands (such as Image Size, Rotate, and Adjust Lighting) and most of the filters are still available. Shortcuts are also available. I really like Quick Fix, and I especially like the ability to easily view before and after versions of your work side by side. What you don't see—and don't have access to—are many of the toolbar tools, including the selection tools, brush tools, shape tools, and eraser tools.

Quick Fix is ideal for many of the image enhancement tasks outlined in this chapter. However, everything you can do in Quick Fix can also be done in Standard Edit—albeit without the handy side-by-side reference. As I go through the steps of improving an image, I'll be sure to note both the Quick Fix and Standard Edit equivalents and let you know when a particular task is best done in one or the other.

I'll also briefly note when a particular editing task can be done in the Organizer. However, keep in mind that when you edit in that workspace, you won't have nearly as many options or the flexibility offered in the Editor. Organizer was originally a separate program, and its very few editing tools are for those wanting to make some quick changes or adjustments without leaving that workspace.

Deciding What Comes When

Quick Fix streamlines your workflow, and like Standard Edit, it doesn't force you into any one way of doing things. When it comes to fixing a typical digital image, however, some tasks are best done before others.

Here is an order I suggest you follow when working on images:

1. Save a copy of your image in the Photoshop file format (File ≻ Save As). Be sure to rename your file to differentiate it from the original. Sometimes a different extension is all that's needed.

2. Rotate the image if it is in the wrong orientation.

3. Use the Smart Fix command. If that doesn't work satisfactorily, use Auto Levels. For even more tonal control, use Levels. (I'll get into the specifics of how to do this shortly.)

4. Apply the Red Eye Removal tool if necessary.

5. Use the Reduce Noise filter to reduce digital-camera–specific noise (Filter ≻ Noise ≻ Reduce Noise).

   (If you are working in Quick Fix, from this point on you'll need to leave and go to Standard Edit.)

6. Use the Clone Stamp tool (🔖) or Spot Healing Brush (✏️) to remove unwanted dust, scratches, and other kinds of flaws.

7. Use File ≻ Save to save the changes to your image.

8. Use the Crop tool (🔲) to crop an image to its essential elements.

9. Resize the image to meet the specific needs of its final destination, be it the Web, a high-resolution inkjet printer, a printed document, or an e-mail attachment.

10. Use the Unsharp Mask filter to sharpen images that were shot out of focus or that look particularly soft for some reason, and to optimize the image for printing.

11. Use File ≻ Save As to save another version of the image. Be sure to rename your file to differentiate it from the copy you saved before resizing, and then select an appropriate file format (JPEG, PSD, TIFF, and so on).

At this point, if you follow my suggestions, you'll have three versions of your image—the original, an "optimized" image, and, finally, an optimized, cropped, resized, and sharpened image. You can vary the order of these tasks slightly. However, whatever order you follow, always keep resizing and sharpening for last. Throughout this chapter, I'll give you exact details about how to perform these tasks.

Note: When I open a digital image, I examine it and make notes about how to improve it. Depending on the inherent size of the image, I do this at 100 percent, 50 percent, or 25 percent. Using other view options, such as 66.7 percent or 33.3 percent, distorts the image on the monitor (↪ "Viewing and Navigation Tools" in Chapter 1).

Setting Proper Orientation

It's difficult and unnecessary to work on an image that is not properly oriented. Look back at the image in Figure 3.1. I shot the photo while in New Zealand and held the camera in the portrait, or vertical, orientation to capture both the water and sky. This is how the image appeared when I first brought it into Photoshop Elements; obviously, it needed rotating before I could move on to other tasks.

To change the orientation of your image, click the Rotate Photo 90 Degrees Counterclockwise icon located at the bottom of the Quick Fix window. Both the Before and After views rotate. If you don't get it right the first time, continue to rotate the image until it's correct.

> **Note:** If your image contains multiple layers, only the selected layers are affected by Quick Fix commands. The exception is the Quick Fix rotate command, which rotates all layers. Also, if you have an active selection, only the selected areas are affected by Quick Fix commands.

You can also rotate an image from the main menu bar regardless of whether you are in Standard Edit or Quick Fix (Image ➤ Rotate). But do beware: If you start with a JPEG file, rotate the image, and then save the rotated version in the JPEG file format, the saved image can become slightly degraded. Although the effect is minimal, it is cumulative—the more times you open, change, and close a JPEG file, the more you'll degrade the image (another reason to leave your original image intact and always do a File ➤ Save As of your edited work). This is not an issue if you save your file as a PSD or TIFF or other lossless file format.

What Do You Do When You Mess Up?

It's comforting to know that when you are working within Photoshop Elements, it's difficult to permanently damage a digital image. There is hardly a mistake you can make that can't be fixed by using the Undo History palette or the Undo command. Even if you accidentally save your work, as long as you haven't closed the file you can revert to a previous version. Here are your choices if—and when—you mess up:

The simplest way to undo an action you've just made is to click the Undo button ( ) in the shortcuts bar or use the keyboard shortcut Ctrl+Z. This button is connected to the Undo History palette, and each time you click it, you move backward through the various recorded states in the Undo History palette (which you can display by choosing Window ➤ Undo History). You can continue stepping backward this way until you reach the beginning of the recorded states in the Undo History palette. To redo the operation, click the Redo button ( ) in the shortcuts bar or use the keyboard shortcut Ctrl+Y (You can customize the keyboard command by choosing Edit ➤ Preferences ➤ General.)

You can also go directly to the Undo History palette to correct mistakes. By default, the Undo History palette records 50 states, or changes, to your image. You can increase this number in the Preferences ("Setting Preferences" in Chapter 1). States are added to the palette from the top down, with the most recent state at the bottom. The name of the tool or command you used is included. To undo a mistake, simply select a state above the one you want to redo, and the Undo History palette reverts your image to that state.

When using almost any tool, it's important to use small steps (release the mouse frequently); that way, you will need to undo only a small amount of work.

As a last recourse, you can always revert to the last saved version. To do this, choose Edit ➤ Revert. If you decide this isn't what you want, you can always undo Revert in the Undo History palette.

Continued on next page

Making Dull Images Shine

Look at the image in Figure 3.3. It's a nicely composed scene, but something is wrong. It looks "flat" and suffers from a poor distribution of tonal values and poor color saturation. The hang glider blends into the sky without strong distinction. In the case of this photo—taken with a digital camera—it's a matter of a wrong exposure. My auto-exposure exposed for the sky and not for the hang glider. Sometimes the quality of light will make a digital image look flat—as if it were shot through fog or haze, whether it was actually shot that way or not.

Figure 3.3: Before applying Smart Fix.

I use one of three methods to improve images that suffer from this "dull" syndrome: Smart Fix, Auto Levels, or Levels. All three methods are available in Quick Fix or Standard Edit.

If you prefer to remain in the Organizer, you can try using Edit ➢ Auto Smart Fix from the Organizer menu bar, or Ctrl+Alt+M. If you don't get satisfying results with this method—and I suspect more often than not this will be the case—switch to either Standard Edit or Quick Fix and try one of the methods outlined later in this section. (In Chapter 10, I'll explain a more powerful, yet complex way of using adjustment layers and masking to fix more problematic images.)

Calibrate Your Display

To get the most out of your digital images, you need to calibrate your monitor and make sure that when it comes to color and brightness, you are at least in the ballpark. How else will you know how much contrast or brightness to add to your carefully optimized image, or how will you know when your colors are right? If the monitor is off, there is no way to predict what the image will look like when it is printed.

If you are really into precision, it pays to spend a few hundred dollars and get a sophisticated calibration device that attaches to your monitor and physically measures the colors and brightness. These products produce a color profile that can be applied to compatible desktop printers for even more consistent results.

The following are two popular products that include a colorimeter and profiling software:

MonacoOPTIX (http://www.xritephoto.com/product/optixxr/) creates monitor profiles for LCDs or CRTs for about $250.

ColorVision ColorPlus (http://pantone.com) is a low-cost solution for around $100.

A less expensive way that requires just software and your own eyes is to use the Adobe Gamma utility that is installed with Elements. This utility walks you step-by-step through the process of calibrating your monitor. You can find Adobe Gamma by opening the Windows Control Panel.

- Set your operating system display preferences to the maximum number of colors, usually 24 or 32 bits.
- If you are using a CRT monitor, let it warm up for at least 30 minutes before performing the calibration.
- Avoid calibrating in a brightly lit room.
- Set your desktop background to a neutral/non-distracting color, preferably midtone gray.
- When adjusting the monitor to the target, it helps to blur your vision by squinting your eyes and leaning back at a distance from the screen.
- Calibrate your monitor regularly, two or three times a month. Settings inadvertently change, and monitors dim with time.

For a useful online calibration tutorial, go to **http://epaperpress.com/monitorcal/**.

Smart Fix

Figure 3.4 (left) shows what happens when I apply Smart Fix and its default settings to the hang glider shot. Smart Fix adjusts for lighting, color, and contrast all at once and can be quite effective for some images but not at all for others.

Figure 3.4: Smart Fix applied at default settings (left). Smart Fix boosted about 130 percent (right).

To apply Smart Fix, use one of these methods:

- In Quick Fix mode, click the Auto button in the Smart Fix section located in the upper right of the Control Center. If you aren't satisfied with the results, click the Reset button located at the top of the After version of your image, or use the keyboard command Ctrl+Z.

- In Standard Edit mode, choose Smart Fix from the Enhance menu (Enhance ➤ Auto Smart Fix).

In this example, there is improvement. But I can do better with Smart Fix by increasing the amount of correction:

- In Quick Fix mode, boost the strength of Smart Fix via the slider located in the Smart Fix section.

- In Standard Edit mode, use the Enhance menu (Enhance ➤ Adjust Smart Fix). In the dialog box, just move the slider over until you get the results you want, or type in a percentage from 0–200 percent. If you select Auto, the fix amount automatically adjusts to 100 percent.

Figure 3.4 (right) shows what happens when I slide the Smart Fix setting in Quick Fix by about 130 percent. Much better. (Each hash mark on the slider is equivalent to 50 percent.) After you determine the proper amount of correction by using the slider, click the Commit button (✓) located at the top of the Smart Fix section, just above the Auto button. If you can't find an adjustment that works, click the Cancel button (⊘). The Commit and Cancel icons appear only after you adjust the slider amount. They are not available when you use the Auto option. If you select any of the other options in the Control Center, your Smart Fix adjustment is automatically committed. Note that the Reset button found above the After view is dimmed until you either Commit or Cancel the Smart Fix adjustment.

Auto Levels

Sometimes, regardless of how much you increase the strength, Smart Fix doesn't do the job. Look at Figure 3.5. I tried using Smart Fix, but it was way off. Instead, I'll try another method—Auto Levels.

Auto Levels finds the darkest and lightest pixels of an image and then remaps the intermediate pixels proportionately. Color casts may be removed or introduced because Auto Levels adjusts the red, green, and blue channels individually.

Figure 3.5: Smart Fix didn't work on this image.

In Standard Edit, you apply Auto Levels via the menu bar (Enhance ➤ Auto Levels) or via the keyboard (Shift+Ctrl+L). In Quick Fix, in the Lighting group in the Control Center, click Auto next to Levels.

That's what I did to this shot, and you can see in Figure 3.6 that it worked. Figure 3.7 shows the image's histogram before and after Auto Levels. Notice that the fixed shot has a much better distribution of tonal values.

Figure 3.6: After Auto Levels.

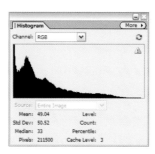

Figure 3.7: The image's histogram before Auto Levels (left): a narrow distribution of tonal values. After Auto Levels (right): a wider distribution of tonal values.

Auto Contrast, by the way—found just under Auto Levels in the Enhance menu and in Quick Fix under Lighting—isn't nearly as useful for color images. It adjusts the overall contrast and mixture of colors, but it does not adjust each color channel (red, green, and blue) individually. I rarely use Auto Contrast, and when I do, it's mostly for grayscale images.

The Lighten Shadows, Darken Highlights, and Midtone Contrast commands found in the Quick Fix Control Center are basically the same commands you get when you choose Enhance ➤ Adjust Lighting ➤ Shadows/Highlights from the main menu bar. These controls are very useful when you want to correct images with a strong backlight and a dark foreground, or vice versa. I'll use these commands later, in Chapters 4, 5, and 6. (When you adjust the Lighten Shadows, Darken Highlights, and Midtone Contrast sliders, Commit and Cancel icons appear next the word Lighting. Select Commit when you are satisfied with the image. Select Cancel if you are not. Until you select either the Commit or Cancel icon, the Reset button located above the After version of your image is dimmed and inoperable.)

More Control: Levels

The Auto Levels command doesn't always work satisfactorily either. The bag on the left in Figure 3.8, shot with a digital camera for a commercial website, lacks color intensity and contrast. But applying Auto Levels makes it look worse. At times like this, I turn to the Levels controls found in the menu bar under Enhance ➤ Adjust Lighting ➤ Levels. (You also have access to Levels from Quick Fix.) The truth is, I probably use Levels more than any other single Photoshop Elements control. It enables me to manually adjust the intensity of my shadow, midtone, or highlight areas. Not only does it give me sophisticated control over the look of my digital images, it is intuitive and relatively easy to use.

Figure 3.8: The original image (left) lacks color intensity and contrast. Auto Levels didn't help (right).

Here is how I used Levels to make the bag look more attractive and saleable:

1. I chose Enhance ➢ Adjust Lighting ➢ Levels. This opened the dialog box shown in Figure 3.9.

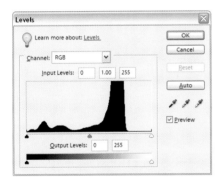

Figure 3.9: Levels graphically shows the distribution of tonal values and provides a means to individually adjust shadows, midtones, or highlights.

2. Looking at the Levels histogram, I saw the problem. Most of the values were to the left, toward the shadow areas. I needed to spread the values across the spectrum and increase the contrast. To do this, I dragged the Input Levels highlights slider (the white triangle at the lower-right corner of the histogram) to the left, toward the edge of the tall black mound. As I did this, I saw the whites, or highlights, in my actual image lighten and the overall contrast increase. (Be sure you have selected the Preview check box in the Levels dialog box. With this option selected, any changes you make in the Levels dialog box are shown in the actual image.)

3. Next, I adjusted the midtones by dragging the Input Levels gray triangle (found in the middle of the bottom edge of the histogram) to the right. This darkened and intensified the midtones. The numbers in the three boxes above the histogram represent numerically, in order, shadows, midtones, and highlight areas. As you move the triangle sliders, you see these values change to reflect the new values. You can also enter numeric values into these boxes, but it's a lot easier to manually slide the sliders.

4. At various points in the process, I found it useful to carefully examine the effects of my changes on detailed parts of the image. For example, when I adjusted the midtones, I wanted to make sure I didn't lose any details in the gold embroidery. Even though the Levels dialog box was open, I could still use my navigation keyboard commands to magnify and scroll around the image. (This works only in Standard Edit, not in Quick Fix.)

5. The shadow areas (represented in the left side of the histogram) looked fine, but I went ahead and moved the shadows slider (the black triangle) anyway. In Figure 3.10, you can see how I adjusted the Levels so that the shadow areas became too dark. At this point I could have slid the black triangle back to its original position, but I decided to start over completely and reset the image to its original state. To do this, click the Reset button in the Levels dialog box.

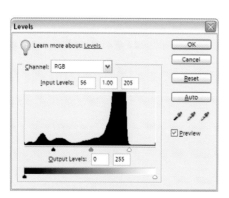

Figure 3.10: Changes made in the Levels dialog box (left) are reflected in the image window (right). In this case, sliding the shadow triangle to the right made the dark areas too dark.

6. I went back and adjusted my highlights and midtones and left the shadows alone. When I was finished, I clicked OK (see Figure 3.11).

Figure 3.11: Corrected image using Levels.

More Levels

If you click Auto in the Levels dialog box, you get the same results as you would using the Auto Levels command. This dialog box also enables you to change the brightness and contrast of the image by dragging the gray slider at the bottom. This affects all the pixels equally and does not affect the color values. You can also choose to work specifically on a red, green, or blue channel by selecting from the Channel drop-down menu at the top of the dialog box. Unless I know one specific color is off, I work in the default composite RGB mode.

The eyedroppers found under the Auto button can also be used to adjust Levels according to a tonal priority. Select the eyedropper on the left and click directly on the area you want to be the darkest area of your image. Observe the changes as Levels forces those areas to black and adjusts the corresponding tonal values accordingly. Select the middle eyedropper and click midtone or gray areas (areas without any color—that is, white, black, or gray) and watch the effect. Select the eyedropper on the right and click on an area you want to be the white area of your image and watch the effect. You can also customize the black, gray, and white targets by double-clicking the corresponding eyedropper tool. This opens the Color Picker, where you can select colors to adjust the three tonal values. This can be useful if you want to adjust the tonal parameters of your image to match the capabilities of your printer. You can always click the Reset button to start over.

Correcting Color

A digital image can contain an unwanted color cast, perhaps because of an improper white balance setting, or a mismatch between film and ambient light, or a poor scan. You can rid a digital image of unwanted colors or make colors truer in several ways by using Photoshop Elements. The easiest way is using the Auto Color Correction command (Enhance ➢ Auto Color Correction, or Color: Auto in Quick Fix). If this doesn't work satisfactorily, and you want more control, try the Color Cast command (Enhance ➢ Adjust Color ➢ Remove Color Cast) or the Color Variations command (Enhance ➢ Adjust Color ➢ Color Variations), both of which I'll describe in this section. (You can also adjust colors individually with Levels, as described earlier.)

Auto Color Correction Command

Auto Color Correction does both independent and composite adjustments of the red, green, and blue channels. Auto Color Correction often does a better job of fixing color cast problems than Auto Levels, which does only an independent adjustment for each color channel.

Here's how to access Auto Color Correction:

- In Quick Fix, Auto Color is found in the Color group in the Control Center.
- In Standard Edit, the command is found in the Enhance menu (Enhance ➢ Auto Color Correction).

Try it, and if it doesn't work, select Undo and then move on to one of the following methods.

Removing an Unwanted Cast with One Click

Figure 3.12 shows a photograph I took of a new MRI scanner at the University of California Medical Center in San Francisco. The balance was off between daylight film (film that was color-balanced for sunlight) and ambient light, and the result was a greenish tint.

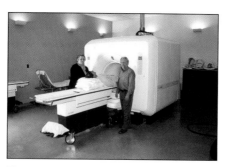

Figure 3.12: A mismatch between film sensitivity and ambient light caused the greenish tint.

It was easy to fix the image by using Photoshop Elements' Color Cast command, which analyzes color samples taken from selective parts of the image and attempts to shift the color cast to a neutral color. Here's what I did:

1. I chose Enhance ➢ Adjust Color ➢ Remove Color Cast to open the dialog box (shown on the left in Figure 3.13). You can do this from within either Standard Edit or Quick Fix.

2. Using the Eyedropper tool ( ), I clicked different areas in the image. I was specifically looking for areas that I knew should be gray, white, or black, but weren't because of the unwanted color cast. The image changed according to the color I selected. When I didn't like a result, I simply clicked another area of my image or clicked on the Reset button, and the image reverted to its original state. The Color Cast eyedropper samples only one pixel at a time, unless you change your Eyedropper Tool sample size in the option bar. To be precise about where you are sampling, you need to magnify your image.

> **Note:** Grays work better than black or white.

3. I poked around until I got what I was looking for, and then I clicked OK. The resulting image is shown on the right in Figure 3.13.

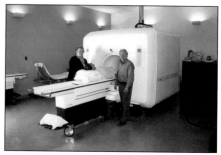

Figure 3.13: The Remove Color Cast command (left) helps remove unwanted color casts. The image with the color cast removed (right).

Shooting Digital: Use the Right Side of Your Brain

When shooting with a digital camera—or, for that matter, any camera—keep in mind that photography is a visual language dependent on light and form. It works best when it speaks to the nonverbal, intuitive side of the brain, complementing words but not necessarily competing with them. A billboard framed against a brilliant blue sky is interesting not only because of the words on the billboard but because of its shape and the way that light strikes it, and the inherent tension between something man-made and something natural. I always tell my students that the best way to learn this language is to take classes and examine images in books and see what works and what doesn't. I tell them to go to exhibitions and art galleries, and by all means, just pay attention to the way the summer light strikes a gnarled old oak tree or glances off a sleeping child's face.

Using Color Variations to Get the Color Right

While on assignment for *Wired* magazine, I used daylight film to shoot the portrait of Cold War warrior and futurist Andrew Marshall in the fluorescent-lit halls of the Pentagon. (Yeah, believe it or not, I still shoot film occasionally.) The mismatch between outdoor film and the indoor lighting caused Marshall to be bathed in an interesting combination of magenta and green light, as you can see in the left of Figure 3.14.

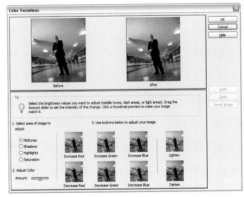

Figure 3.14: The colors in this photo (left) needed to be adjusted. The Color Variations command (right) is a good way to visually adjust color, contrast, and saturation.

To tone down the strong casts, I used Photoshop Elements' Color Variations command. The Color Variations command lets you adjust the color balance, contrast, and saturation of an image by showing you thumbnails of alternatives. Like the Color Cast command, Color Variations is most useful for images that don't require precise color adjustments.

I followed these steps:

1. I chose Enhance ➤ Adjust Color ➤ Color Variations to create the adjustment thumbnails (see on the right of Figure 3.14). Color Variations is also available while working in Quick Fix. The thumbnail in the top-left corner of the dialog box shows the original image (Before). As I made adjustments, the After thumbnail on the right changed to reflect my choices. When I went too far and wanted to revert to my original, I simply clicked the Before thumbnail or the Reset Image button. You can also click Undo to step backward through your changes. In the lower-left corner of the Color Variations dialog box, dragging the Amount slider determines the amount of each adjustment. Also, by selecting one of the Shadows, Midtones, or Highlights radio buttons before making adjustments, you can emphasize adjustment of the dark, middle, or light areas. (Midtones is the default setting.) To change the degree of hue in the image, select Saturation.

2. I didn't need to adjust the brightness of this particular image, but I could have by clicking the Lighten or Darken thumbnails on the right side of the dialog box. Instead, I adjusted the color by clicking the Decrease Green thumbnail. That took care of some of the green cast. Next, I clicked the Increase Blue thumbnail, and that took care of some of the magenta cast. Neither adjustment removed all the magenta or green cast, but I still liked the result

3. When I was finished, I clicked OK. Figure 3.15 shows the adjusted image.

Figure 3.15: The adjusted image.

Scanning Digital: Scanning Old Black-and-White Photos

When scanning old black-and-white photos, keep your scanning software set at RGB. Don't scan in grayscale even though that might seem like the logical way to go. Most old photos contain subtle colors or tints, caused by the aging process or the characteristics of the photographic paper. It's these colors that make the image look authentic.

CHAPTER 3: YOUR IMAGES: GLOBAL SOLUTIONS

Tinting Images

I like grayscale images. I really do. But sometimes they benefit from a color tint. The tint need not be overwhelming. In fact, sometimes a subtle shade of yellow or red is all it takes to give a grayscale image an added pop so that it jumps from a page.

Take, for example, the 1761 engraving from a Russian bath shown in Figure 3.16. The image was published in black-and-white in a book I wrote on bathing. It looked fine. However, when I went to place the image on my website, it was lacking. It needed to stand out more.

Figure 3.16: The original grayscale image.

This is what I did:

1. I opened the Hue/Saturation dialog box (Enhance ➢ Adjust Color ➢ Adjust Hue/Saturation), shown on the left in Figure 3.17.

> **Note:** This will not work if you are in Grayscale or Bitmap mode—it works only if you are in RGB or Indexed Color mode. If you need to, choose Image ➢ Mode ➢ RGB. (It's best to avoid Indexed Color mode unless you have a specific application that calls for it.)

2. I selected Colorize. The image was converted to the hue of the current foreground color—in this case, red.
3. I then slid the Hue and Saturation sliders to select variations of color.
4. When I got the tint I wanted, I clicked OK. The tinted image is shown in Figure 3.17.

Figure 3.17: To tint, make sure the Colorize option is selected in the Hue/Saturation dialog box (left). The tinted image (right).

You can tint an image using the Hue/Saturation dialog box (Enhance ➢ Adjust Color ➢ Adjust Hue/Saturation) from within Quick Fix as well. You may want to set a foreground color in the Editor first, since this determines the tint when you click Colorize. You can also use the Quick Fix Color group. Start by sliding the Saturation slider completely to the left. Then adjust the Tint slider to introduce a tint. You can then use the Hue slider to introduce new tints. (When you adjust the Saturation, Hue, Temperature, and Tint sliders, the Commit and Cancel icons appear next to the word Color. Select Commit when you are satisfied with the image. Select Cancel if you are not. Until you select either the Commit or Cancel icon, the Reset button located above the After version of your image is dimmed and inoperable.)

Eliminating or Diminishing Dust, Scratches, and Electronic Noise

Most digital images suffer from dust, scratches, or other marks, or electronic "noise." High JPEG compression can also cause unwanted artifacts, which show up as "blocks" and are especially obvious in areas of continuous tone such as a vast blue sky or skin, and can appear as chunky blocks of pixels. Any of these flaws can detract from the look of a digital image. With smaller prints, or when viewed on a monitor, these artifacts are not as noticeable, but as prints get larger—or if an image is magnified over 100 percent—these artifacts can be quite visible. Fortunately, Photoshop Elements offers several tools for getting rid of them.

Reduce Noise Filter

A most useful tool in the Photoshop Elements arsenal is the Reduce Noise filter. The filter can be applied from either Quick Fix or Standard Edit. Look at Figure 3.18 (left), and you'll see a shot I took in extremely low light. I managed to get the shot without using a flash by boosting my digital camera's ISO setting to 1600. I got the shot, but increasing the ISO introduced a lot of "noise" or "grain" into the image. Figure 3.18 (right) shows a magnified view and reveals the noise more clearly.

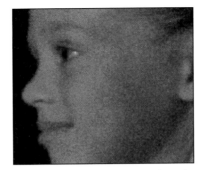

Figure 3.18: I shot this photo in low light without a flash by boosting my digital camera's ISO to 1600 (left). The magnified view shows the noise clearly (right).

To reduce the noise, I used the Reduce Noise filter (Filters ➤ Noise ➤ Reduce Noise). The filter is available in both Standard Edit and Quick Fix. Figure 3.19 shows my settings.

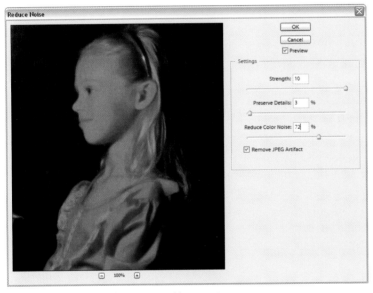

Figure 3.19: My Reduce Noise filter settings.

Settings of Strength = 10, Preserve Details = 3, and Reduce Color Noise = 72% gave much better results. To get those values, I just used trial and error until I got something that looked less "noisy" but still maintained edge detail as well. I also checked the new Remove JPEG Artifact box. JPEG artifacts usually show up as square blocks, especially in areas of solid color, and they result from lossy compression. The artifact removal feature is aimed at reducing these defects.

Spot Healing

Sometimes flaws are not global but specific. The flaws you see in Figure 3.20, for example, were caused by dust accumulating on the electronic sensor of my Nikon D100. Similar artifacts can be caused by a smudge or speck of dust on the lens. A dirty scanner glass will also produce similar results.

Figure 3.20: The flaws on this image were caused by dust on the electronic sensor.

The Spot Healing Brush ( ) is especially effective in removing these kinds of image flaws. To use this brush, you'll need to be in Standard Edit.

The Spot Healing Brush tool is found in the same location on the toolbar as the Healing Brush tool (use the keyboard command J) and is easy to use. You don't need to establish a sample area (as you need to do by Alt+clicking with the Healing Brush and Clone Stamp tools). You only need to select a brush, position your cursor, and click over an area you wish to heal. You can also click and hold the mouse and drag to "paint" over a complex shape. After you stop painting and release the mouse, the Spot Healing Brush tool goes to work. Like the Healing Brush tool, it automatically samples the areas outside the selection and blends the results with the area within the selection.

For the photo in Figure 3.20, the Spot Healing Brush worked great. This is what I did:

1. I selected the Spot Healing Brush tool from the toolbar.
2. I chose a Hard Round 30 pixels from the options bar. I chose this size because it was about 20 percent larger than the area I wished to remove. Using a brush 10–30 percent larger than the area you wish to remove is a good rule of thumb to follow. (You can play around with a soft- or hard-edged brush. In most cases, hard is the way to go, but sometimes a soft brush produces a smoother edge transition.)
3. I set the Type to Proximity Match. (Create Texture generates an obvious pattern, which isn't appropriate if you are trying to seamlessly remove a flaw.)
4. I placed my cursor over the large flaw in the middle and clicked. I then selected a smaller, Hard Round 20 pixels brush and clicked the smaller flaws sprinkled throughout the image. Done.

   The result is shown in Figure 3.21.

If you try the Spot Healing Brush on large flaws—say, over 100 pixels—you'll quickly see why it is called a "spot" healing brush. The tool seems to get confused, and produces unpredictable and often unsatisfactory results. You'll also find it works best when the area around the objects you are trying to remove is surrounded by uniform color or texture.

Figure 3.21: Flaw fixed with the Spot Healing Brush.

Combining Tools and Techniques

Sometimes you'll want to use a combination of tools to fix a particularly challenging job. For this example, I used a combination of the Dust & Scratches filter, a selection tool, and the Clone Stamp tool to fix the 50-year-old photo shown in Figure 3.22.

Figure 3.22: This 50-year-old photo is full of scratches and other artifacts of age.

In Standard Edit, here's what I did:

1. I cropped the edges of the scan by using the Crop command (↝ "Cropping to the Essential Parts" later in this chapter).
2. I applied Auto Levels to optimize the colors and tone (↝ "Making Dull Images Shine" earlier in this chapter).
3. At a magnification level of 300 percent, I noticed the sky was filled with dust, scratches, and other artifacts of age (see the left side of Figure 3.23). As I scrolled around, I saw there were also patterns caused by the scanning process. Glass against glass often causes a swirling pattern, called "Newton's rings," to form. The old transparency was sandwiched between two pieces of glass. I was tempted to use the Dust & Scratches filter (Filter ➤ Other ➤ Dust & Scratches) to clean up the entire image, but I knew this wasn't a good idea because it

would blur the image. Instead, I selected the sky by using the Lasso selection tool () and applied the filter only to this selected area. I set the Radius at 4 and the Threshold at 0 (see the right side of Figure 3.23). In general, higher Radius values effectively remove more dust and scratches but they blur other pixels in the image as well. Depending on the image, you can still remove dust and scratches but diminish the blur caused by higher Radius values by selecting higher Threshold values.

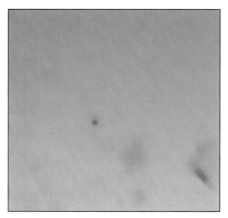

Figure 3.23: A magnification of 300 percent reveals the details of the problem (left). Applying the Dust & Scratches filter (right) to the selected background removed many of the artifacts and left the foreground area sharp.

4. Although the filter got rid of most of the smaller artifacts, the larger ones remained. To get rid of these, I selected the Clone Stamp tool (📷) from the toolbox. In the options bar, I selected the following options for the Clone Stamp tool:

    Brush: Soft Round 100 pixels

    Mode: Normal

    Opacity: 100 percent

    Aligned: selected

    Use All Layers: selected

    I positioned the cursor slightly to the side of a scratch or smudge, in an area of the sky devoid of spots. While holding the Alt key, I clicked and sampled. Then I clicked and "stamped" over a flawed area, careful not to drag and smear the pixels and cause an unnatural-looking blur.

5. After deselecting the sky (Ctrl+D), I turned to the foreground and to the woman on the road (see the left side of Figure 3.24). This area wasn't as bad as the sky, but it still needed some cleaning up. Again, I used the Clone Stamp tool to selectively rid the woman's arm and face of spots, this time using a smaller brush setting for the smaller areas.

This was a particularly difficult image, and, frankly, I had to draw the line at how much time I was going to put into it. I could have continued to use the Clone Stamp tool to make each and every detail perfect. However, I was satisfied with cleaning up the sky and most of the woman. After all, it is a historical photo, and I wanted to keep some of its authenticity. The final image is shown on the right in Figure 3.24.

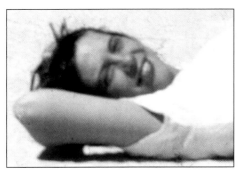

Figure 3.24: I used the Clone Stamp tool to selectively clean up the woman (left). The final image (right), after applying the Dust & Scratches filter and using the Clone Stamp tool for extensive cloning.

Converting Color Images to Black-and-White

Beyond the obvious—a black-and-white picture is often simply more beautiful than a color version—there are several reasons why you might convert a color image to black-and-white: Black-and-white images stand out in a world saturated with color images; they can be more economical to print; and, if you save an image in Photoshop Elements' Grayscale mode, they take up less file space.

The image in Figure 3.25 (left) was shot by San Francisco resident Julie Christensen for a local newspaper. The newspaper prints only black-and-white photos, and Julie gave me a color print to scan and convert.

I scanned the print in color and converted it to black-and-white simply by choosing Enhance ➤ Adjust Color ➤ Remove Color (see the right-hand image in Figure 3.25). This simple command converted the colors in the image to gray values, assigning equal red, green, and blue values to each pixel in the RGB image. The lightness value of each pixel did not change, and, because the image remained in RGB mode, the file size didn't change either.

Figure 3.25: The original image (left). Quickly convert to black-and-white (right) by choosing Enhance ➤ Adjust Color ➤ Remove Color. (Photo by Julie Christensen)

If you want to keep your file size down, I suggest you convert an image to black-and-white by simply changing modes from RGB to Grayscale (Image ➢ Mode ➢ Grayscale). If you use this method, you won't have access to many Photoshop Elements filters and effects, which work only in RGB mode. But because grayscale images are only 8 bits per pixel, versus 24 bits per pixel, your file size will be about 66 percent smaller.

Cropping to the Essential Parts

Cropping is one of the most important ways to improve your digital image. Not only does cropping strengthen the composition of an image, it also reduces the overall size with no degradation in quality. In Photoshop Elements, using the Crop tool or Crop command is one of the easiest things you can do.

This is a good time to emphasize the value of working on a copy of your original digital image. I can't tell you how many times I've cropped an image to what I thought was an optimal composition but then later decided I needed more sky or more foreground. I would have been in trouble if I didn't have the original to go back to.

In Figure 3.26 you'll see how with a little cropping, I emphasized the child and her day care provider, and made a more compelling image.

Figure 3.26: Before cropping, the image is unnecessarily large and not as effective. The shaded area outside the bounding box denotes the area that will be cropped.

This is what I did:

1. I selected the Crop tool (▯). In Quick Fix—shown here—it's located to the far left of the window. In Standard Edit, it's in the toolbox.

2. I clicked and dragged over the part of the image I wanted to keep—in this case, the child and day care provider. When I released the mouse button, the crop marquee appeared as a bounding box with handles at the corners and sides.

3. The area to be cropped appears gray by default, which makes it easier to visualize how my image will look after it is cropped.

> **Note:** The Crop tool's default shield color, gray—or more precisely, black at 75 percent opacity—is fine for most images. However, if you are working with images that contain large dark expanses, the gray shield may not be visible. In such cases, you can choose a lighter color and opacity in the Display & Cursors preferences panel.

4. I then adjusted the size of the crop marquee by dragging the corner handle. You can move the marquee to another position by clicking inside the bounding box and dragging. To rotate the marquee, just position the pointer outside the bounding box—the pointer turns into a curved arrow—and drag. You can constrain the proportions by holding down the Shift key as you drag a corner handle. If you hold the Ctrl key while dragging the bounding box near the edge of an image, you can avoid the "snap to edge" effect. Now when you drag, the transition will go smoothly. Holding the Alt key while dragging any handle causes the crop window to grow from the middle. If you use the Shift and Alt keys together, you can draw a symmetrical crop window from the center. You can press these either before or after you start to drag. The center is where you first clicked.

5. A new feature in Elements 4 is that you can use the options bar to change the aspect ratio Preset while cropping. Be sure to set it to No Restriction if you want to drag one of the sides.

6. After I finished, I clicked the Commit side of the button ( ) just under the crop marquee. I could have instead double-clicked inside the crop marquee, or selected a different tool, or pressed Enter/Return. If I had decided not to crop, I could have clicked the Cancel side of the button ( ) or pressed the Esc key.

In Standard Edit, I also could have cropped this image by using the Crop command on the Image menu. In that case, I would have had to do the following:

1. Select the part of the image I wanted to keep by using any of the marquee selection tools ("Selection Tools" in Chapter 1). Keep in mind that regardless of the shape of your selection, the final cropped shape will always be rectangular, based on the outermost parameter of the selection.

2. Choose Image ➢ Crop from the menu bar.

> **Note:** Remember to back up your images before you get too adventurous with the Crop tool, or make sure you are working on a copy of your image.

At times you'll want to crop to a specific resolution and size. Figure 3.27 (top) shows a series of thumbnail shots that I created for Newsweek.com. I started with literally hundreds of screen-sized images, all of which required a smaller, thumbnail version to be used as a navigation device. The job was so big that any extra steps added unwanted time to the process. Instead of cropping and then resizing each cropped image, I simply put the required size and resolution values of the thumbnail version into the Width Height or Resolution text boxes in the options bar. The options bar is shown in Figure 3.27 (bottom). I then followed the preceding steps that were used in the day care example. After I finished making my cropping selection, I clicked Commit (✓⊘) and ended up with exactly the size and resolution I needed—in this case, 30×30 pixels at 72 dots per inch (dpi).

Figure 3.27: The Crop tool can be set to crop to a specific size and resolution (top). (Photos by Peter Turnley, with permission from Newsweek, Inc.) The Crop tool options bar (bottom).

Although this procedure saved time, there was a tradeoff in quality. By resizing so radically in one jump, I degraded the final image more than I would have if I had taken it down slowly in increments of, say, 50 percent.

There may be times when you want to crop an image and have the result be a specific resolution as well as a specific size. When you crop, you not only can specify the dimension of the cropped image, you can specify the resulting image resolution. This allows you to crop and resample in a single step if you choose to. For example, assume you are starting with a typical five-megapixel image and want to crop a small portion of it to an 8×10. The result will be an 8×10 image at some very low resolution, too low for printing. Using the Resolution box, you can have the resulting image have a specific resolution. Here's how to do this:

1. Assume that you want to end up with an image that will print an 8×10 at 200 pixels per inch. (200 to 300 pixels per inch is a good range for most inkjet printers.) Also, assume that the image is in the landscape orientation. If not, reverse the Width and Height numbers in step 2.

2. Select the Crop tool and enter **10 in** in the Width box and **8 in** in the Height box and **200 pixels/inch** in the Resolution box. The *in* represents inches.

3. Drag the Crop tool to select the area that you want to keep and click Commit or press the Enter key.

4. The resulting image will be 10 inches $\times$ 8 inches pixels with a resolution of 200 pixels per inch. This can be checked by selecting Image ➤ Resize ➤ Image Size. You can also check the resolution in the status bar below the image to see the final results. Click the black arrow to the right of the bar to select Document Dimensions.

Remember, however, when you crop and resample like this, you may be enlarging a portion of the image to such an extent that a print of it will be pixilated. Examine the image before printing.

Knowing Your File Size

Just as you wouldn't lift something without knowing its weight for fear of injuring your back, you shouldn't begin working on a digital image without knowing its pixel dimensions. Why? The larger the image, the more the pixels, and the more "processing" power it takes to do even the simplest tasks.

How do you determine file size?

Choose Window ➤ Info from the menu bar. Look at the bottom of the Info window. Click the More button and choose Palette Options. Make sure there is a check mark in the Document Sizes box. The number to the left is the approximate size of the saved, flattened file in the Photoshop format. The number next to it is the file's approximate size, including layers. If an image contains only one layer, the two numbers will be the same. (The same information shown in the Info palette is available in the status bar below the image.)

These numbers are useful to know when working on an image within Photoshop Elements. However, the numbers aren't representative of the file size of the image if it is saved in other file formats such as JPEG or GIF. For that, you'll have to either leave the program and check the file size where it's stored, or go to the Organizer, select the image in question, and then choose Window ➤ Properties. You can also use Photoshop Elements' Save for Web plug-in and check the file size in the lower-left corner. Finally, just click File ➤ Open from the menu bar and in the resulting dialog box, select the image in question and get the file size.

Note: ↩ Globally resizing an image to match the needs of a particular print size is explained in Chapter 11.

Sharpening

If you have a digital image that appears soft or blurry, Photoshop Elements gives you several options for sharpening it. The Sharpen filter globally increases the contrast of adjacent pixels, whereas the Sharpen Edges filter sharpens only the areas of a major brightness change and leaves smooth areas untouched. The toolbox also has a Sharpen tool, which sharpens specific areas of an image. Quick Fix's Sharpen command has an auto-sharpen feature plus amount controls.

But the tool I consistently use is the Unsharp Mask filter, which can be accessed from either Standard Edit or Quick Fix. This filter is based on a traditional film compositing technique that creates a blurred negative version of the image. It then averages this copy with the original, and through three controls—Amount (percentage), Threshold, and Radius—gives you precise control over the amount of sharpening and the way the sharpening is applied.

Note: Quick Fix's Sharpen command uses the Unsharp Mask filter, but without Threshold and Radius controls. When you adjust the Sharpen Amount slider, Commit and Cancel icons appear. Select Commit when you are satisfied with the amount of sharpening. Select Cancel if you are not. Until you select one of these icons, the Reset button located above the After version of your image is dimmed and inoperable.

Here's how I used the Unsharp Mask filter to improve the photo (1700 × 1680 pixels, 72 pixels/inch) shown on the left in Figure 3.28:

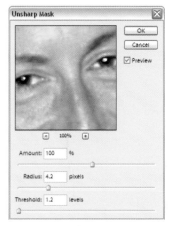

Figure 3.28: The original image (left) is lacking sharpness. The Unsharp Mask dialog box (right). Your settings will vary depending on the size and content of the image.

1. I chose Filter ➤ Sharpen ➤ Unsharp Mask and made sure the Preview check box was selected.
2. I then dragged the Amount slider until it reached 100 percent.
3. I set the Threshold at 12. (Setting the Threshold slider at a higher value forces the Unsharp Mask filter to leave the flesh tones, or other areas containing contiguous pixels of similar tonal values, relatively alone. Leaving the Threshold set at 0 forces the filter to sharpen all the pixels in the image equally and may introduce unwanted artifacts in flat-colored areas such as the skin.)
4. I then slid the Radius slider until I was visually happy with the amount of sharpening. In the case of this image, a value of 4.2 was just about right.

Note: If the Preview check box is selected, you can see the effects of the Unsharp Mask on the image in the document window. Selecting and deselecting the Preview option gives you a way to toggle back and forth between a sharpened and unsharpened version of your image. You can also view the effect of the Unsharp Mask in the dialog box's small preview window. If you click the image in the preview window, you'll see how the image looks without the effect of the Unsharp Mask. In the preview window, you can also drag to see different parts of the image and click the plus sign (+) or the minus sign (−) to zoom in or out. To see a particular spot in your image in the preview, just click it in the image window. You may have to move the Unsharp Mask window out of the way to do this.

5. I clicked OK. Figure 3.29 shows the resulting image.

Figure 3.29: Image sharpened with the Unsharp Mask filter.

The values that you use for your image will vary depending on such factors as the image's content, size, and final destination. For an average-sized image that contains a lot of detail—say an architectural shot at 1600 × 1800 pixels—try setting your percentage at 150 percent and your Radius at 2. For these kinds of images, I generally leave the Threshold setting at 0, which forces the Unsharp Mask filter to sharpen all the pixels equally.

For an image of the same size that contains expanses of color and tone, such as a face, I recommend setting your Amount at 100 percent, your Radius between 0.5 and 1, and your Threshold between 2 and 15. Playing with your Threshold setting helps you avoid introducing noise in the flat areas of color. Increase these numbers if you are working with larger images. Decrease them for smaller images.

Choosing a File Format

Before you begin optimizing your digital images for the Web, for printing, or for other electronic presentations created using applications such as PowerPoint, you'll need to decide on a file format. Photoshop Elements, not surprisingly, offers many choices of file formats, available when you choose File ➤ Save or File ➤ Save As from the menu bar in the Editor.

You can also save files in different formats via the Organizer workspace by choosing File ➤ Export to Computer from the Organizer menu bar. Be sure to select your images first, or the Organizer will attempt to export all of your images. Here you have fewer file type options, but in return, there is a convenient option for choosing a photo size. In Figure 3.30, I chose a JPEG file with a 1024 × 768 pixel size of medium quality. By selecting multiple images in the Organizer or by using the Add button in the lower left of the export window, you can perform this operation on multiple images.

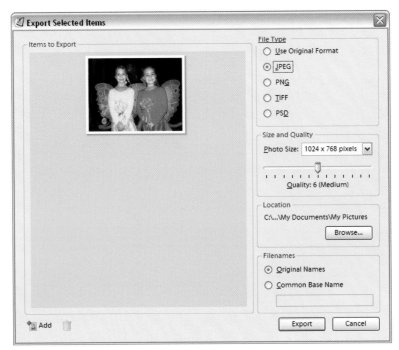

Figure 3.30: Exporting an image from the Organizer.

So which file format should you choose? Take a look at the most relevant formats and decide:

JPEG It's remarkable that the term *JPEG* has made it into the popular vernacular. "Just JPEG it to me" has become almost as common as "Send me an e-mail" or "Just Photoshop it." Its popularity is for good reason. The JPEG (Joint Photographic Experts Group) file format shrinks full-color or grayscale digital images to a manageable size. And just as Visa and MasterCard are household names in the financial world, JPEGs are universally accepted by most applications and web browsers.

The JPEG file format supports millions of colors and compresses an image much more than a GIF ever could. However, with the JPEG file format, you don't have precise control over the individual colors, and because data is actually thrown away (this is known as *lossy compression*), there is some reduction in quality. The loss of quality is especially noticeable in images that contain a lot of detail. That's why the JPEG format is generally not used on images that contain type or where precise detail is critical.

GIF The GIF (Graphics Interchange Format) file format supports only up to 256 colors. It can simulate more colors through a process called *dithering*, but this often results in a grainy or rough-looking image. Most digital images consist of millions of colors, so you can see right away that GIF is not necessarily the best choice for a photograph or continuous-tone image. On the other hand, GIF gives you precise control over which colors you choose to use. This can be important, for example, if your image is a graphic containing large expanses of a few colors that you want to blend seamlessly into an HTML-designated background color. It's also possible with the GIF file format to define selected areas as transparent, which can make an irregularly shaped graphic or image appear to float without a rectangular border on a web page. Finally, you can use the GIF file format to create simple animations. ☞ "Creating Animation with GIFs" later in this chapter.

TIFF TIFF (Tagged Image File Format) isn't supported by web browsers, so it's not a viable format for the Web. However, the TIFF format is capable of saving millions of colors and is supported by most presentation and slideshow applications. TIFF is cross-platform, which means you can view it on both Mac and Windows computers. It is also a *lossless* format, which means no data is lost or pixels altered when you save your image file. File size is primarily controlled by resizing your image, but some lossless compression is also possible. In terms of capabilities, there really isn't that much difference between the TIFF and PSD file format. In fact, an advanced TIFF format can even save layers.

PSD PSD is the Photoshop native file format and is mainly for use with Adobe Photoshop Elements or Adobe Photoshop. If you want to save an image with layers and/or selections intact, this is the best format. It's not a good format for e-mail attachments, web pages, or sharing, however, since the file sizes can be quite large. A PSD file can always be flattened and saved as a JPEG, for example, for these uses.

The Bottom Line

For the sake of simplicity, I'll say this:

- Use JPEG for photographic images and continuous-tone art destined for the Web or other electronic format via just about any imaginable application.
- Use GIF when you want universal support for graphics that contain type or a limited number of colors, or for those special situations when you want transparency or an animation.
- Use TIFF for applications such as Microsoft's PowerPoint, when file size isn't such a big issue and quality is.
- Use PSD as long as there is a chance that you may want to re-visit a particular layer or selection in an image.

Creating Animation with GIFs

You can create simple animations by using the GIF file format and the Save for Web plug-in. Individual animation frames are created from Photoshop Elements layers. You can open an existing GIF animation file and view each frame as a layer in Photoshop Elements. This round-trip GIF animation capability is especially handy if you want to change and edit your animation.

I'll show you how to create an animated GIF by using four frames from a video clip. It was less than 150KB, much smaller than a video and almost as effective and easily e-mailable.

This is what I did:

1. I selected File ➢ Import ➢ Frame from Video from the menu bar. This brought up the dialog box shown in Figure 3.31.

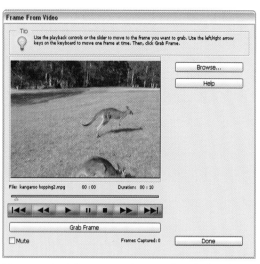

Figure 3.31: The Frame from Video dialog box. From here you can grab as many frames as you wish.

2. I selected Browse, and selected and opened the video. (Photoshop Elements reads just about anything the Microsoft Media Player supports—AVI, WMV, ASF, and MPEG, but not MOV). Using the VCR-like controls, I found a frame at the beginning of the sequence. I selected Grab Frame. Then I stepped forward to a frame in the middle of the sequence, paused, and selected Grab Frame. I repeated this two more times at different intervals. When I was finished, I selected Done.

3. Photoshop Elements numbers the frame grabs in sequence. I selected the second frame grab, copied the selection from frame grab 2, and pasted it onto frame grab 1. I selected frame 3, copied, and pasted it on frame grab 1. I selected frame grab 4, copied, and then pasted it on frame grab 1. Now I had one file with four layers, as shown in Figure 3.32. The order of the layers is important because it determines the animated sequence.

Figure 3.32: My Layers palette showing the four layers that will make up my animated GIF.

4. Next, I selected the Save for Web plug-in by choosing File ➢ Save for Web from the menu bar. I selected GIF as the file format, chose the Selective palette, chose 256 colors, and selected the Animate check box. In the Animation settings, I selected Loop so my animation would play continuously, and I experimented with the frame rate settings until I got the look I wanted. You can step frame by frame through an animation by using the Animation controls in the Save for Web dialog box. However, to view the animation in action, you need to click the Preview In check box and view your animation in a selected web browser.

My GIF animation is available for download on this book's companion website. The original Photoshop Elements file, complete with layers, is also there.

Adding a Photo Credit

By walking step-by-step through the process of creating a personalized photo credit (see Figure 3.33), you'll see how the Type tool works. It's a fairly intuitive tool to use, especially if you are familiar with word processing software. However, please take a minute to read the sidebars that accompany this otherwise simple step-by-step example. Until you've grasped some of the basic concepts behind the Type tool and used it a few times, it won't always work the way you might expect it to.

Figure 3.33: To create a photo credit, find an area with similar tones and then use a contrasting color and an easy-to-read font.

Here's how I created the photo credit text:

1. I selected the Type tool (T.) from the toolbox. If I click and hold the Type tool icon, or right-click it, four choices appear: Horizontal Type Tool, Vertical Type Tool, Horizontal Type Mask Tool, and Vertical Type Mask Tool. I chose Horizontal for this example, but the choice is not critical because I can always go back and change the orientation later in the options bar.

> **Note:** Type is fully editable as long as it remains as a type layer. If you simplify the type layer, the type becomes rasterized and has the same properties as any other bitmap element in your image. You can simplify a layer via the Layers palette pop-up menu or by selecting Layer ➢ Simplify Layer from the menu bar. Why simplify a type layer? There are certain things you can't do to a type layer, such as apply Perspective and Distort commands or use any of the filters or paint tools. I suggest that you make a copy of your type layer and simplify the copied layer. That way, you can always go back to the original type layer and make changes.

2. Before I typed, I had to choose a font and a font style, size, and color from the options bar. I also checked that the other options in the Type tool options bar

were appropriate. For example, I wanted to be sure that I didn't inadvertently select the Horizontal or Vertical Type. (Photoshop Elements 4 also offers control over the amount of space between lines of type. This is called *leading*, and most of the time the Auto setting in the pop-up menu is the way to go. The higher the leading value—measured in points—the greater the distance between the baseline of one line of type to the baseline of the next line.) Here are the settings I used:

Font: Arial. This is a sans serif type that is legible even when it's small.

Font Style: Regular. I want the type to be readable but not necessarily dominant. The other options—Bold, Italic, and Bold Italic—draw more attention to the type.

Font Size: 14pt. The size you use depends on the size of your image. As a rule of thumb, 72pt type is approximately one inch high in an image that is 72dpi. My image is 144dpi, so the pixels are packed relatively tighter, which reduces 72pt type to about half an inch. Having said this, the fact is I'm never exactly sure how big my type will look. I experimented until I get the size I want.

Font Color: Black. I chose a contrasting color to the underlying tonal values. You can change the color at any time by clicking the color swatch located in the options bar. (In earlier versions of Photoshop Elements, you couldn't change colors while typing without changing the color of the previous type.)

Anti-aliased: Selected. This smoothes the edges of the type. It also adds more colors and therefore adds file size. The increased file size is inconsequential unless your image is destined for the Web.

Choosing Fonts and Styles

You must have the bold, italic, and bold italic versions of your font loaded in your system for these options to be available. You can always choose a faux bold or faux italic from the options bar. Keep in mind that these faux fonts are only crude approximations of actual fonts and are machine-made, without considering nuances such as spacing and aesthetics.

Before adding type to your digital image, consider your choice of fonts. If you plan to use small type, say as a photo credit or caption, use a font that holds up and is still readable when small. Usually, so-called *sans serif* fonts are best for this because they are simpler and don't contain decorative flourishes, or *serifs*, at the top or bottom of a character. Two popular and commonly available sans serif fonts are Arial and Helvetica. If you are using type as a headline for a poster or flyer, the font can be either serif or sans serif as long as it is readable from a distance. Latin Wide and Copperplate are popular headline fonts. If you plan to fill your type with an image or texture, use the bold version of a heavy font such as Verdana, Myriad (both sans serif), or Georgia (serif). It's a good rule of thumb not to mix more than two fonts on a single image. If you've chosen an appropriate font, you won't need to embellish it with too much color or gaudy effects. Photoshop Elements uses the fonts installed in your system folder. The actual fonts that are available to you will vary.

3. After selecting my options, I placed my cursor on the upper-right side of the image and clicked. I chose an area consisting of light, flat tones so my black type would be easily visible. When I clicked my mouse, an insertion bar in the shape of an I-beam

appeared at the point of clicking. I then typed in my letters. The baseline of my type lined up, with the small line through the bottom of the I-beam. The I-beam also marked a point of reference for any alignment choices I made in the options bar.

4. As you can see in Figure 3.34, when my letters came to the edge of the image, they didn't automatically wrap to another line; they continued off the edge. I could have pressed the Enter key when I got to the edge of the picture, which would have created a new line, but instead I continued typing. When I was finished, I pulled the cursor away from the type until it turned into the Move tool (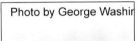), at which time I dragged the type into position. You can also move type in one-pixel increments by using the arrow keys. To move the type in 10-pixel increments, hold down the Shift key while using the arrow keys.

Photo by George Washir

Figure 3.34: Type does not wrap to the next line as it does with conventional word processing software. It continues off the edge of the image unless you press the Enter key. In this case, I just dragged the single line of type into position.

Understanding Type States

Photoshop Elements type can exist in one of three basic states: edit, committed, and simplified. When type is in the *edit* state, all you can do is edit it; you can't use other layer commands from the Layer menu. After type is *committed*, you can edit and apply just about any Photoshop Elements tool or command, including a layer effect. However, in order to use any of the painting tools or filters, you must first *simplify* the type layer.

If you have committed your type, you can quickly change the color of your type by double-clicking the *T* in the type layer in the layer palette, or by selecting the Type tool from the toolbar and the layer containing the type you wish to change and clicking the color swatch found in the options bar. Click a new color, and the type changes accordingly. You can also use either of these shortcuts: Alt+Backspace fills the type with the foreground color. Ctrl+Backspace fills it with the background color.

After type has been committed, you can drag it at any time into different positions. Just select the Move tool ( ) from the toolbox and click the type to automatically select the type layer. A bounding box appears around the selected type. Clicking outside the bounding box deselects the type. Place the pointer inside the bounding box and drag the type into position. Be sure that the Auto Select Layer and Show Bounding Box options are selected in the Move tool options bar.

How do you know which state your type is in? One way is to look at the Layers palette. If the layer thumbnail contains a *T*, the type is in either edit or committed state. If the layer thumbnail doesn't contain a *T*, it is a simplified layer. If the Cancel and Commit buttons are showing in the Type tool options bar, the type is in the edit state. If not, it has been committed. If your type has been simplified and you try to use the Type tool on it, the Type tool just creates a new type layer. You can't edit simplified type.

Moving the type automatically committed it. I could have committed it before this, however, by clicking the Commit button (✓) in the options bar. I also could have clicked the Cancel button (⊘), which would have discarded the type layer. Clicking the Cancel button discards a type layer only if the type has not been previously committed.

What do you do if you want to go back and change your type? Here's what I did to add a copyright symbol and date to the photo credit in Figure 3.36:

1. I made sure the Type tool was selected.

2. I placed the cursor over the type I wished to edit. The cursor turned into an I-beam insertion point. I placed the insertion point at the end of the word *Washington* and clicked. This automatically selected the type layer and put me back into the edit state. I then typed a copyright (©) symbol and 2004. (The copyright symbol is typed by pressing Num Lock on the numeric keypad, holding down the Alt key, and typing 0169 on the numeric keypad.) At this point, I could have selected all my type and chosen a new font or font style or even changed the color of the type in the options bar. I also could have changed the orientation from horizontal type to vertical by selecting the Text Orientation button (⊥T) from the options bar, but I didn't. (Only selected type changes if you choose a new font, size, or color. You do not need to select any type to change the orientation.)

Note: To select all the type on a type layer, select the text tool and either triple-click anywhere on the type itself, or use the keyboard shortcut Ctrl+A, or, in the Layers palette, on the type layer, double-click the *T*. Additionally, double-clicking a word selects all the letters in that word. You can select individual characters by clicking and dragging the cursor over them, or by using the Shift+arrow keys. To delete individual characters, position the insertion point in front of the character you wish to delete, click, and then press the Delete key. You can also select one or more characters and press Delete.

3. When I was finished, I moved the cursor away from the text and moved the type into position. Doing this automatically committed my new type.

The edited text is shown in Figure 3.35.

> Photo by George Washington © 2004

Figure 3.35: Edit your type by selecting the Type tool and clicking the type.

Adding a Copyright Watermark

To guard against unwanted commercial usage of an image, photo agencies and professional photographers often imprint a faint, but noticeable © symbol over an entire image. This imprint lives with the image in print or electronic form, telling the viewer not to use the image for commercial purposes without getting permission—and an unaltered version of the image—from the photographer.

Here's how to create a copyright watermark:

1. With the image open, select the Shape tool by pressing the letter U on the keyboard.

2. In the Shape tool options bar, click the Custom Shape tool icon (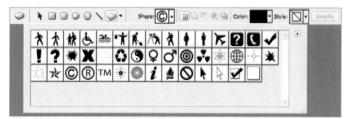). Then click the arrow next to the word *Shape* to call up the Custom Shape Picker.

3. Click the arrow at the top right of the Custom Shape Picker, and from the resulting list, select Symbols. This brings up the choices shown in Figure 3.36.

Figure 3.36: In the Shape tool options bar, I selected Custom Shape and Symbols, which displays these choices.

4. Choose the shape to create; I selected the © shape.

5. Drag across your image to define the area you'd like the shape to appear in. I held the Shift key to constrain the scale and then clicked in the upper-left corner of my image and dragged my cursor all the way to the bottom of the image, filling the screen with the © shape.

6. In the Layers palette, set the blend mode to Soft Light and opacity to 50 percent. These settings allow most of the image to show through the shape, as illustrated in Figure 3.37. You can choose other blending modes and opacities depending on how obvious you want to make the symbol.

Figure 3.37: A copyright watermark helps prevent unwanted commercial use of your image.

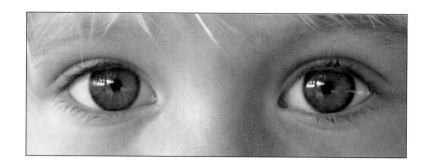

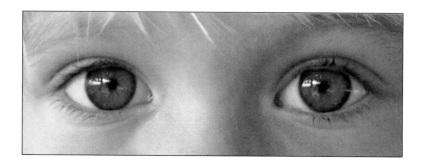

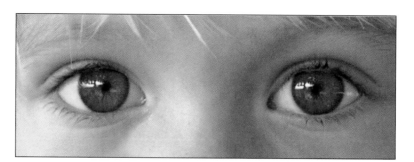

Better Faces

How many times have you seen someone look at a picture and heard him or her say, "That doesn't look like me!" You may even have said it as you stared at a picture of yourself. Sometimes the criticism is based entirely on vanity. But often the fault lies with the photograph. Blame it on the camera, the lens, the lighting— or even more likely, the photographer. With the help of Photoshop Elements—and especially with the Healing Brush tool—there are no more excuses. You can make better faces. This chapter shows you simple tips and techniques for using Photoshop Elements to intensify eyes, eliminate red eye, reduce wrinkles, and otherwise improve digital images of the human face.

4

Chapter Contents

What Comes First

Before starting to work on a face or faces, I usually begin by cropping the image to its essential parts and optimizing the tonal values (↷ "Cropping to the Essential Parts" in Chapter 3). What I do next depends on the image, the person depicted in the image, and where it is ultimately going to be shown or published.

Many times a face needs only a little tweaking to get it just right. Sometimes this means removing red eye with the Red Eye Removal tool, whitening the white part of the eyes and teeth, slightly increasing the color saturation of the eyes and lips, or selectively diminishing wrinkles with Photoshop Elements' amazing Healing Brush tool. Other relatively easy tasks include selective burning and dodging, and applying a digital fill flash.

Some faces are more challenging than others. For example, when a face is distorted because of natural or unnatural causes, I use various Transform commands or the Liquify filter to get it right. Although it is relatively easy to change the color of hair, or to lighten or darken hair, removing or adding hair requires a little more work, and for this I almost exclusively use the Clone Stamp tool. Blurring a distracting background can also improve a portrait, and for this I use a combination of selection tools and the Gaussian Blur filter.

The last things you'll ever do to a digital image are resize and sharpen it to the needs of your final destination (↷ "Resizing" and "Sharpening" sections in Chapter 3). Be sure to keep an original, full-sized version of your image for future purposes.

Note: How far do you want to go? The possibilities for improving or changing a face by using Photoshop Elements are almost unlimited. That's why I suggest you ask yourself how far you want to go and how much time you want to spend. There are no easy answers, and no hard rules to follow. The answers to these questions invariably depend on the wishes of your subject and the final destination of the image. If the picture is just for fun and the person in the picture has a good sense of humor, well, anything goes. If you are preparing an image for a corporate brochure or other serious purpose, tread lightly and make subtle changes.

Whatever you do, please keep in mind that it's a special day when the subject of your work actually likes his or her own portrait. Unless you've really messed up their face, you can chalk up any complaints to vanity and human nature!

Working the Eyes

The first thing we usually notice about someone is his or her eyes. Are they bright, dull, or shiny? Red? Bloodshot? Yellow? Sick? The eyes are the gateway to the soul, and that is where I usually start.

Eliminating Red Eye

Red eye occurs when light from an on-camera flash reflects off the blood vessels in the back of the eye, giving someone a demonic look (see Figure 4.1). Red eye is such a common problem in color images that Photoshop Elements 4 includes an easy-to-use tool devoted to fixing the problem: the Red Eye Removal tool.

Figure 4.1: Before using the Red Eye Removal tool. Note the position of the cursor in the middle of the pupil.

Here is what I did to get rid of the red eye shown in Figure 4.1:

1. I selected the Red Eye Removal tool (🔴) from the toolbar.
2. I placed my cursor—which turned into a plus sign—on the center of the pupil and clicked. Depending on the image, you need not be precise where you click. Sometimes you can even get away with clicking anywhere in the vicinity of the eye, and the tool automatically differentiates between the eye and other parts of the face and applies the appropriate red eye removal. In one instance I accidentally clicked a nose, and the red eye was removed!
3. When the red eye was removed from one eye, I turned to the other eye and repeated step 2. (The tool is smart, but not smart enough to do both eyes at once!)

Done. That's all I did to get the results for both eyes shown in Figure 4.2.

Figure 4.2: After using the Red Eye Removal tool and the one-click-per-eye method.

It's remarkable how well the one-click method worked on this image. Sometimes, however, the one-click method doesn't do the trick. There is no hard-and-fast rule to follow, but I've noticed problems with the one-click method when the edge of the red is less defined and the color spills randomly across the iris. In any case, if it doesn't work, you can use another method. You use the same tool, just a different method.

This is what I did to get rid of the red eye shown in Figure 4.3:

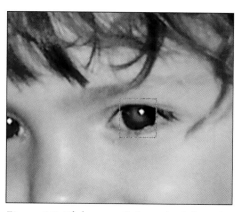

Figure 4.3: If the one-click method doesn't work satisfactorily, try defining a parameter for the Red Eye Removal tool by clicking and holding the mouse and dragging a selection around the iris.

1. I selected the Red Eye Removal tool ( ) from the toolbar.

2. I clicked and held the mouse and dragged a rectangular selection with my cursor just outside the parameter of the iris, as you can see in Figure 4.3. When I released the cursor, the tool went to work and nearly instantly gave me the results you see in Figure 4.4. Varying the size and position of the selection will affect the outcome, and once again, you may need to experiment to get it right.

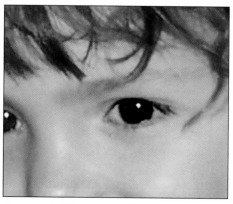

Figure 4.4: The results of clicking and holding while dragging a selection.

Although I used the Red Eye Removal tool for both the one-click and click/hold/drag methods, these two methods employ fundamentally different mathematical algorithms to do the job. You can tell they are different just by comparing the amount of time the methods take to remove red eye. The one-click method takes longer because it first identifies the eye and *then* removes the red. The click/hold/drag method is much faster because you define the work area with a selection. (There are other, more technical reasons why the methods are different, but I'll spare you the details.) I suggest you try the one-click method and if that doesn't work to your satisfaction, try the click/hold/drag method. Experiment and figure out which is best for a particular image.

Regardless of which method you use, you can fine-tune the results with two options available in the Red Eye Removal tool options bar, shown in Figure 4.5(a). Note the default setting for Pupil Size is 50 percent, and the default setting for Darken Amount is also 50 percent. Using these settings, I got the results shown in image (b). Image (c) shows what happened when I increased the Pupil Size to 100 percent and increased the Darken Amount to 100 percent: the pupil is larger, and the density of the black is increased. Image (d) shows what happened when I set the Pupil Size to 1 percent and the Darken Amount to 1 percent. I think you get the idea. Again, you'll have to experiment to find the right settings for your particular image.

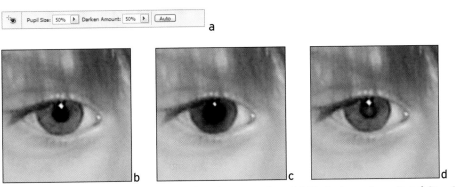

Figure 4.5: (a) The Red Eye Removal tool options bar. (b) Default settings: Pupil Size 50 percent and Darken Amount 50 percent. (c) Increasing Pupil Size and Darken Amount to 100 percent. (d) Setting both Pupil Size and Darken Amount to 1 percent.

Notice in Figure 4.5 that Elements 4 adds a button to the options bar labeled Auto. I have tried this feature on several images containing red eye and have found that it works some of the time. You might try this first since it's likely to repair both eyes at the same time. If this doesn't work, one of the two methods described in this section surely will.

In addition, Elements 4 can now remove red eye from images as they are being imported into the Organizer (↯ Chapter 2).

However, my recommendation for the best method is to use the Red Eye Removal tool—in the Editor or Quick Fix mode—and drag a rectangle around the red eye. This seems to give the most consistent results.

Eliminating Dog Eye

And you thought this chapter was only about people! *Dog eye* occurs when you use a flash to take a picture of a dog. Dog eye is similar to red eye in people, but much worse. For better night vision, dogs—like cats and many other animals—have extra cells behind the retina that act like a mirror. This mirror reflects light back, giving the rods and cones a second chance to pick up the small amount of light available at night. This is what makes cats' and dogs' eyes seem to glow in the dark. It's also what gives their eyes a hellish glow when photographed with a flash.

Recently I received an e-mail from reader John Howell who attached a picture of his dog Reuben displaying a classic case of dog eye (see Figure 4.6). He wanted to know how to fix the shot.

Figure 4.6: Dog eye can't be fixed with the Red Eye Removal tool.

Photoshop Elements' Red Eye Removal tool isn't much use for this kind of problem. No matter which method you use—one-click or click/hold/drag—the tool looks only for variations of the color red. If the variations aren't there, the tool doesn't do anything.

I suggested John try two other methods, which I'll share here.

Method 1 is the simplest way I can imagine to make Reuben appear less threatening:

1. Magnify and zoom in on one of the eyes by using the Zoom tool found in the toolbar.
2. Select the Paint Bucket tool ( ) from the toolbar.
3. Make sure the foreground color in the color swatch at the bottom of the toolbar is set to black.
4. Position the Paint Bucket tool over the blown-out highlights of one eye and click.
5. Repeat steps 1–4 for the other eye.

This fills the white area with black. It's certainly not a perfect solution, but if you zoom out or print the shot small, it doesn't look too bad, as you can see in Figure 4.7.

Figure 4.7: Using the Paint Bucket tool is the simplest solution.

Method 2 results in a more realistic-looking image, shown in Figure 4.8.

Figure 4.8: Adding a "glass" eye is more realistic.

1. Magnify and zoom in on the dog's eye by using the Zoom tool.
2. With the Magic Wand tool ( )—or the selection tool of your choice—make a selection of the blown-out areas of the eye. Slightly feather the selection 2–3 pixels (Select ➤ Feather).
3. In the Layers palette, make a new layer (Layer ➤ New ➤ Layer).
4. With the new layer active, fill your selection with black or another color (Edit ➤ Fill or use the Paint Bucket tool as described in method 1).
5. In the Styles and Effects palette located in the palette bin, select Layer Styles and Glass Buttons from the pop-up menus.
6. Choose a "glass" color. (I chose Black Glass.) If you're satisfied with black, you can stop here; the remaining few steps show you how to change the color to anything you want.
7. Flatten the layers (Layer ➤ Flatten Image).
8. Select the Color Replacement tool ( ) from the toolbar. (It shares the same spot on the toolbar with the Brush tool, which uses keyboard shortcut B; repeatedly hitting the B key cycles through the brushes.) In the options bar, choose the following options:

    Mode: Color
    Sampling: Continuous. For some images, the Once option also works fine. Background Swatch is not appropriate for this example.
    Limits: Contiguous. Discontiguous can work too if you paint carefully.
    Tolerance: 30 percent. A higher percentage replaces adjacent pixels with a broader range of color values. A lower percentage replaces only a few adjacent pixels with similar color values.
9. Select a color from the foreground color swatch at the bottom of the toolbar. (Click the foreground color swatch, and the Color Picker will open.) I chose blue.
10. Click the area you want to change and then "paint" the replacement color over it.

Figure 4.9 shows the results.

Figure 4.9: Change to any color by using the Color Replacement tool.

Whitening the Whites

Both of the methods I use to whiten the whites of the eyes use the Dodge tool. One method is slightly quicker than the other but less precise.

Here's method 1:

1. Select the Dodge tool ( ) from the toolbox; it shares the same place on the toolbar as the Sponge and Burn tools. Press the letter O on your keyboard and repeatedly hit the O key to cycle through the three tools.

2. In the options bar, select Midtones from the Range menu and 50 percent from the Exposure menu. (Remember that no one has perfectly white whites, and at 100 percent exposure, it's easy to overdo the amount of whitening. I chose 50 percent exposure because it gives me more control over the amount of dodging.)

3. Select an appropriate brush size. (To alter the image shown on the left in Figure 4.10, I chose a Soft Round 35 pixels brush, which fit nicely in the space between the eyelids and the pupils.) The brush size that works in your image will depend on the size of your image and the white space itself.

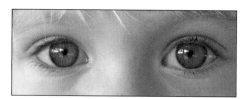 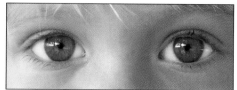

Figure 4.10: Before dodging (left). After dodging (right).

 Note: I often talk about an "appropriate" brush size. This is, of course, subjective—it's one place where I can't tell you exactly what number to input. An appropriate brush size is based on the resolution of an image and the size of the area you wish to work on.

4. Start by clicking and dragging carefully over the parts of the eye that you want to whiten. If you need a better view of the area you are working on, magnify the image by using one of the View tools. Dodge incrementally, dragging over a small area and then releasing the mouse button. By doing this, you can undo incrementally as well. If you do all your dodging in one click, the Undo command will undo all your work to the point of that first click.

5. When you achieve the look you want, stop. Remember, it's tempting to go too far and make the white perfectly white. Don't. It won't look natural. My final shot is shown on the right in Figure 4.10.

The second method I use is similar to the first one, but this time I create a selection that protects the non-white areas from the effects of the dodging. This way, the size of my brush isn't so important and I don't need to be nearly as precise when I dodge.

Here's method 2:

1. Select the Lasso selection tool (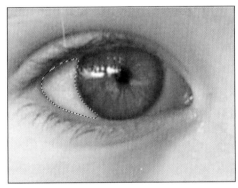) from the toolbox. In the options bar, make sure that the Anti-aliasing check box is selected. I also set the Feather option to 3 pixels. Anti-aliasing softens the color transition between most non-linear edge pixels and background pixels and smooths the jagged edges of a selection. Feathering softens the edge of the selection, but when you apply the Dodge tool, feathering also creates a smooth transition between the white and adjacent areas.

2. Carefully select one white area, as shown in Figure 4.11. Then, while holding down the Shift key, select the white area on the other side of the pupil. A plus sign appears next to the pointer. While holding down the Shift key again, select the whites in the other eye.

Figure 4.11: A selection protects the non-white areas from the effects of the Dodge tool.

Note: You can also add selections by clicking the Add to Selection icon () in the options bar.

3. Select the Dodge tool from the toolbar. This time you can choose a fairly large brush because the selection will protect the rest of the image. Then dodge incrementally, just as in the first example, until you get the effect you want.

4. To deselect the selection, use the keyboard command Ctrl+D. You can also deselect a selection by choosing Select ➢ Deselect from the menu bar or by clicking anywhere in the image outside the selected area.

Note: You can control the size of the brush by pressing the left or right bracket keys.

Enhancing the Color

It's easy to enhance the color of the eyes. I use a method similar to the one I just described, but instead of using the Dodge tool on the white areas of the eye, I use the Sponge tool to saturate the colors of the iris (see Figure 4.12).

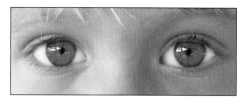

Figure 4.12: Use the Sponge tool to saturate the colors.

To create this effect, I did the following:

1. I selected the Sponge tool ( ) from the toolbox. It shares a place in the toolbar with the Burn and Dodge tools.
2. In the options bar, I selected Saturate from the Mode menu and 50 percent from the Pressure menu.
3. I then selected an appropriate brush size. For this image, I chose a Soft Round 65 pixels brush.
4. I started by clicking and dragging carefully over the parts of the eye that I wanted to enhance. I saturated incrementally, dragging over a small area and then releasing the mouse button.
5. When I got the saturation I wanted, I stopped. It's easy to go too far and make the eyes look unnatural.

If you want to be more precise, you can also make a selection as described in the preceding section and then saturate only the selection.

Changing the Color

It's easy to change the color of the eyes from, say, green to blue. Although there are other ways of doing this, I recommend a simple yet effective method using the Color Replacement tool. I outlined a similar method earlier in this chapter to change the color of a dog's eye from black to blue. Take a look at Figure 4.13.

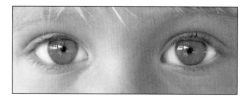

Figure 4.13: Change color by using the Color Replacement tool.

This is what I did to change the color of the eyes:

1. I selected the Color Replacement tool ( ) from the toolbar.
2. I chose a brush size from the pop-up palette in the options bar. I chose a Soft Round 75 pixels brush, but the brush you choose will depend on the specifics of your particular image.

3. I set my options in the Color Replacement tool options bar to the following:

> **Mode: Color**
>
> **Sampling: Once.** This tells Elements to only replace colors where you started to drag. It constrains the tool to only replace a few colors at a time. You may have to click and drag several times, since most eyes contain several different colors. Elements 4 now uses buttons for selecting the Sampling Mode, as shown in Figure 4.14. From left to right, the options are Continuous, Once, and Background Swatch.

Figure 4.14: New Color Replacement options bar.

> **Limits: Contiguous.** (Affects consecutively touching pixels meeting the mode, sampling, and tolerance requirements.) The Discontiguous option can work too if you paint carefully.
>
> **Tolerance: 30 percent.** A higher percentage replaces adjacent pixels with a broader range of color values. A lower percentage replaces only a few adjacent pixels with similar color values.

4. I specified a replacement color by selecting a light blue from the Color Picker. (Click the foreground color swatch found at the bottom of the toolbar; then, when the Color Picker opens, select the color of your choice.)

5. I clicked the iris. This set a "target" color. Then I dragged over the irises. The parts of the eye that matched the target color were colorized with the light blue. To sample new target colors, I simply released the mouse and clicked again on another part of the iris. If you find the color spilling over to other areas of the eye, reduce the Tolerance setting; if the color isn't flowing evenly, you may need to increase Tolerance. For some images, you may find that no matter what Tolerance setting you choose, the color still spills onto unwanted areas of the eye, for example, the eyelashes. If this happens, make a selection around the iris and then apply the Color Replacement tool.

Enlarging the Eyes

Portrait painters learned long ago that they could make their wealthy patrons happy by slightly enlarging the eyes of their female subjects. Enlarged eyes evoke youth, innocence, and receptiveness. When it's appropriate, you can easily do something similar by using the Liquify filter. The Liquify filter enables you to warp, twirl, expand, contract, shift, and reflect areas of your image. It's as if your image were turned into easily manipulated molten pixels (☞ "Liquify Filter" in Chapter 1). I used the Liquify filter to enlarge the eyes shown in Figure 4.15.

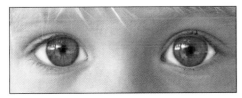

Figure 4.15: Use the Liquify filter to enlarge the eyes.

Here's what I did:

1. I chose the Liquify filter (Filter ➤ Distort ➤ Liquify). This opened the dialog box shown in Figure 4.16. Keep in mind that the Liquify filter works on the selected layer of an image. In my case, the image had only one layer, so selecting a layer wasn't an option.

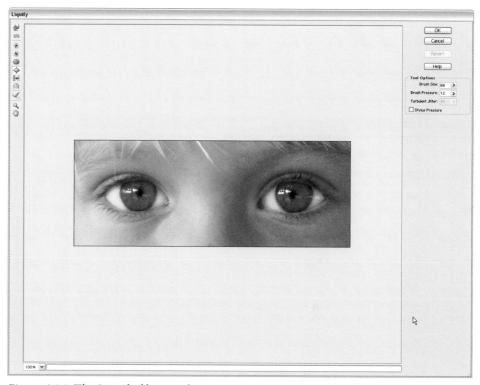

Figure 4.16: The Liquify filter work area.

2. I selected the Bloat tool (🔘) and then adjusted the brush size so the brush would fit over the entire eye. I then adjusted the brush pressure. I chose a low brush pressure so that changes occurred more slowly and it was easier to stop when I got what I wanted.

3. I placed the brush over one of the eyes and then clicked and held the mouse without moving the cursor. The Bloat tool moved pixels away from the center of the brush, effectively making the eye bigger.

Note: If you go too far, you have a few choices: You can revert to the original version by clicking Revert. You can also Alt+click the Cancel button and it turns into Reset. Or you can use the Reconstruct tool (✅) and hold down the mouse button and drag over the distorted areas.

4. When the first eye looked the way that I wanted it to, I did the same to the other eye, making sure to apply the same amount of enlarging. Then I clicked OK.

Sometimes it's enough to slightly enlarge the pupil, or the dark part of the eye. To do this, simply choose a smaller brush size and apply the Bloat tool to just that area.

Working on Lips

After the eyes, the next area I work on is the lips. Again, a lot of what I do is very subtle and yet very effective. Mostly, I slightly enhance the color of the lips by using the Sponge tool in the Saturate mode. Sometimes it's fun to change the color of the lips as well. To perform either of these tasks, I suggest you follow the step-by-step instructions used earlier in this chapter to enhance eyes (☞ "Enhancing the Color" and "Changing the Color"). Just focus on the lips instead of the eyes. If you want to imitate a Julia Roberts look, use the Liquify filter to add fullness. Here is how to produce the results shown in Figure 4.17:

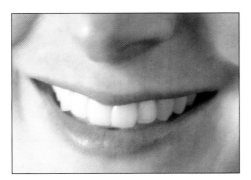 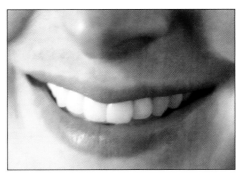

Figure 4.17: Before the Liquify filter (left). After the Liquify filter and increased saturation (right).

1. Select the mouth by using any of the selection tools.
2. Choose Filter ➢ Distort ➢ Liquify.
3. Select the Bloat tool (⬥) and choose an appropriately sized brush and a relatively low brush pressure.
4. Place the brush over the lips. Click and selectively add fullness. If you don't overdo it, the effect can look realistic. Go too far, and it's pretty outrageous!

Whitening and Fixing Teeth

People spend a lot of money making their teeth look good. After the eyes and the lips, teeth are probably the most noticed part of the face. You can do someone a big favor by removing years of coffee or tobacco stains with a few selective brush strokes. Whatever you do, don't go too far. Teeth that are perfectly white look unnatural.

To use the Dodge tool to whiten teeth, take these steps:

1. Select the Dodge tool (🔍) from the toolbox.
2. In the options bar, select Midtones from the Range menu and 50 percent from the Exposure menu.
3. Select an appropriate brush size.
4. Click and drag carefully over the parts of the teeth that you want to whiten. Magnify your image if needed. Dodge incrementally, dragging over a small area and then releasing the mouse button.
5. Stop when you get the look you want. You've gone too far if the teeth look unnatural or if you lose the texture of the teeth. Figure 4.18 shows before and after shots.

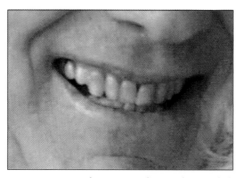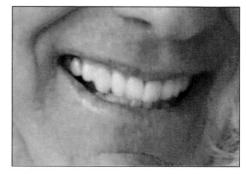

Figure 4.18: Before using the Dodge tool (left). After using the Dodge tool (right).

To use the Brush tool to whiten teeth, take these steps:

1. Choose a color to paint with by selecting the Eyedropper tool ( ) from the toolbar. Click the lightest section of a tooth. Now click the foreground color swatch ( ) in the toolbar, which now contains your sampled color. This opens the Color Picker. Select a color that is brighter than the sampled color. On the left in Figure 4.19, you can see the sampled color shown in a small circle. The larger circle shown above and to the left of the sampled color is the mouse cursor, which you can move around to select a lighter color. When you click the cursor on a color, that color appears in the upper half of the color rectangle to the right of the color slider, with the sampled color appearing in the lower half of the rectangle.

2. Select the Brush tool ( ) from the toolbar.

3. Select an appropriately sized soft-edged brush from the options bar. Set the Mode to Lighten and the Opacity to 15–20 percent.

4. Paint carefully over the teeth until you get the effect you want.

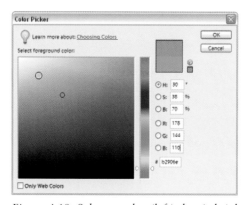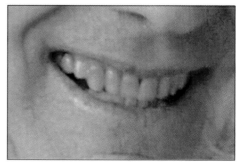

Figure 4.19: Select a color (left) that is brighter than the tooth (right).

Here is how you fix a tooth with the Liquify filter:

1. Make a selection around the area you want to fix.

2. Choose Liquify from the Filter menu (Filter ➢ Distort ➢ Liquify).

3. Select the Bloat tool ( ) if you want to enlarge a tooth, the Pucker tool ( ) if you want to shrink one, or the Warp tool ( ) if you want to straighten one. Choose an appropriate brush size and a relatively low brush pressure.

4. Place the brush over the area you want to fix. It will take some experimentation, but you can shrink the gaps between teeth, fill in a missing piece of enamel, or straighten a crooked tooth.

In Figure 4.20 you can see how I've fixed two teeth by using the Liquify filter and the Bloat tool.

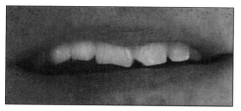 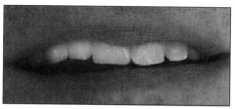

Figure 4.20: Before applying the Liquify filter (left) and after (right).

Selectively Removing Wrinkles and Blemishes with the Healing Brush

Personally, I like wrinkles; they show character and maturity. However, I know that not all wrinkles are caused by age and character. Many times they are unwanted artifacts of a high-speed contrasty film or harsh lighting.

Getting rid of wrinkles and removing blemishes and other unwanted artifacts from the face is especially easy with Photoshop Elements' Healing Brush tool, which is similar in practice to the Clone Stamp tool. You start by clicking and defining a source. Then you "paint" over the area you wish to replace or "heal." But the Healing Brush tool does much more than simply duplicate and replace pixels. It matches the texture, lighting, transparency, and shading of the sampled pixels to the source pixels. The result is often a seamless blend that leaves little or no trace of the original underlying flaw.

To use the Healing Brush tool to eliminate wrinkles or other small skin blemishes, take these steps:

1. Select the Healing Brush tool ( ) from the toolbar (it's under the Spot Healing Brush).

2. In the options bar, select a brush size. The brush size will vary depending on the target. In general, it's a good idea to pick a size 30 percent or so larger than the crease of the wrinkle or the circumference of the blemish. Hard-edged brushes are usually more effective than soft-edged ones. The Healing Brush tool applies a complex blending algorithm to the edges of the brush, and a soft-edged brush adds a variable to the equation that makes the results unpredictable.

3. From the Healing Brush tool's options bar, set the remaining options as follows:

   Mode: Normal. Choosing Replace basically turns the Healing Brush tool into a Clone Stamp tool, which isn't what you want for this exercise.

   Source: Sampled. The Pattern choice blends a chosen pattern over the target area, which isn't useful for this kind of cosmetic healing.

   Aligned. You can go either way with this setting depending on the size and location of the flaw you are healing. Selecting Aligned means pixels are sampled continuously, always at a relative distance from the target. Deselecting Aligned means that after you click to define a source, Photoshop Elements will use that initial source point as a reference when you click and paint with the Healing Brush—no matter where you move on the image. It will continue to use the original defined source even if you release the mouse button and click another target area.

   Sample All Layers. Select this if you want to sample data from all visible layers. Sample All Layers is particularly useful if you want to keep your original image untouched. In this case, simply create a new layer (Layer ➤ New ➤ Layer), make it active, and follow the subsequent steps for using the Healing Brush tool. The healing will occur on the new layer, leaving the underlying layer untouched. When you are completely satisfied with your results, you can choose Layer ➤ Merge Down or Layer ➤ Flatten Image. Or you can save the layered PSD file.

4. Pick an area adjacent to the wrinkle or blemish and sample it by holding down the Alt key and clicking. Now click and hold the mouse, and paint over the wrinkle or blemish. When you release the mouse, the Healing Brush goes to work. If the area you painted over is large, it may take time to complete the healing process. If the healing is acceptable, you are finished. If not, use the Undo command (Ctrl+Z, or Edit ➤ Undo) and start over. Often it is just a matter of changing the brush size to get it right. Sometimes, if the area you want to heal is adjacent to a detail with strong contrast—for example, an eyelid or a lip—you'll need to isolate the target area with a selection and then apply the Healing Brush tool.

I used this method to remove the wrinkles shown in Figure 4.21 and to remove the blemishes shown in Figure 4.22.

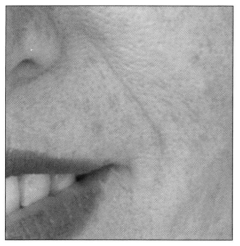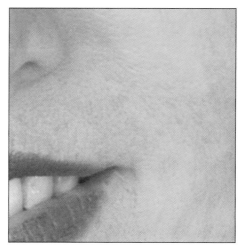

Figure 4.21: Before (left) and after (right) using the Healing Brush tool.

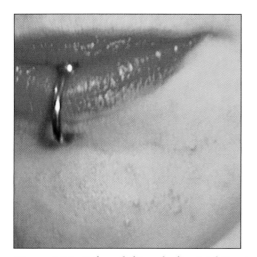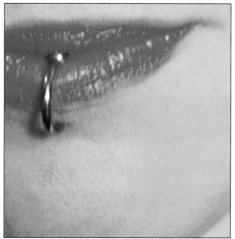

Figure 4.22: Before (left) and after (right) using the Healing Brush tool.

Keep in mind that wrinkles are technically shadows on a digital image. If you want to diminish their appearance—and not get rid of them completely—you can just lighten them up.

To use the Dodge tool to reduce wrinkles, take these steps:

1. Select the Dodge tool ( ) from the toolbar. Set it to Midtones and use an appropriately sized, soft-edged brush. If needed, magnify your image so the wrinkles fill the screen.

2. With a very low exposure—say 10–20 percent—gently stroke the wrinkle away with the brush. Don't go too far. Before you make a final judgment, zoom back to normal magnification. That way, you'll have a more objective view of your work.

Diminishing and Straightening the Nose

Wide-angle lenses or oblique camera angles can make a nose seem much larger than it is. Again, the Liquify filter is a good way to diminish an unnaturally large nose—or to straighten a crooked one.

Here's how to use the Liquify filter to diminish or straighten a nose:

1. Select the nose by using any of the selection tools.
2. Choose Liquify from the Filter menu (Filter ➤ Distort ➤ Liquify).
3. To diminish a nose, select the Pucker tool ( ). Pick a brush size that fits over the entire nose. Select a brush pressure less than 50. Hold the cursor over the nose and click incrementally until you get the effect you want.
4. To straighten a nose, select the Warp tool ( ). Click and drag to shift the nose into a straighter position.

I used a combination of these techniques to achieve the effects shown in Figures 4.23 and 4.24.

Figure 4.23: Before applying the Liquify filter (left). After applying the Liquify filter (right).

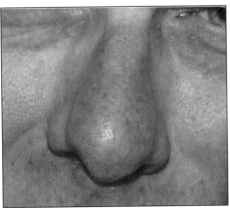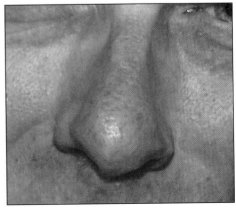

Figure 4.24: Before applying the Liquify filter (left). After applying the Liquify filter (right).

Making People Glow

In the "old days," I used to stretch a nylon stocking over my darkroom enlarger lens to give a portrait a glamorous, dreamy glow. It's easy to simulate this look with Photoshop Elements.

Look at the difference between the images in Figure 4.25.

Figure 4.25: The original photo (left). It's easy to create a softer look (right).

Here's what I did to create the softer effect:

1. I selected and made a copy of the background layer and named it **Blur**. You can copy a selected layer by choosing the Duplicate Layer command either from the Layer menu on the main menu bar or from the Layers palette menu. You can also duplicate a layer by selecting it and dragging it to the New Layer button (▣) at the top of the Layers palette. You can also right-click the active layer—but not the thumbnail—and choose Duplicate Layer from the pop-up menu.

2. With the **Blur** layer selected, I applied a strong Gaussian blur (Filter ➤ Blur ➤ Gaussian Blur). The exact amount of blurring will depend on the size of your image. In the case of this image, I chose a Radius of 30 pixels from the Gaussian Blur filter dialog box.

3. In the Layers palette, I selected Overlay from the Blending Mode menu (see the left-hand image in Figure 4.26). (You can also experiment with the Soft Light, Hard Light, and Screen blending options.) I diminished the Opacity setting in the Layers palette to 90 percent, which gave me the effect I wanted. Again, the exact opacity that looks the best will depend on your image.

Figure 4.26: The soft look is created with a combination of blurring and different Layers settings (left). The blur effect is selectively removed from the neck and chest area with the Eraser tool (right).

4. I liked the effect of the blurring on the face. However, I wasn't pleased with the way the effect blurred the clothes. To selectively remove the effect from that area, I chose the Eraser tool ( ) from the toolbox and selected an appropriately sized, soft-edged brush. With the **Blur** layer selected, I used the eraser to remove the blur effect from the tie and shirt (see the right-hand image in Figure 4.26).

As you can see in Figure 4.27, the effect also works well in grayscale. To soften this image, I followed the same steps; however, before I began, I desaturated the image by choosing Enhance ➢ Adjust Color ➢ Remove Color from the main menu bar. I also chose Screen, instead of Soft Light, from the Blending Mode menu and dropped the Opacity setting to 25 percent. I also could have turned the color image into black-and-white by changing the mode from RGB to Grayscale (Image ➢ Mode ➢ Grayscale from the main menu).

Figure 4.27: The soft-focus effects work with a black-and-white image as well.

Correcting Skin Tones

Depending on the lighting conditions or your camera's white balance settings, you may end up with skin tones that need correcting. This happened to me while in a market in St. Petersburg, Russia. I shot a photo of a typical local shopper (shown in Figure 4.28), and her face had that unflattering pale washed-out look. Elements 4 makes this easy to correct.

Figure 4.28: I started with the original pale-skinned image (left) and easily corrected it using the new Adjust Skin Tone feature (right).

Here's what I did:

1. In Standard Edit, I chose Enhance ➢ Adjust Color ➢ Adjust Color for Skin Tone. (This is the same in Quick Fix.)
2. I clicked on her forehead in several different locations until I liked the result. I experimented with the sliders but left them in the original position.
3. When I was finished, I clicked OK.

Creating a Digital Fill Flash

It's common to take a picture of a person against a bright background. However, if you don't use a fill flash or specifically expose for the skin tones, a face will turn into a silhouette (see Figure 4.29). Photoshop Elements includes a useful Shadows/Highlights command that does a good job of creating a digital fill flash, balancing the foreground with the background.

Figure 4.29: Before applying Shadows/Highlights, the face is too dark (left). After applying Shadows/Highlights (right), both the face and the background are fine.

Here is what I did to fix this picture of San Francisco Giants slugger Barry Bonds:

1. I selected Shadows/Highlights from the Enhance menu (Enhance ➢ Adjust Lighting ➢ Shadows/Highlights).

2. I set the Lighten Shadows slider settings at 50 percent, which made the face look right. I left the other settings alone.

3. I clicked OK. That's all. It was that easy.

Note: One of the most effective ways of emphasizing the features of someone is to isolate their face from the background. If you shoot a portrait with a longer than normal focal length and a wide f-stop, the background will naturally fade out of focus. However, when shooting this way isn't possible, or if you inherit a photo with a distracting background, you can use Photoshop Elements to save the day. Later in this book I'll show you how to use the Gaussian Blur filter to isolate an object from its background. (☞ Chapter 5, "Adding Selective Focus.")

Fixing Hair

You can do a lot to hair with the help of Photoshop Elements. You can tint it, you can change the color entirely, you can shape it, and you can even add or delete it. As usual, a subtle approach is the most realistic.

Adding Hair

Hair, or the lack of it, can be a sensitive subject. I want to thank another friend, Jonathan, for agreeing to let me use a before and after shot of him and his family to illustrate what Photoshop Elements can do to … well, to add hair. Check out Figure 4.30.

Figure 4.30: Jonathan and his family before (left). Jonathan and his family after (right).

Here is what I did to go from the before shot to the after shot:

1. I made a new layer and named this layer **Hair** (Layer ➤ New ➤ Layer).

2. I selected the Clone Stamp tool (🔲) and chose an appropriately sized, soft-edged brush from the options bar. I set the Mode to Normal and the Opacity to 80 percent. I made sure that Sample All Layers was selected in the options bar.

3. With the **Hair** layer selected, I sampled Jonathan's son's hair with the Clone Stamp tool. (To take a sample, click the desired area while holding the Alt.) I then brushed Jonathan's head, filling it with the hair from his son. This new set of hair was painted on its own layer, keeping the real Jonathan intact for future reference (see Figure 4.31).

Figure 4.31: The new hair is on its own layer.

4. When I was finished, I selected the background layer containing Jonathan and his family and, using the Burn tool (), I burned in his beard.

> **Note:** If you are getting serious about retouching and restoring photographs, I highly recommend Katrin Eismann's *Photoshop Restoration & Retouching* (New Riders, third edition, 2005). It's written with Photoshop in mind rather than Photoshop Elements, but it is a very practical book that will give you easy-to-follow techniques for resurrecting old photos, improving portraits, and touching up glamour shots. I also highly recommend the website of my tech editor Doug Nelson, **www.retouchpro.com**.

Shooting Digital: Making a Better Portrait

Getting a person to relax is essential to taking a good portrait. And before they can relax, you must relax too. If you are nervous or unsure of yourself, your subject will respond accordingly. Make an effort to smile, be confident, and at least act like you know what you're doing. It helps also to know ahead of time where you will be shooting the picture. Scout out a quiet spot with good light (natural light outside or by a window works well) and a simple, uncluttered background. Many digital cameras enable you to instantly view a picture on an electronic display. Show your subject a few shots and engage them in the process. Before you know it, that fake smile will disappear and be replaced by a real one.

Changing Color, Tinting, and Trimming Hair

My hairdresser, Robert, tells me that most of the colorizing he does is really lightening and darkening certain parts of the hair to model or mold it. The secret, he says, is to lighten the front part so it creates a glow around the face while darkening the back to bring out the highlights in the front. He also adds streaks of light and dark to give the hair a sense of depth. All of this is easy to do in Photoshop Elements. Look at the difference between the images in Figure 4.32.

Figure 4.32: Before (left) and after (right) adding highlights.

Here is what I did to add the highlights:

1. I created a new layer from the Layer menu (Layer ➢ New ➢ Layer). This opened the dialog box shown in Figure 4.33. Here I chose Color Dodge from the Mode pop-up menu and selected Fill with Color-Dodge-Neutral Color (Black). I named this layer **Highlights**. Then I clicked OK.

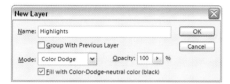

Figure 4.33: By selecting a new layer with these settings, you can literally paint highlights onto an image.

2. I selected the Brush tool () from the toolbar and then selected the Airbrush icon in the toolbar ( ). I selected an appropriately sized, soft-edged brush from the options bar and set the Mode to Normal and the Opacity to 4 percent. In the Color Picker at the bottom of the toolbox, I selected white for the foreground. On the layer called **Highlights**, I applied the Airbrush to the hair in the front, airbrushing lightly until I got the right amount of "modeling."

> **Note:** Why Airbrush? I like the pressure control. That's a matter of preference.

3. To enhance the shadows, I created another new layer (Layer ➢ New ➢ Layer). This time in the dialog box, I chose Color Burn from the Mode pop-up menu and selected Fill with Color-Dodge-Neutral Color (White). I named this layer **Shadow**. I applied the Airbrush tool to this layer, but this time I painted the back of the hair with a black foreground color instead of white. Figure 4.34 shows all my layers after painting with the Airbrush.

Figure 4.34: Highlights and shadows are painted onto their own layers.

It's also easy to add color to hair by using the Color Replacement tool. Compare the two images in Figure 4.35.

Figure 4.35: Hair before using the Color Replacement tool (left) and after using Color Replacement (right).

Here's what I did to go from the first image to the second:

1. I chose the Color Replacement tool ( ) from the toolbar. In the options bar, I chose the following:

    Mode: Color

    Sampling: Continuous

    Limits: Contiguous. Discontiguous will work too.

    Tolerance: 30 percent. A higher percentage replaces adjacent pixels with a broader range of color values. A lower percentage replaces only a few adjacent pixels with similar color values.

2. I clicked the foreground color swatch in the toolbar to access the Color Picker. I used the Eyedropper ( ) to sample a color from the bird. (The cursor changes to the Eyedropper when moved outside the Color Picker. You can also choose a color directly from the Color Picker.) After selecting my color, I clicked OK.

3. Then I simply used the Color Replacement tool and broad strokes with my brush to apply the color to the hair.

My friend Tracy took the photo on the left in Figure 4.36 of her husband, Chris, in their backyard in Chico, California. Tracy told me that she wanted to see her husband without the gray. "And, oh, by the way," she asked, "Could you trim his beard as well?"

Figure 4.36: Chris in real life (left). Chris with his beard trimmed and all of the gray removed (right).

This is what I did:

1. I selected the Burn tool ( ) from the toolbar.
2. I selected an appropriately sized, soft-edged brush and set the Range to Midtones and the Opacity to 50 percent.
3. I burned until the beard was the right shade.
4. I selected the Clone Stamp tool ( ), sampled areas outside Chris's beard and carefully "trimmed" the edges.

   The results are shown on the right in Figure 4.36.

Better Outside Shots

Outside shots depend a lot on the undependable. The weather may not cooperate. Power lines, telephone poles, or even people can get in the way. It may be the wrong time of year or the wrong time of day. It may even be day when you really want night. You lose a lot of control when a picture is taken outside, but with the help of Photoshop Elements, you can get some of that control back.

Chapter Contents

Intensifying the Sky

Many outside shots benefit from a dramatic sky filled with intense colors or interesting cloud patterns. Techniques I described earlier in this book will help many skies reach their full potential ($\curvearrowleft$ "Making Dull Images Shine" in Chapter 3). However, if your digital image inherently suffers from a boring sky, you can use some other simple Photoshop Elements' techniques to "clone" a dramatic sky from one digital image and place it instead on another.

Cloning Clouds

On the left in Figure 5.1 is a photograph I took on the Spanish island of Menorca. It's not a bad photograph, but a dramatic sky would make it a lot better. By using Photos hop Elements, and working in the Standard Edit mode, I was able to create the new image shown on the right. You can apply these techniques to make your own dramatic sky.

Figure 5.1: By cloning a sky from another image, this photo (left) will become a lot more interesting. The same photo with a new sky (right).

This is what I did to create the new image:

1. I opened the image shown in Figure 5.1 and another image containing a dramatic sky, shown in Figure 5.2. Both of these images came from a Kodak Photo CD and were opened at 1536 × 1024 pixels at 144 pixels/inch. (If your images have resolutions that are different from each other, you should resample the image containing the dramatic sky to match the resolution of your target image. To resample, choose Image ➢ Resize ➢ Image Size and type in the matching pixel values. Be sure to check Resample Image at the bottom of the dialog box.)

Figure 5.2: These clouds will liven up almost any sky.

2. In the image containing the man and the horse, I created a new layer and called it **Clouds** (Layer ➤ New ➤ Layer). I did this because I wanted to clone the new sky to its own layer and keep the old sky intact.

3. I selected the Clone Stamp tool () from the toolbar and selected the image containing the dramatic sky. In the options bar, I selected the following:

   Brush: Soft Round 300 pixels
   Mode: Normal
   Opacity: 100 percent
   Aligned: selected
   Use All Layers: selected

   (The brush size you choose will depend on your image.)

4. I positioned the cursor at the top far left of the dramatic sky and, while holding the Alt key, I clicked and sampled.

5. I placed the cursor on the top far left of the image of the man and the horse and "painted" the new sky. I started with a horizontal stroke, going from left to right, filling in the top 33 percent of the sky. Then, and this is very important, I changed the opacity of the Clone Stamp tool in the options bar to 65 percent. I painted another horizontal layer of sky, this one just under the one that was painted at 100 percent opacity. I painted about 40 percent of the sky this way and stopped just above the top of the horse and the top of the rock talus. At this point, I wasn't very precise and some of the clone spilled over the horse and the rock talus. However, it didn't matter because the new sky was actually going on its own layer (see Figure 5.3), the layer I called **Clouds**, and I would go back later and fix the overlapping areas.

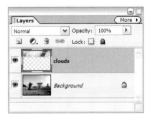

Figure 5.3: By keeping **Clouds** *as its own layer, I can go back and edit or enhance it at any time.*

6. When I finished cloning the new sky onto the old, I selected the Move tool (⊹) from the toolbar. With the layer called **Clouds** still selected, I put my cursor on the image window, and clicked and dragged the sky around until it was positioned exactly as I wanted.

7. I chose the Eraser tool (🖉) from the toolbar. I selected the following options from the options bar:

    Brush: Soft Round 100 pixels
    Mode: Brush
    Opacity: 100 percent

    On the layer called **Clouds**, I carefully erased the clouds and sky away from the horse, the man, and the rock. (For the detailed areas, I used a Soft Round 35 pixels and a Soft Round 17 pixels brush.)

8. I enhanced the clouds by applying Levels to the **Clouds** layer only (Enhance ≻ Adjust Lighting ≻ Levels). Finally, I used the Crop tool (🔲) to crop off a small part of the right side of the image, where the cloned sky didn't fit quite to the edge.

9. At this point, I could have flattened my image (Layer ≻ Flatten Image, or Flatten Image from the Layers palette menu), or just saved my image with the two layers intact. Keeping the two layers increases the file size, but I kept them because I wanted the option of going back and tweaking my image, or even restoring the original sky if I wanted.

In some cases, when you are transferring an entire sky from one image to another, it's not a bad idea to use a copy-and-paste technique rather than using the Clone Stamp tool. For this particular image, however, I needed to gradually blend the two skies. The Clone Stamp tool enabled me to do this by giving me the ability to change the opacity as I painted.

Changing the Time of Day

Photographers and artists love morning and evening light. It's when the sun is angled to the horizon and the shadows are long and dramatic. Sunset light is especially pleasing when the light passes through a thick layer of particulates, such as smog, moisture, or dust. Midday light, on the other hand, is much more difficult to work with. Depending on the time of year and the place, the light is harsh, and shadows are short and intense.

With Photoshop Elements, you can imitate the golden light of a sunset or even change day to night. Here are some specific examples with techniques you can use on your own digital images.

Midday to Sunset

Figure 5.4 shows a beautiful scene taken in San Francisco around 3 PM by professional photographer Monica Lee and a shot of the Manhattan skyline taken by me.

Figure 5.4: These photos are beautiful, but they could benefit from warm sunset light. (Photo by Monica Lee (left) and the author (right).)

I thought both photos might benefit from warmer, more golden sunset light. Here are two ways to do this with Photoshop Elements. The first method requires a few more steps but gives you more control. (It also prepares you for using a similar method in the example following this one, "Morning to Sunset.") The second method uses one of Photoshop Elements's photo filters. Both methods require working in the Standard Edit mode.

Method 1:

1. I opened the image and made a new layer called **Sunset Light** (Layer ➤ New ➤ Layer). I set my layer Opacity to 56 percent and the Mode to Color Burn.
2. I selected an appropriate color for my warm tint. I did this by clicking the foreground color selection box in the toolbox. This brought up the Color Picker, where I chose a color with the following RGB values (see Figure 5.5):

    Red = 255

    Green = 204

    Blue = 102

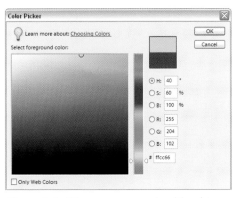

Figure 5.5: Choose a warm tint like this one from the Color Picker.

3. I selected the Gradient tool ( ) from the toolbox. I chose the following settings from the options bar (see Figure 5.6):

    Gradient Picker: Foreground to Transparent

    Type of Gradient: Linear Gradient

    Mode: Normal

    Opacity: 100 percent

Then, with the empty **Sunset Light** layer selected, I applied Linear Gradient (▣) to the image. I did this by holding the Shift key and dragging the cursor from the bottom of the image window halfway up, just past the top of the row of houses. Holding the Shift key while I did this constrained the angle to multiples of 45 degrees. (I used Linear Gradient to apply the warm tint, but you can instead apply the tint selectively by using the Brush tool (✐). Just be sure to apply the color to a layer of its own, using the color values from step 2 and the **Sunset Light** layer specifications from step 1.)

Figure 5.6: Set the Gradient tool options as shown.

4. After I applied the warm tint, I noticed that the sky looked too light for the late hour I was trying to imitate. To darken the sky, I created a Levels adjustment layer and adjusted the entire image so the background darkened appropriately. I then selected the Gradient tool and kept the same settings as described in step 3. However, I clicked the Default Colors icon (◼) (you can also use the shortcut key D) to set the colors in the color selection box to their default colors in the toolbox, and reset my foreground and background colors to black-and-white. I then used the Gradient tool on the adjustment layer to create a mask that prevented the Levels adjustment from affecting the foreground (see the left side of Figure 5.7). More information on this technique is provided later in this book (☞ "Layer Adjustments with Masks" in Chapter 10). The result is shown on the right in Figure 5.7.

*Figure 5.7: Note the Layers palette options for **Sunset Light** and the adjustment layer mask (left). The new image is now bathed in sunset light (right).*

Method 2:

1. I opened the image and made a copy of the background layer (Layer ➤ Duplicate Layer).

2. On the duplicate layer I applied a photo filter (Filter ➤ Adjustments ➤ Photo Filter). I chose Warming Filter (85) from the Filter pop-up menu; I set Density to 76 and kept Preserve Luminosity selected. (You can also apply the photo filter as

an adjustment layer and forgo step 1. However, you'll see shortly why I chose to apply it as a normal filter to a copy of the background layer.)

3. At this point, for some images, all you need to do is select OK, and you're done. The filter does the job. However, for this image, the filter made the sky look strange, as you can see in Figure 5.8. To correct this, I selected the Magic Eraser tool ( ) from the toolbar and after a little experimentation, I set the Tolerance to 40 in the options bar. I left Contiguous selected. (Tolerance settings depend on how wide a range of similar colors you want to erase and will vary depending on the image. Selecting Contiguous ensures that only pixels sharing a boundary or touching each other will be erased.)

Figure 5.8: The photo filter gave the buildings the glow I was looking for, but they didn't do a good job on the sky.

4. On the duplicate layer, I clicked the sky. The Magic Eraser erased most of the sky on the duplicate layer. (The Layers palette and final image are shown in Figure 5.9.) Now the original sky—which was OK without the filter—shows through from the layer below. (If I had applied the photo filter as an adjustment layer, I couldn't have conveniently used the Magic Eraser selectively on the sky area.)

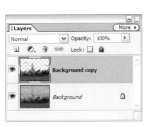

Figure 5.9: Note how the Magic Eraser selectively deleted the sky in the top, duplicate layer (left). This enables the sky from the background layer to show through (right).

Morning to Sunset

The image on the left in Figure 5.10 is a shot I took of the ancient Mayan ruins in Tikal, Guatemala. Even though it was early morning and the jungle mist hadn't cleared, the light had a bluish tint.

Figure 5.10: This jungle scene (left) lacked warmth. I used the layer blending and Opacity settings (right) to make it more tropical.

I wanted the image to feel warmer, more tropical, so I did the following:

1. With the Tikal image open, I made two copies of my background layer and named these layers **Sharpen** and **Blur**. I created a new layer and called it **Tint**. My Layers palette is shown on the right in Figure 5.10. The layer order is important.

Note: The easiest way to duplicate a layer is to select the layer in the Layers palette and drag it to the New Layer button (⬚) at the top of the Layers palette. The easiest way to create a new layer is to click that button. Remember, the Layers palette is located by default in the palette bin. However, by clicking/holding/dragging on the top tab of the palette you can move the palette anywhere you want on the screen.

2. To the layer called **Blur**, I applied a strong Gaussian blur (Filter ➢ Blur ➢ Gaussian Blur) and set the Radius setting to 5.7. I left the **Blur** layer blending Mode to Normal and set the layer Opacity to 58 percent.

3. To the layer called **Sharpen**, I applied an Unsharp Mask (Filter ➢ Sharpen ➢ Unsharp Mask). I used the following settings:

   Amount: 100 percent
   Radius: 1.9 pixels
   Threshold: 0 Levels

   (With other images, depending on the content and resolution, these numbers will vary. You'll want to experiment to get it right.)

   I then set the **Sharpen** layer Opacity to 61 percent and left the blending Mode at Normal.

Note: Chapter 3 goes into detail on using the Unsharp Mask.

4. I filled the **Tint** layer with a light orange tint. To do this, I clicked the foreground color selection box in the toolbox to open the Color Picker, and then I selected a color with the following RGB values:

   Red = 255
   Green = 204
   Blue = 102

   I chose Fill Layer from the Edit menu and chose the settings from the dialog box shown on the left in Figure 5.11. You can also use the Paint Bucket tool ( ) to fill the **Tint** layer. Just be sure your Fill option in the option bar is set to Foreground and not Pattern. (I want to acknowledge Photoshop master Brad Johnson for concocting this particular tint, which I use often.)

Figure 5.11: Fill settings (left). The final image (right).

5. I set the Mode of the **Tint** layer to Color Burn and the Opacity to 44 percent, and I was done. The final image is shown on the right in Figure 5.11.

It may seem counterintuitive to apply both a Sharpen and Blur effect to the same image, but rather than canceling each other, the combination of the two effects gave my image a soft, dreamy look and yet kept much of the sharpness in some of the detailed areas. I also could have modified the effects of these two layers by using the Eraser tool ( ) and selectively erasing each effect from certain areas.

Shooting Digital: The Rules of Good Composition

Regardless of whether you are shooting a digital camera or a film camera, the rules of good composition remain the same. Somewhere in your picture there should be a focal point. This can mean arranging your shot to include a blooming branch in the foreground, a large rock in the middle ground, or a dramatic sky in the background. Don't make the common mistake of assuming that, simply because a scene looks breathtaking to the eye, it will work as a photograph. Without a strong focal point, the camera translates the scene into a mush of small objects that are visually boring.

Day to Night

Figure 5.12 is a still frame grabbed from a Lexus TV ad. The shot was taken during the day, but the director, Melinda Wolf, decided afterward that it should have been shot during the night. Special-effects wizard Michael Angelo was called. Before working on the actual footage, Michael used digital editing to show the director what the scene might look like at night. Michael used Photoshop to create this image originally, but he kindly modified his procedure to show how it could be done using Photoshop Elements.

Figure 5.12: This is how the shot looked during the day (left). This is how it would have looked at night (right).

This is what Michael did to get the results shown on the right in Figure 5.12:

1. He made a duplicate layer and called it **Night**. To duplicate a layer, select the layer and drag it to the New Layer button ( ) at the top of the Layers palette.

2. With the **Night** layer selected, Michael removed the color by choosing Enhance ➢ Adjust Color ➢ Remove Color. Then he selected Enhance ➢ Adjust Color ➢ Adjust Hue/Saturation and selected the Colorize option in the dialog box. He tinted the image blue by sliding the Hue slider to the right. He left the Saturation in the middle, set at 50. Then he darkened the overall image by sliding the Lightness slider to the left. Because he selected Preview in the dialog box, all his changes were visible on the actual image, and he could easily modify his settings to get exactly what he wanted (see Figure 5.13).

Figure 5.13: Michael's Hue/Saturation settings (left). Settings for the Lens Flare filter (right).

3. He created a duplicate layer of **Night** and called it **Lens Flare**.

4. To the **Lens Flare** layer, he applied the Lens Flare filter (Filter ➢ Render ➢ Lens Flare). See Figure 5.13 for the settings he used. He dragged the flare over one of the headlights and selected OK. He repeated these steps, selecting the Lens Flare filter again to apply another "headlight."

5. He duplicated the **Lens Flare** layer and called this layer **Final**. On this layer, he used the Dodge tool (⬛) from the toolbox to paint the reflection of the headlights in the pavement.

The conversion of a single frame from day to night was a piece of cake for Michael compared to what he had to do to convert the entire film footage into night. That was a task for another program and a subject for another book!

Making Weather

If you don't like the weather, use a Photoshop Elements effect and make some of your own. That's what I did to turn the relatively calm day shown on the left in Figure 5.14 into the blizzard shown on the right.

Figure 5.14: All it takes is a Blizzard effect to add drama to the image on the left.

To do this, simply choose Effects and Image Effects from the pop-up menus in the Styles and Effects palette, located by default in the palette bin. Then select and apply the Image Effect called Blizzard. (To apply the effect, double-click its icon, or click and drag the icon on top of the image window.)

Remember, all effects can be easily removed and sometimes altered. To remove an effect, you can either choose Edit ➢ Undo Blizzard (Ctrl+Z), or select the effect layer in the Layers palette and click the trash can at the top of the palette. For the Blizzard effect, try varying the blending and Opacity settings found at the top of the Layers palette. Color Dodge and Soft Light blending choices work well.

Working with the Midday Sun

The image on the left in Figure 5.15 shows a field of wheat shot in the middle of the day by field biologist Laura Laverdiere of the Syngenta Crop Protection company. She used a digital camera to document the effects of different fertilizers and insecticides.

The midday sun washed out much of the color, making it more difficult to see the difference between the healthy and unhealthy plants. The right side of the figure shows the same field after Laura used Photoshop Elements to fix the shot.

Figure 5.15: The midday sun washes out color (left). With a little help from Photoshop Elements, this is now a useful image (right). (Photo by Laura Laverdiere)

Making this right was a simple matter: Laura applied Auto Levels to her image (Enhance ➤ Auto Levels). Then she slightly increased the saturation (Enhance ➤ Adjust Color ➤ Adjust Hue/Saturation).

Adding Lighting Effects

Look at the image on the left in Figure 5.16. The light is flat and monotonous. If we could just part the gray veil and bring out the sun, it might help. Well, with Photoshop Elements and its Lighting Effects filter, we can do just that.

Figure 5.16: This photo (left) is waiting for a little divine intervention. The sun (right), thanks to the Lighting Effects filter. (Photos by Monica Lee)

Here is what I did to create the final image shown on the right in the figure:

1. I made a copy of the background layer.
2. I selected the Lighting Effects filter (Filter ➤ Render ➤ Lighting Effects, or select Filters and Render from the pop-up menus in the Styles and Effects palette, located by default in the palette bin). This brought up the dialog box shown in Figure 5.17.

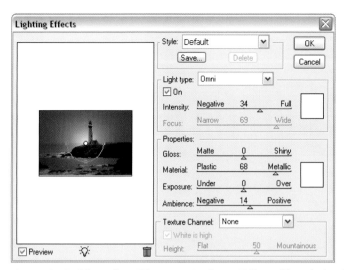

Figure 5.17: Photoshop Elements' Lighting Effects filter dialog box.

3. For Style, I chose Default.

4. For Light Type, I chose Omni, which created a light that shone in all directions. I selected the On check box (below the Light Type) and an Intensity of 34. Still, in the Light Type section of the dialog box, I clicked in the color box and then chose white from the Color Picker.

5. I adjusted the Omni light by dragging the center circle in the preview window just over the top of the lighthouse. I played with the size of the light by dragging one of the handles defining the edges of the light until I got what I wanted.

6. To set the light properties, I dragged the corresponding sliders and chose the following:

- For Gloss (which determines how much a surface area reflects), I left the slider at a neutral 0. (Matte creates a dull reflection, whereas Shiny creates a high reflectance.)
- For Material, I slid the slider more toward Metallic.
- I kept Exposure at 0.
- For Ambience, I moved the slider toward the positive, which increased the overall brightness of my image.
- I left the color of the Ambience light white. (To change the ambient color, click the color box to the right of the Ambience slider and use the Color Picker that appears.)

These settings took some trial and error. Any time I made a choice, the image in the preview window changed, reflecting that choice. I played around until I got the quality of light that looked appropriate.

7. After I was finished, I clicked OK.

As you can see, the Lighting Effects filter offers many options for changing the quality and direction of light in your digital image. It takes some time and experimentation to fully master its potential, but the extra effort is worth it.

Removing Unwanted Objects

Many times a picture is perfect except for a power line or an unwanted sign or, for that matter, an unwanted person who wanders into your shot. Sometimes all it takes to get the picture right is a little Photoshop Elements blur here, or a burn there. Other times you'll need to remove the object entirely, and that's when other techniques come in handy. In Chapter 6 I'll show you how to use the Clone Stamp and Healing Brush tools to remove annoying power lines that often appear in outdoor shots. In this section, I'll show you a couple of ways to remove other kinds of unwanted objects.

Removing a Tarp from the Golden Gate Bridge

Photographer Monica Lee needed a shot of the Golden Gate Bridge, but on the day she picked to shoot it, the Highway and Transportation District wasn't cooperating. As you can see in Figure 5.18, they placed a yellow tarp right in the middle of the bridge. Monica got the shot, and I helped her remove the unwanted blemish.

Figure 5.18: Who put that yellow tarp in the middle of my picture? (Photo by Monica Lee)

This is what I did:

1. I made a selection from a nearby part of the bridge by using the Rectangular Marquee tool (⬚), as shown in Figure 5.19. I copied this selection and pasted it on a layer that I called **Fix**.

Figure 5.19: I made a selection from a clean part of the bridge.

2. I used the Move tool (⛨) from the toolbox to slide the fix into place over the yellow tarp. It didn't match up perfectly, so I selected the Free Transform command (Image ➢ Transform ➢ Free Transform) and turned the fix slightly so it did fit (see Figure 5.20).

Figure 5.20: I used the Free Transform command to position the pasted fix (left), and then used the Clone Stamp tool to clean it up. The fixed image (right).

3. I then used the Clone Stamp tool (🔖) to remove the last bits of yellow on the bottom.

The results are shown on the right in Figure 5.20.

Removing a Person

My wife, Rebecca, writes and photographs for a monthly column in *Parents' Press*. Mostly she takes pictures of our daughters and the daughter of her coauthor, or photos of other known kids. If an unknown child slips into a photograph, Rebecca is required by the magazine to get a model release before the magazine can use the picture. Occasionally she gets a shot that she wants to submit but that doesn't have a model release.

That's what happened on the left in Figure 5.21. The person sliding down the slide is our daughter, so there's no problem using her image for the magazine, but who is the person behind her? Using Photoshop Elements, I made the image publishable, as shown on the right.

Figure 5.21: The child in the background is recognizable (left). After using the Burn tool, the background child is no longer recognizable (right).

Here's what I did to remove the unknown person: I first made a duplicate layer of the background. Then I selected the Burn tool (⬚) from the toolbox and selectively darkened the boy's face until it was unrecognizable.

For other pictures that contained unwanted or unusable faces, I've used the Blur tool (⬚) to achieve a similar goal. You can also use the Mosaic filter (Filter ➤ Pixelate ➤ Mosaic) to achieve the blurred-face look used on real-life television shows to protect someone's privacy.

Adding Selective Focus

Field biologist Laura Laverdiere is hindered not only by the difficulties of shooting under a midday sun. The digital camera she uses doesn't give her much creative control. For example, the camera is fully automatic, and it's impossible for her to choose a lens aperture and thereby increase or decrease the depth of focus. She gets around this limitation by using Photoshop Elements' Gaussian Blur filter selectively to create a sense of depth. By doing this, she calls attention visually to the critical parts of her image.

In the photo shown on the left in Figure 5.22, Laura wanted the chemically damaged leaf to stand out.

Figure 5.22: A narrower depth of focus would be helpful (left). Now the damaged leaf jumps out (right). (Photos by Laura Laverdiere)

To emphasize the leaf, she did the following:

1. She created a duplicate layer and called this layer **Blur**.
2. With the Lasso tool (![lasso]), she made an outline around the chemically damaged leaf and feathered this selection by 3 pixels (Select ➢ Feather). Then she chose Select ➢ Inverse from the menu bar.
3. She applied a strong Gaussian blur with a 4.4 pixel setting to the selection (Filter ➢ Blur ➢ Gaussian Blur). She then deselected her selection (Select ➢ Deselect, or Ctrl+D). The results are shown on the right in Figure 5.22.

This is a perfect example of a time when the Selection Brush might be used instead of the Lasso tool for making a selection. Simply click the Selection Brush in the toolbar (![brush]) and "paint" your selection over the plant. After you do this, follow the rest of the steps in this procedure to feather and inverse the selection and then move on to step 3. To make the Selection Brush tool feel even more like painting, choose Mode: Mask from the menu bar, and the selected area will appear "masked" in the overlay color of your choice. If you use the Mask mode, however, keep in mind that you do not need to inverse your selection. Mask mode works the opposite way from Selection mode. What you paint over is "protected" or "masked" as if you used masking tape, and not "selected." In other words, by painting over the damaged leaf in Mask mode, you've automatically protected it from the effect of the Gaussian blur—so you don't need to inverse your selection as you would otherwise. (For more on the Selection Brush, ☞ "Selection Tools" in Chapter 1.)

By working on a duplicate layer, Laura kept her original image intact. Also, if she wanted to selectively remove the Gaussian blur effect, all she had to do was use the Eraser tool ( ) selectively on the Blur layer, and the unblurred areas in the background layer would be revealed.

Creating a Large-Scale Digital Fill Flash

I used Photoshop Elements' Shadows/Highlights command elsewhere in this book to illuminate a person and a room (☞ "Creating a Digital Fill Flash Effect" in Chapter 4, and "Balancing the Light" in Chapter 6). Shadows/Highlights also works well as a large-scale digital fill flash on outdoor objects, as shown in Figure 5.23.

Figure 5.23: Before Shadows/Highlights is applied (left). After Shadows/Highlights is applied (right).

To get this kind of effect without software help would have required a powerful off-camera strobe or large reflector to fill in the shadows—neither of which I usually carry in my camera bag. Also, if you try to correct this image with Levels or other Enhance controls, you can't control either the shadow or highlights independently and get satisfactory results.

To fix the photo (taken at California's Morro Bay State Park), I opened it, selected Enhance ➤ Adjust Lighting ➤ Shadows/Highlights, and adjusted the sliders using the settings shown in Figure 5.24.

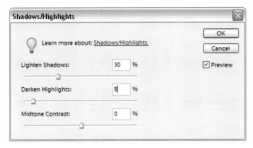

Figure 5.24: My Shadows/Highlights settings.

As you can see, I adjusted the Shadows slider to "open" up the shadows and I also darkened the highlights slightly with the Highlights slider. Often, with images like this, I get away with adjusting only the Shadows. Just experiment. As long as you have the Preview check box selected, you'll get instant feedback.

Exteriors and Interiors

If you are selling, renting, or swapping a building, you'll be amazed at all the things Photoshop Elements can do to help bring out desirable features and diminish or remove detractive ones. Even if you aren't in the real estate business and just appreciate a good picture, the techniques you learn in this chapter will be extremely useful.

Chapter Contents

Straightening a Slanted-Looking Facade

Look at just about any real estate magazine or newspaper section, and you'll see photos of buildings with sides that appear to converge rather than remain parallel. This is an effect called *keystoning*, and it occurs when the plane of the camera and the plane of the building are not parallel to each other.

You can avoid keystoning by positioning your camera so that it is even with the plane of the building. However, this isn't always possible, and Figure 6.1 illustrates my point. I shot it with a Canon Digital Rebel aimed up from the sidewalk. Notice how the pillars appear to converge, when in reality they are parallel. In some photographs, keystoning isn't bothersome. But in others, it can be so extreme that it disorients the viewer and leaves an impression that something is profoundly wrong with the building. Fortunately, it's not hard to fix shots like this with Photoshop Elements and the Perspective command (Image ➤ Transform ➤ Perspective).

Figure 6.1: The pillars of this building appear to converge.

Here's what I did to straighten the building:

1. I copied the background layer containing the building (Layer ➤ Duplicate Layer). I turned the visibility of my original background layer off so it wouldn't confuse me later when I applied the Perspective command. (You can turn a layer's visibility off by deselecting the eye icon in the leftmost side of the Layers palette.) I created a copy for a couple of reasons: First, I wanted to keep my original image intact, and second, Transform commands aren't an option when you are working on a background layer.

2. After duplicating the layer, I made sure all of my image fit on the screen and was visible by double-clicking the Hand tool ( ).

3. I then selected View ➤ Grid to give me a series of 90-degree vertical references. The grid makes it a lot easier to determine when the lines of the building are straight. Figure 6.2 shows the grid, which I customized. Using the grid is an alternative to another method I'll describe in the next chapter, when I'll use the Pencil tool to draw a 90-degree reference line on a separate layer (☞ "Fixing Keystoning" in Chapter 7).

Figure 6.2: A grid provides a series of 90-degree lines, which I can use as reference points when I try to straighten the building.

Note: To change the pattern and color of the grid, choose Edit ➤ Preferences ➤ Grid. You can select a preset color or a custom color. You can choose solid, dashed, or dotted lines. You can also vary the spacing of the major grid lines and the frequency of minor grid lines.

4. I selected the Perspective command (Image ▷ Transform ▷ Perspective) and kept the default Transform settings found in the options bar. In the Transform options bar, Rotate ( ) selects the Rotate transform, Scale (▣) selects the Scale transform, and Skew (◿) selects the Skew transform.

5. I dragged the top-right corner of the bounding box outward until the pillars were parallel.

6. When I was finished, I clicked the Commit button (✔) in the options bar. You can alternatively press Enter.

Note: Once you're in Transform mode, you can switch to a different type of transform by right-clicking anywhere in the image window and making a choice from the contextual menu.

To better illustrate how the Perspective command works, I'll give you an example of using it in the wrong way. On the left in Figure 6.3, you can see what happens when I place the pointer on the bounding box handle in the upper right and click and drag it inward. On the right, you can see what happens when I change the perspective by dragging the opposite way.

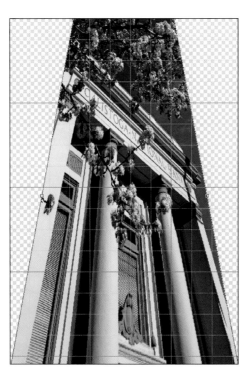

Figure 6.3: The image on the left shows what happens when I drag the bounding box inward. The image on the right shows what happens when I drag the bounding box too far the other way. Notice that I've expanded the image window, as signified by the gray. Now the bounding boxes are visible.

Figure 6.4 shows the correct adjustment, as confirmed by the vertical grid lines. In the second and third attempt it was necessary for me to slightly expand my image window. I did this by placing my cursor over the lower-right corner of the image window and clicking and dragging to the right. This made it possible to see the perspective control bounding boxes even as I dragged them beyond the edges of my image.

Figure 6.4:By aligning the sides of the pillars with the grid lines, I can see that this is about right.

Transforming a Kitchen

When the real estate market is hot, Jeanne Zimmermann shoots hundreds of photos a month with a digital camera. She documents property from both an indoor perspective and an outdoor one. She shoots big buildings and small buildings, commercial and residential. As soon as she is finished shooting, the images are quickly downloaded into her computer and prepared for newspaper ads, flyers, and the Web. (Her website is **www.loftsunlimited.com**. You'll also find her work under the name Sally Rogers.) Jeanne's job is demanding because it requires attention to both quality and speed. She does her best to get the shot right in the first place, but that's not always possible considering her schedule.

Figure 6.5 shows a not-so-uncommon mistake: the picture wasn't framed properly. In the days before she owned Photoshop Elements, Jeanne would have had to live with the mistake, reshoot, or decide that the kitchen wasn't that important after all. Nowadays she just starts up her computer and gets to work.

Note: Just about all real estate shots can benefit from the basic image-processing techniques described earlier in this book (↩ Chapter 3 and Chapter 5). Another relevant topic is how to make panoramas from a sequence of photos (↩ Chapter 9). ↩ Chapter 10 contains several useful advanced digital photography techniques such as extending exposure latitude.

Figure 6.5:This kitchen looks like it was in an earthquake. (Photo by Jeanne Zimmermann)

Here is what Jeanne did to straighten the kitchen:

1. She made a copy of the background layer, turned off the visibility of the original layer, and turned on the grid, just as I did in the preceding procedure.

2. She then selected Image ➤ Transform ➤ Free Transform (Ctrl+T) from the main menu bar.

3. As she positioned the pointer in the upper-right bounding box, it turned into a curved arrow (⟳). She rotated the image until the lines in the cabinet lined up with the vertical lines of her grid. Rotating some images like this can rotate parts of the image off the edge of the canvas. If this happens, enlarge your canvas area (Image ➤ Resize ➤ Canvas Size) before applying the Transform command or, even easier, use Image ➤ Resize ➤ Reveal All *after* you apply the Transform command.

4. When she was finished, she clicked the Commit button (✓) in the options bar. You can also press Enter.

5. As you can see on the left in Figure 6.6, the rotation fixed the kitchen but created a skewed image frame. She used the Crop tool to crop the image, as shown on the right in Figure 6.6.

Figure 6.6:After using the Free Transform command, the kitchen appears mostly level (left). Jeanne used the Crop tool (right) as a final step.

Elements 4 includes the new Straighten tool that aligns an image to any line that you draw. It does not provide as much control as the preceding procedure, but it works well on many images, especially those that have correct perspective. Here are the steps for using it:

1. With your image open, select the Straighten tool from the toolbox (   ).
2. If your image has several layers and you wish to straighten them all, select Rotate All Layers in the options bar.
3. Select one of the Canvas Options in the options bar. The results from the first option (Grow Canvas to Fit) and third option (Crop to Original Size) depend on your background, since the added canvas uses that color.
4. Draw a line in the image with the Straighten tool representing the new straight horizontal line. If you hold the Ctrl key while drawing the line, Elements assumes that the line represents the new straight vertical line. If the image rotates 90 degrees unexpectedly, it's most likely because you didn't use the Ctrl key.

Note: ↝ In Chapter 11, I'll show you how to automatically create a web photo gallery of images.

Removing a Construction Sign

Jeanne does her best to shoot around clutter or objects that detract from the property. In the case of Figure 6.7, she couldn't avoid the bright red construction sign in front, which gave the false impression that the building was still under construction.

Figure 6.7: The red construction sign is distracting. (Photo by Jeanne Zimmermann)

Here is what she did to remove the sign:

1. She created a duplicate of her background layer. She'll work on the duplicate and save the original layer for future reference.

2. She selected the Clone Stamp tool ( ) from the toolbox and magnified her image 400 percent. She positioned the red construction sign in the middle of her image window. (If an image is larger than the image window, you can move it around by holding down the spacebar. The cursor turns into a hand. Then, when you click and drag, the image moves with your cursor.)

3. She used a Soft Round 13 pixels brush and started on the red cones, sampling or "cloning" parts of the road and sidewalk by holding the Alt key while clicking them, and then painting the sampled areas over the cones (shown on the left in Figure 6.8). Then she sampled parts of the wall and the sidewalk and painted them over the sandwich sign, this time using a Hard Round 5 pixels brush, because the work in this area required her to be more precise. Next, she turned to the sign itself, sampling and using parts of the window and window frame to cover it. At times, the clone didn't look quite right. Ctrl+Z quickly reverted the step. As a final step in removing the sign, Jeanne selected a Soft Round 35 pixels brush and a Soft Round 9 pixels brush and cloned the intact tree trunk over what remained of the sign (shown on the right in Figure 6.8).

Figure 6.8:Jeanne started with the red cones, using the Clone Stamp tool to replace them with parts of the sidewalk and street (left). She then cloned the tree on the left side of the image over the area where the red sign used to be (right).

4. She then zoomed back to 100 percent magnification (by double-clicking the Zoom tool) and tightly cropped the image. Using the Levels controls, she adjusted the contrast of her image by choosing Enhance ➢ Adjust Lighting ➢ Levels or by pressing Ctrl+L.

5. She then used the Hue/Saturation controls to increase the saturation by choosing Enhance ➢ Adjust Color ➢ Adjust Hue/Saturation or by pressing Ctrl+U until she got what she wanted, as shown in Figure 6.9.

If you zoomed in tightly, you'd see that the clone job isn't perfect. Zoomed out, however, most people wouldn't notice.

Figure 6.9:The final image after cropping, applying Levels, and increasing saturation.

Note: The secret to using the Clone Stamp tool is not to get too caught up in the details. Zoom in to see what you're doing. But then periodically zoom out to see how your work looks in a normal view. It's also useful to turn away from the monitor from time to time. When you look back, you'll have a different perspective. The fact is, after spending so much time working with the Clone Stamp tool, you'll be tuned into every tiny imperfection–things that most people probably won't even notice.

Smart-Blurring a Background

In the photo shown on the left in Figure 6.10, Jeanne wanted to highlight the staircase, not emphasize the view out the windows. Shooting-wise, there wasn't much Jeanne could do except cover the windows completely. At first, she tried selecting the entire window area and applying a Gaussian blur (Filter ➢ Blur ➢ Gaussian Blur). She got what you see on the right in Figure 6.10. The Gaussian blur blurred everything, including the window frame. She considered selecting each glass part of the window individually and applying the Gaussian blur, but that would have taken too much time. Instead, she turned to the Smart Blur filter, which gave her a lot more control over the blur, enabling her to blur the background and leave the window frame alone.

Figure 6.10:Jeanne wanted to diminish the view out the windows (left). A Gaussian blur blurred everything, including the window frame (right). (Photos by Jeanne Zimmermann)

To use the Smart Blur filter, she did the following:

1. She used the Polygonal Lasso tool (⬚) to select the window areas on both sides of the staircase. (Remember, you add to a selection by selecting the Add to Selection icon in the options bar.)

2. She selected the Smart Blur filter (Filters ➢ Blur ➢ Smart Blur). By playing with the relationship between the Radius and Threshold settings, she got the effect she was looking for.

Jeanne's Smart Blur settings are shown on the left in Figure 6.11. The final effect is shown on the right.

If you look closely at the staircase, specifically at the handrail and the wire mesh below it, you can see that this image isn't perfect. The Smart Blur actually blurred the thin wire mesh as well as the background. Because this particular image was destined to run small on a website, this imperfection was acceptable. It's possible to be more precise by first selecting the area around the wire mesh and choosing a smaller Smart Blur Radius such as 1.0. The smaller Radius protects the thin wire mesh and still slightly blurs the background. After applying the Smart Blur to the selected area, deselect the first selection (Ctrl+D) and then select the other window areas with the Polygonal Lasso. Finally, apply the Smart Blur and stronger settings shown in Figure 6.11.

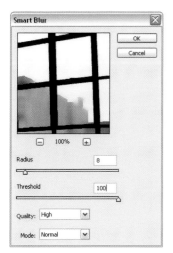 

Figure 6.11:Jeanne's Smart Blur settings (left). The result after applying the Smart Blur filter (right).

Note: The Smart Blur filter's Radius setting specifies the area the filter covers when looking for pixels of dissimilar values. In some cases, a higher number doesn't produce more blur as you might expect. It all depends on the value of adjacent pixels and your Threshold setting. Increasing or decreasing the Threshold setting determines how different the pixel values must be before they are affected by the Radius setting. You can also choose between speed and quality with the Quality setting. The High setting slows the processing but produces a better result. Normal mode is the default, but for special effects you can also choose Edge Only and Overlay Edge.

Balancing the Light

Figure 6.12 shows a dark living room with a lot of light pouring in from a window. Getting a proper exposure in this kind of situation is tricky—especially considering the limits of the relatively inexpensive digital camera Jeanne was using. To balance the light and bring out the details of the room, Jeanne used one of the most useful commands in Photoshop Elements: Shadows/Highlights (Enhance ➢ Adjust Lighting ➢ Shadows/ Highlights). Not only can you lighten the darkest areas of an image independent of the light areas, but also you can use the Highlights control to darken the lighter colors independent of the dark ones.

Figure 6.12:The light needs balancing in this photo. (Photo by Jeanne Zimmermann)

Note: Architects use "before and after" photo-montage techniques to help create visual references for clients and approval boards. An example of these kinds of composites appears in a later chapter (☜ "Pre-visualizing a Scene" in Chapter 8).

This is what Jeanne did to balance the light:

1. She chose Enhance ➤ Adjust Lighting ➤ Shadows/Highlights.
2. She used the settings shown on the left in Figure 6.13. Note that she adjusted only the Lighten Shadows slider. She left the Darken Highlights slider at 0 percent, and the Midtone Contrast slider at 0.

   The results are shown on the right in Figure 6.13.

Jeanne, of course, could have adjusted the lighting of this image by using other methods. For example, she could have used a selection tool to select the brightly lit window area, and then inverted the selection (Select ➤ Inverse) and used Levels controls to adjust the tonal values of the dark areas only. This would have worked fine; however, it would have taken more time than simply using the Shadows/Highlights command.

Figure 6.13:The Shadows/Highlights settings (left) and the results (right).

Creating a Warm and Inviting Atmosphere

Figure 6.14 shows a living room photographed by Jeanne Zimmermann. The cold blue cast is the result of an improper white balance setting and doesn't show the room as it really is. It is easy to apply a warm cast to this image, making it much more inviting to a potential buyer.

Figure 6.14:The original photo has a cold, blue cast. (Photo by Jeanne Zimmermann)

Here is what she did to produce the effect shown in Figure 6.15:

1. She chose Filter ➢ Adjustments ➢ Photo Filter. (You can also apply Photo Filter as an adjustment layer. Just click on the adjustment layer icon located at the top of the Layers palette and select Photo Filter from the pop-up menu.)
2. She selected Filter: Warming Filter (85) from the dialog box shown on the right in Figure 6.15.
3. She set the Density slider to 85 percent.
4. She clicked OK.

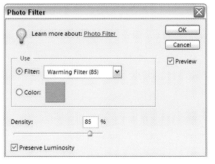

Figure 6.15:The Photo Filter's warming filter makes the room more inviting (left). The Photo Filter's settings (right).

That's all. It's that easy to apply a warm tint to just about any image. If you look at the Photo Filter's pop-up options, you'll also find a collection of other photo filters loosely based on traditional film camera filters. Warming Filter (81), for example, produces a slightly less warm effect, while Cooling Filter (80) produces a pronounced blue, or cool, cast. (Jeanne uses the Cooling Filter on some images when she wants to produce a more industrial or high-tech effect.) You can also customize the Photo Filter by selecting Color from the dialog box and clicking the color swatch to the right. This brings up a color picker, and any color you choose forms the basis for the effect. Sliding the Density slider to a greater percentage increases the effect of the filter.

Sure, there are other ways to use Photoshop Elements to change the tint of any image. Choose Enhance ➤ Adjust Color ➤ Remove Color Cast, for example, or Enhance ➤ Adjust Color ➤ Color Variations. I suggest you start with Photo Filter—it's so easy. If that doesn't work, try one of the other methods.

Removing Wires

Telephone or electric lines are just about everywhere, and it's nearly impossible to shoot a home or building in such a way as to avoid them. Sometimes these lines can be removed easily by using the Clone Stamp or Healing Brush tool, or by using a "Nudge" technique that I'll explain shortly. I say "removed easily" with the following qualification: our eyes are very sensitive to horizontal lines. Take a telephone line that runs horizontally in an image and rotate it so it is vertical, and it's less likely that you'll even notice it. Our innate sensitivity to horizontal lines also means that if you try to remove such a line from your image, you must do it carefully, in a way that leaves no trace. I suggest that if you have a choice between doing the job poorly and leaving a vestige of our modern life, choose the latter.

Having said all this, let's look at two simple techniques for removing the pair of horizontal wires shown in Figure 6.16.

Figure 6.16:Power and telephone lines are hard to avoid but easy to remove.

The first method requires either the Clone Stamp tool or the Healing Brush tool. I'll start with the wires on the left side of the image and use the Clone Stamp tool to remove them. If you choose to use the Healing Brush tool, the method is basically the same. However, with the Healing Brush tool, you are blending—not replacing—pixels, and the results are more unpredictable. You can make the Healing Brush tool act like the Clone Stamp tool by selecting Replace from the Mode's pop-up menu in the options bar.

> **Note:** I don't recommend using the Spot Healing Brush tool for this kind of job. It's easy to use because it doesn't require establishing a sampling area, only a target. However, the results are often unpredictable, especially with larger targets.

Here are the steps for the first method:

1. I selected the Clone Stamp tool (⬛) from the toolbox and kept the default settings in the options bar.

2. I started with a Hard Round 19 pixels brush and then changed to Hard Round 5 pixels as I worked on the wire near the windowsill and the wire near the top of the roof. I chose a hard-edged brush because I wanted to keep the texture of the stucco intact. A soft-edged brush would have diffused the edges and blurred some of the details.

Remember, both the Clone Stamp tool and the Healing Brush tool require you to first place your cursor over the area you wish to clone from. Alt+click then establishes the sampling point. After establishing the sampling point, move the cursor to the target you wish to clone to, click, and paint with your cursor. With the Clone Stamp tool, the results are almost immediate. With the Healing Brush tool, the results are somewhat delayed because the Healing Brush tool does more than just replace pixels; it actually blends texture, lighting, and shading of the sample and target areas.

When working with the Clone Stamp tool (or any other brush tool), get near-instant access to the brush palette by right-clicking anywhere in the image window area. The palette appears on the screen, and you can choose a new brush. This method is especially handy because you can easily match the size of your brush to the area you're working on.

The Clone Stamp tool worked great, as you can see in the close-up in Figure 6.17. I could have kept using it—or the Healing Brush tool—to remove the rest of the wires. To demonstrate a slightly faster alternative, however, I'll use the Nudge method to remove the rest of the lines.

Figure 6.17:I used the Clone Stamp tool to remove the wires that crossed the building.

To use the Nudge method, I followed these steps:

1.   I selected both wires by using the Polygonal Lasso tool. I feathered this selection 5 pixels (Select ➢ Feather or Ctrl+Alt+D), as shown on the left in Figure 6.18. I used the arrow keys on my keyboard to move just the selection outline slightly below the power lines, as shown on the right of Figure 6.18.

 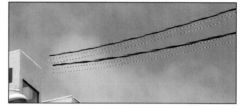

Figure 6.18:I made a selection by using the Polygonal Lasso tool and feathered it 5 pixels (left). Then I used the arrow keys to move the selection down (right).

2.   While holding the Ctrl+Alt keys, I used the arrow keys to nudge up the selection of the sky. This copied my selection and offset the duplicate by 1 pixel (shown on the left in Figure 6.19). I kept nudging the selection until the power lines were replaced by sky. There was a little streaking in the clouds, but after deselecting my selection, I went back and quickly fixed it with the Clone Stamp tool. The final image is shown on the right in Figure 6.19.

Figure 6.19:Holding the Ctrl+Alt keys while using the arrow keys duplicates a selection and offsets it by 1 pixel (left). On the right, you can see the final results.

The Nudge method works especially well when the line to be removed crosses areas of continuous tones. It doesn't work so well in complex areas, where the copying and shifting of pixels are more noticeable.

Shooting Digital: Successfully Shooting Buildings and Rooms

You can do a lot with Photoshop Elements to fix a photograph that is lacking. However, you can save time by shooting interiors or exteriors with certain points in mind in the first place. Here are a few tips:

- If you are using a typical digital camera, you can avoid keystoning by shooting a building straight-on level. This may require the use of a ladder, or it may mean scouting out a higher vantage point, such as the roof of another building or a hill.

- When shooting, focus on desirable aspects of the property, such as hardwood floors, new appliances, a beautiful deck, or a view.

- To avoid window glare, use a polarizing filter. You'll need to rotate the filter until the glare is gone. With digital single lens reflex (SLR) cameras, you can view the effects through the viewfinder. With other digital cameras offering a live image preview, you can see the results in the LCD window. Remember that polarizing filters are most effective when used at a 90-degree angle off axis to the sun. This means the lens is less effective if the sun is directly behind you or in front of you, and most effective when the sun is to the left or right. Polarizing filters can also help increase color saturation in many outdoor shots.

- Shoot around clutter or just remove it before shooting. If your camera has manual aperture and focus controls, you can control the depth of focus and blur a distracting background or foreground.

- Because you are shooting with a digital camera and film costs are not an issue, shoot the same scene from several angles. You can edit the best shot later.

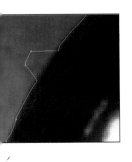

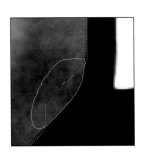

CHAPTER 7: BETTER PRODUCT SHOTS ■

Better Product Shots

7

It doesn't matter if you are selling a camera on eBay or a vintage sports car through a community bulletin board. A professional-looking image will help sell your stuff. Sure, it helps to have a fancy photo studio or a high-end advertisement budget. But you can make a product shot taken with a consumer digital camera in your living room look significantly better just by using various Photoshop Elements tricks and techniques. In this chapter, you'll learn how.

Chapter Contents

Separating a Product from Its Background

Just about anything you do to enhance or fix a product shot begins by using various selection or eraser tools to separate the product from its background. Only after you do this can you effectively do the following:

- Fix or replace a distracting background.
- Colorize, texturize, or add motion blur to the product.
- Add depth through a drop shadow or other layer effect.

How hard is it to use Photoshop Elements to do this? It depends. I've been handed digital photos of products taken against a white or single-color background and with a few clicks of the Magic Eraser tool, I finished the job in a few seconds. Other times, I've been handed a shot of a product placed against a busy background and spent way too much time using many of Photoshop Elements' selection and eraser tools to get the job done right.

Don't be discouraged if your results are less than perfect or if you feel you are taking an inordinate amount of time. The whole time you are trying, you are building skills and experience that will make the job easier next time. If you become really frustrated—and that is an appropriate response—you might even consider reshooting the product against a plain-colored background, which will make your Photoshop Elements work go easier and faster.

Note: When you choose and apply one of the several selection tools to an active layer, you'll get a dotted border that looks like an army of marching ants. Technically, this dotted border is called a *selection marquee*, but I like to think of the little dots as protective ants, keeping the outside at bay. Any tool or task that you apply while the ants are in place will affect only the selected areas. For example, if you choose a Gaussian blur, the effect will apply only to the area that is bounded by the selection marquee. You can easily reverse the selection by choosing Select ➤ Inverse from the menu bar or by using the keyboard command Ctrl+Shift+I. Then, for example, when you apply a Gaussian blur, it will affect only the areas outside your original selection.

The relevant selection tools for this chapter include

- The Rectangular Marquee tool ( )
- The Elliptical Marquee tool ( )
- The Lasso tool ( )
- The Polygonal Lasso tool ( )
- The Magnetic Lasso tool ( )
- The Magic Wand tool ( )

More details on these and the Selection Brush ( ), which gives you a choice between viewing a selection marquee or a colored mask, are provided earlier in this book ("Selection Tools" in Chapter 1).

When It's Easy

The image shown in Figure 7.1 makes me smile with joy. It's a shot taken with a digital camera of a 1940s-style film camera against a single-color background. All it needs is a few clicks with the Magic Eraser tool to remove similar pixels within a predetermined range. This will separate the vintage camera from its background, and I can then add a drop shadow, swap the background, or apply a myriad of other image effects that are possible only when there is a transparent background.

Figure 7.1: It's relatively easy to remove a background when it's a single color. It doesn't matter if the color is slightly graduated.

Here's what I did to remove the background:

1. I chose the Magic Eraser ( ) from the toolbox. The Magic Eraser shares toolbox space with the Background Eraser ( ) and the standard Eraser tool ( ). You can flip through the eraser tools by using the E key on the keyboard.

2. In the options bar, I used the following settings:

   Tolerance: 45. I came up with this number after some trial and error. The default setting is 32, but when I used this number, the Magic Eraser sampled too few variations of color and erased only a part of the background. When I tried a Tolerance of 100, it sampled too many colors and actually ate away, or erased, some of the foreground object as well as the background. See Figure 7.2.

Figure 7.2: A Tolerance setting of 32 was too little (left). A Tolerance setting of 100 was too much (right).

A tolerance of 45 wasn't perfect because it still required a few clicks in different parts of the background to do the job, but it was close enough. Theoretically, if my background had been exactly one color, a Tolerance setting of 1 would have removed all of the background with one click. However, I've noticed that making a photo with no color or tonal variations in the background is difficult. Even when you use a perfectly white or single-color background, the slightest variations in lighting result in different tonal values.

Anti-alias: Selected. This keeps a smooth transition between erased and non-erased parts.

Contiguous: Selected. This setting, which is the default, is very important. If I hadn't kept this setting, the Magic Eraser would have assumed that I wanted to erase all similar pixels in the image, not just pixels contiguous to the one I clicked. This means that if there had been a similar color anywhere in the image, even within the boundaries of the camera, these colors would have been erased as well (regardless of the Tolerance setting).

Sample All Layers: Selected. In this case I had only one layer, so it didn't matter whether I selected this option. However, it would have made a difference if I had had more than one layer and wanted to sample the erased color by using data combined from all visible layers.

Opacity: 100 percent. I wanted to erase completely to transparency. A lower opacity would have erased the pixels to partial transparency. Frankly, for the purposes of erasing a background in preparation for other tasks, I can't think of a reason why you should choose anything less than 100 percent.

3. After I set my options, I clicked first on the top part of the image. As you can see on the left in Figure 7.3, this only partially erased the background. Next, I reset the tolerance to 20 and clicked lower in the image, and to the left in the

shadow areas, until I got what you see on the right of Figure 7.3. I lowered my tolerance to 20, because the higher setting actually erased part of the camera. I also used the standard Eraser tool () to clean up some stray pixels at the very bottom of the camera that weren't erased by the Magic Eraser.

Figure 7.3: One click of the Magic Eraser erased part of the background (left). More clicks with a lower tolerance setting erased the rest of the background (right).

When you use the Magic Eraser (or Background Eraser) on a background layer, as I did, you'll notice that the name in the Layers palette is automatically changed from **Background** to **Layer 0**. That's because a background layer can't contain transparency, and by changing its name, its properties are also changed.

> **Note:** What is a *transparent layer*? It's helpful to think of an illustration in a physiology book that shows the various parts of the human body in several translucent overlays. Viewed together, the layers make up the complete human body. But lift the layers and you can view each component—skin, muscles, skeleton, and internal organs—separately as well. This is basically what's happening when you place an object on a Photoshop Elements' transparent layer. The object—or technically, the grouping of pixels—is surrounded by a sea of transparency that is designated by a translucent checkered pattern. This pattern can be removed or changed to make the transparent areas more or less obvious (Edit ➤ Preferences ➤ Transparency). If the layer that contains transparency sits above another layer, the non-transparent areas of the lower layer show through.

In this chapter, I'll show you ways to create and use layers that contain transparency. Keep in mind that a background layer cannot contain transparency. If you cut or delete from a background layer, it will fill with the background color as defined in the color selection box located at the bottom of the toolbox. If you have a background layer and want transparency in that layer, you'll need to change the name of the background layer to something else. To do this, double-click the layer in the Layers palette and either leave the default name, **Layer 0**, or type something else and click OK. You can also choose Layer ➢ New ➢ Layer from Background from the menu bar.

By the way, what is the difference between the Magic Eraser and the Magic Wand (✎)? Not much. The Magic Eraser finds pixels of similar value and automatically erases them, either to transparency or—if the transparency is locked in the Layers palette—to the selected background color. The Magic Wand finds pixels of similar value and selects them.

In the preceding example, I could have used the Magic Wand to select the background and then pressed the Delete key or chosen Edit ➢ Cut from the menu bar, and I would have gotten the same effect (➥ "Selection Tools" in Chapter 1). Because one click of the Magic Wand wouldn't have been enough, just as it wasn't enough with the Magic Eraser, I then would have held the Shift key while clicking on other areas, thereby adding new selections without deselecting the preceding ones. Of course, to cut to transparency, I also would have had to rename my background layer.

When It's a Little More Difficult

Look at the image on the left in Figure 7.4. The designer of the wine label, Lisa Friedman, didn't want me to get rid of the background; she just wanted me to tone it down a little so she could use the image to promote her design work. Because the background is filled with texture, this image is more difficult to work with than the preceding one.

Figure 7.4: The bottles and the background aren't very distinct (left). No matter what I did, I couldn't get the Magic Wand to select just the background (right).

Just for fun, try using the Magic Wand to select the background. (Forget the Magic Eraser, because Lisa basically liked the background and didn't want to replace it.) I tried various Tolerance settings, but the Magic Wand always seemed to select pixels inside the bottle as well. There were just too many similarities in tone between the bottles and the background for the tool to work efficiently. On the right in Figure 7.4 you can see the results when I chose a tolerance of 44.

Because the Magic Wand wasn't so useful, I decided to use a combination of two other selection tools, the Magnetic Lasso and the Lasso, which share a spot in the toolbox.

I started with the bottle on the right and the Magnetic Lasso tool. Because the edges of this bottle are fairly well defined, the Magnetic Lasso's selection border should easily and automatically snap into place.

This is what I did to select the bottle on the right:

1. I selected the Magnetic Lasso tool (⬚) from the toolbox and chose the following options from the options bar:

   Feather: 0. This is the default setting and I wanted the selection to tightly hug the edge of the bottle, so I left the setting at 0.

   Anti-aliased: Selected. This is also the default setting and will produce a smooth transition between the bottle and its background.

   Width: 40. The range here is 1–40, and I chose 40 because the image is relatively simple and has well-defined edges. With this setting, the Lasso is looking in a 40-pixel radius from the cursor for edge values. In other words, I don't need to be right up close to the edge I wish to select with the cursor. I can be within a 40-pixel range, and the cursor will still find the edge. This means I can be looser with the cursor and work a lot faster. Lower width values are critical when you are working on images with soft edges that are adjacent to other soft edges. In those cases, if you use a higher value, the Magnetic Lasso easily gets "confused" and places anchor points on edges that you didn't want selected. With lower values, you need to be very precise in placing the cursor, and that definitely will slow you down.

   Edge Contrast: 30. The range here is 1–100 percent, and I chose 30 percent after some trial and error. Higher values are usually fine for well-defined edges. I chose a relatively low number because the shadow areas around the top and bottom of the bottle were less defined, and when I selected a higher percent, the Magnetic Lasso didn't do a good job of finding the edges.

   Frequency: 57. I left this at its default. This specifies the rate at which the Magnetic Lasso sets fastening points. A higher value anchors the selection border in place more quickly.

2. I started on the lower-right side of the bottle by clicking the mouse. This set the first fastening point, which anchored the selection border in place. Next, I moved the pointer along the edge of the bottle. As I moved the pointer, the active segment snapped to the strongest edge in the image based on my Width settings. As you can see on the left in Figure 7.5, fastening points were periodically set based on my Frequency setting. (You can remove a previously set anchor by simply hitting the Delete or Backspace key.) I also set fastening points

manually by clicking the mouse. For a close-up view, I used Ctrl+spacebar+click to magnify my image and then held the spacebar to activate the Hand tool so I could scroll around the image.

A couple of times, as I was moving the Magnetic Lasso around a corner, my fastening point jumped way off the edge (you can see this on the right in Figure 7.5). I did one of two things: I simply hit the Delete key, which brought me back to the last fastening point, where I tried again. Or I just left the mistake alone, knowing I was going back later to fine-tune the selection.

 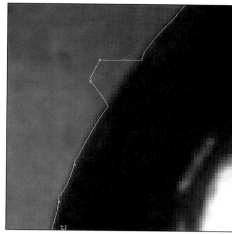

Figure 7.5: This magnified view (left) shows the fastening points and selection border of the Magnetic Lasso tool. I've increased the contrast of the image so you can see the points and border better. A more closely magnified view (right) shows a fastening point gone awry. I'll go back later and fix it with the Lasso tool.

3. After I circled the bottle and was ready to close the selection border, I double-clicked. (You can also press Enter, or watch for the cursor to change when you arrive back at the origin point—a small circle appears—and then click.)

4. To refine the selection, I selected the Lasso tool (🔾) from the toolbox. Because I wanted to subtract from the selection, I clicked the Subtract from Selection icon (🔲) on the options bar. You can also hold down the Alt key. A minus sign (–) appears next to the pointer.

Note: To add to a selection, either choose Add to Selection from the options bar or hold down the Shift key. A plus sign (+) will appear next to the pointer.

5. I then clicked and dragged the cursor around the area that I wanted to subtract, following the edge of the bottle closely. After I released the cursor, the selection was updated to reflect the boundaries of my new selection. See Figure 7.6.

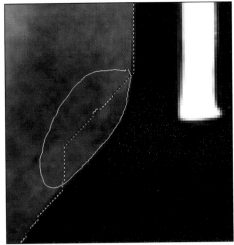

Figure 7.6: Subtract from a selection by choosing Subtract from Selection or holding down the Alt key and circling the area you want deselected.

I like the Magnetic Lasso a lot, but it takes getting used to. The first time I used it, I had no trouble. I was working on an image with clearly defined edges. However, not long after that I had a really frustrating experience with it. I was working on an image that didn't have clearly defined edges, and the selection border was constantly snapping into the wrong place. I didn't seem to have any control over where it was going; I felt I had stuck my fingers into a wad of bubble gum and couldn't shake it loose. I suggest that you spend some time getting to know more about this tool in the Adobe Online Help or elsewhere in this book (☞ "Selection Tools" in Chapter 1).

Extracting Part of an Image

Photoshop Elements 4 has introduced a new tool called the Magic Extractor. This is a neat feature for extracting an object from its background. It isn't flawless, but it's a great tool to have in your arsenal. I started with the image of the two wine bottles shown earlier and wanted to copy the label from the bottle on the right to the bottle on the left.

Here's what I did:

1. With the image of the wine bottles open, I duplicated the background layer (Layer ➤ Duplicate Layer).
2. With the duplicate layer selected, I chose the Magic Extractor (Image ➤ Magic Extractor).
3. In the Magic Extractor window, I used the Foreground Brush tool (at the top of the tool box on the left) to draw several lines on the white label that indicated this was the object I wanted to keep. See Figure 7.7.

Figure 7.7: The Magic Extractor window on the left with red lines indicating what should be extracted and a blue circle indicating what should be eliminated. The preview is shown in the middle, with the final result on the right.

4. I then chose the Background Brush tool—the next tool down—and drew an outline around the area I wanted eliminated. You can use a combination of spots and lines if you wish.

Note: Adobe recommends using lines for the foreground (the portion of the image you want to keep) and spots for the background (the portion you want to erase). In this example, I used an outline around the portion I wanted to erase and it worked fine. It pays to experiment.

5. I then selected the Preview button, and the results showed up after a few seconds. If you make a mistake, press the Reset button at the bottom. This will allow you to easily start over without closing the Magic Extractor window.

6. Since I was happy with the preview, as shown above in the middle of Figure 7.7, I selected OK.

7. The extracted label is now on top of the original background layer. With the Move tool, I dragged the label over to the bottle on the left to get the results shown on the right in Figure 7.7. If I needed to resize the label, I would use the Move tool to drag the handles.

The image now has two layers. I saved it as a PSD file in case I wanted to work on it later or flatten it to save as a TIFF for printing. To copy this label to another image with a bottle in it, I could drag the extracted label layer to the other image, resizing the label or bottle to get them to line up.

Note: Extracting the label on the right was quite easy for Elements. The label on the left is quite difficult, however, since the dark label blends into the bottle. Most other extractions will fall somewhere in between these two, but at least you have an example from both ends of the difficulty scale.

Changing a Product's Color

With a product selected or its background deleted, changing the product's color is easy. Let's try this on the plastic toy image shown in Figure 7.8. The background of this shot was deleted using the Magic Eraser, and the plastic toy is alone on a transparent layer (&r "Separating a Product from Its Background" earlier in this chapter).

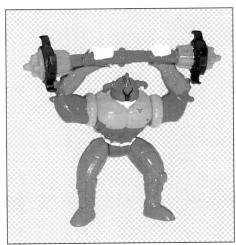

Figure 7.8: Changing the color of this toy is easy. Note that the toy is surrounded by a sea of transparency.

Changing Color via the Hue/Saturation Command

Figure 7.9 shows the effect of changing the colors via the Hue/Saturation controls (Enhance ➢ Adjust Color ➢ Adjust Hue/Saturation). All I did was slide the Hue slider until I got the colors I wanted. Obviously, this method is easy and provides immediate gratification, but it's useful only if you are trying to globally change or shift colors. If you want to change just one color or a specific range of colors, you'll find the following method a lot more useful.

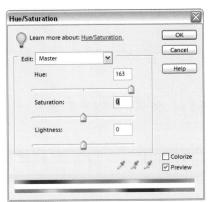

Figure 7.9: Globally change color with the Hue/Saturation controls (left). Slide the Hue slider (right) to change the color.

Changing Color via the Replace Color Command

Figure 7.10 shows the effect of selectively changing the color via the Replace Color command. This method is much more precise than the Hue/Saturation command, because it enables you to create a mask around specific colors and then replace those colors in the image. You can change the saturation and lightness of the masked area as well.

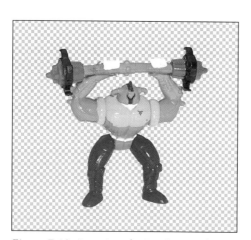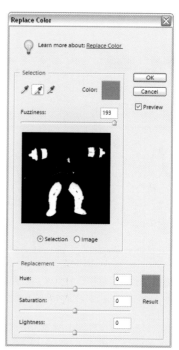

Figure 7.10: By using the Replace Color command, I could selectively replace the pink with purple (left). The Replace Color dialog box (right).

This is how I used the Replace Color command:

1. I selected the Replace Color command (Enhance ➢ Adjust Color ➢ Replace Color).

2. In the Replace Color dialog box shown on the right in Figure 7.10, I used the Eyedropper tool ( ) to select the pink colors in the legs and barbell. The black areas in the preview window are the masked areas. I expanded the tolerance of the mask slightly to include more than the sampled colors by dragging the Fuzziness slider. The black areas in the preview window expanded accordingly. (You can add distinctly different colors to your selection by clicking the Add to Sample eyedropper ( ) found in the Replace Color dialog box.)

3. When I was satisfied that I had masked the areas I wanted, I dragged the Hue slider to change the color just as I wanted. Then I added some saturation with the Saturation slider.

Changing Color via Painting

You can also selectively paint different colors with the brush tools. Before you do this, however, you must select the object so the painting or fill area doesn't spill over into the transparent areas.

To select the object in the Layers palette, on the layer containing your product and transparency, Ctrl+click the layer thumbnail. Another way to prevent color bleeding is to lock the transparent pixels. To do this, click the Lock Transparent Pixels button (▣) in the upper part of the Layers palette.

The left side of Figure 7.11 shows what happens when the plastic toy isn't selected or the transparency isn't locked. The blue paint spills all over the canvas. On the right in Figure 7.11, you can see how selecting or locking the transparency confines the paint to the plastic toy.

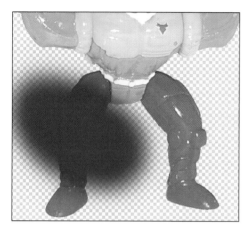 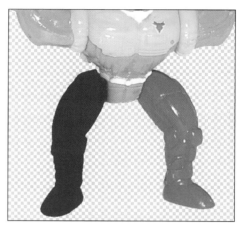

Figure 7.11: Paint spills all over if you don't select or lock the transparency of your image (left). With the object selected or transparency locked, the paint goes only where you want it to go (right).

There are many things to consider when you use a brush tool to change or alter the colors. For example, you'll probably want to experiment with different Mode and Opacity settings. If you leave your settings at their defaults (Mode: Normal, Opacity: 100 percent), you will replace an area that has tonal variations with a single, flat color, which may not be what you want. This is what happened in Figure 7.11.

Here is one simple way to use a brush to change or add colors and still maintain control over how the new paint blends with the old:

1. Assuming that the object you want to paint is already on a transparent layer, select it by Ctrl+clicking the layer thumbnail.

2. Create a new layer and name it **Color** (Layer ➢ New ➢ Layer). Make sure this layer sits above the layer containing the figure you want to color.

3. Select the Brush tool (✐) from the toolbox and if you wish, select the Airbrush option (✍) on the options bar. Pick a brush size from the options bar. Keep the Option settings at their defaults. Select a color to work with from the foreground color box at the bottom of the toolbox.

4. Paint on the layer called **Color**. Make sure the selection from step 1 is still visible. If it's not, your paint will spill all over the layer and not be confined to the parts of the object you want to paint.

5. When you are finished painting, while keeping the **Color** layer active, experiment with different Mode and Opacity settings in the Layers palette.

The advantage of using this method is obvious. Because you are painting on a separate layer, your original image remains intact. If you don't like what you have, just delete the **Color** layer and start over. Also, you are not confined to one Mode or Opacity setting. You can go back and change these settings at any time until you get just the right blending of new and old colors. (Remember, these are the settings accessible via the top of the Layers palette.)

Changing Color via the Paint Bucket Tool

Another simple way to replace color is via the Paint Bucket tool. Figure 7.12 shows an example of a product prototype created by product designer Marcia Briggs for L.L. Bean. Marcia made the line drawing by hand and then scanned it into her computer to create the image on the left. Because the client wanted to see the product in various colors, Marcia left the original drawing uncolored, knowing how easy it is to use the Paint Bucket tool to create several versions.

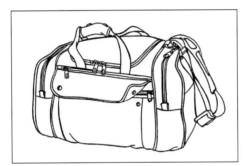 

Figure 7.12: Marcia drew this product prototype and scanned it into the computer (left). She then filled the bag with color (right) using the Paint Bucket tool.

This is what she did to color the bag:

1. She selected the Paint Bucket tool ( ) from the toolbox.
2. She left all the options in the options bar set at their defaults. Because she was working with a line drawing with basically no color variations to take into consideration, the Tolerance settings didn't matter. (The Paint Bucket tool looks for adjacent pixels that are similar in color value. The more colors you want to replace, the higher you must set the Tolerance values.)
3. She specified a foreground color from the foreground color box at the bottom of the toolbox. She clicked inside the area where she wanted the color. Then she chose another color and clicked inside another area. She did this until she got the results shown on the right.

By the way, even though Marcia was working with essentially a bitmap image, which is an image that contains only black or white, she stayed in the RGB mode (Image ➤ Mode ➤ RGB Color). Otherwise, she wouldn't have access to any other colors. Also, the Paint Bucket tool doesn't work in Bitmap mode.

Changing a Product's Texture

It's easy to change the texture of a product or add a pattern after you have selected it or separated it from its background. You can try a variety of Photoshop Elements tools, filters, and fills and see what you come up with.

Adding a Pattern via the Paint Bucket Tool

Let's go back to Marcia's bag. With her permission, I've applied a series of patterns by using the Paint Bucket tool. I also changed some of the colors (see Figure 7.13).

Figure 7.13: These patterns were created by using the Paint Bucket tool and setting the Fill option to Pattern.

Here's all I did to produce the patterns shown in this image:

1. I selected the Paint Bucket tool ( ) from the toolbox.
2. In the options bar, I changed Marcia's Fill setting from Foreground to Pattern and then chose a pattern from the Pattern menu.
3. I clicked inside an area where I wanted the first fill pattern. Then I chose another fill pattern and clicked inside another area. I did this until I had I totally ruined a perfectly good bag.

Adding a Pattern via the Fill Command

Look at the pattern shown in Figure 7.14.

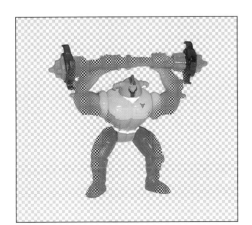 

Figure 7.14: To create this pattern, I used the Fill command and selectively erased (left). With the plastic toy selected, I created a new layer, called it Pattern, and made it active (right).

To create this pattern, I first removed the toy from its background with the Magic Eraser. Then I did the following:

1. I selected the plastic toy by Ctrl+clicking the layer thumbnail.

2. I created a new layer and named it **Pattern** (Layer ➢ New ➢ Layer). I made sure that this layer sat above **Layer 0,** which contained the plastic toy (see Figure 7.14).

3. I chose Edit ➢ Fill Selection from the menu bar, making sure that the layer called **Pattern** was active.

4. I selected Pattern in the Use list and selected the fill of my choice in the Custom Pattern box, shown on the left in Figure 7.15.

Figure 7.15: From the Use list, I chose Pattern (left). The Pattern filled the plastic toy (right). I used the Eraser tool to selectively remove it where I wanted the original colors to show through.

5. I clicked OK. The pattern totally filled the plastic toy, as shown on the right in Figure 7.15.

6. To selectively remove the pattern, I selected the Eraser tool () from the toolbox and selected a soft-edged brush from the options bar. On the layer called **Pattern,** I applied the Eraser to various parts of the toy where I wanted to remove the pattern.

Another variation of this procedure is to apply a Texture or Image Effect from the Styles and Effects palette located in the palette bin. (Select Effects from the left drop-down menu, and select either Textures or Image Effects from the drop-down menu on the right. Choices, represented by icons, appear below the drop-down menus.) If you use one of these effects, follow the procedure I just outlined, but after step 1, drag and drop the effect you want from the Styles and Effects palette onto the image window. You can also double-click the effect's thumbnail. You don't need to make a new layer; a new layer is created automatically when you apply the effect. Just remember to avoid using any textures whose name is followed by the word *layer.* For example, if you use the Sunset (Layer) effect, the effect won't fill your selection—it'll fill the entire layer.

Adding Pattern via a Fill Layer

You can also apply a pattern (or for that matter, a solid color or gradient) via a fill layer. Not only is a fill layer nondestructive, it can be easily changed at any time.

To use a fill layer for applying a pattern, take these steps:

1. Select your object by Ctrl+clicking the layer thumbnail. This is important. If you don't select your object, the fill will completely fill a layer.

2. Choose Layer ➤ New Fill Layer ➤ Pattern (or Solid Color or Gradient). After you follow the prompts and create a new layer, you will see the choices shown in Figure 7.16. Alternatively, you can select Pattern (or Solid Color or Gradient) directly from the Layers palette. Just click the Create New Fill or Adjustment Layer icon ( ) at the top of the Layers palette, and you'll go directly to the Pattern Fill options.

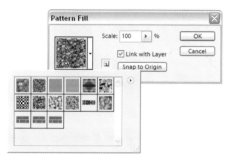

Figure 7.16: After you select New Fill Layer ➤ Pattern and follow the prompts to create a new layer, you get the choices shown here.

3. Choose from the various palette choices.

4. After you select your fill, you can go back later and edit the mask to selectively apply the fill (↪ "Making Dull Images Shine" in Chapter 3). Figure 7.17 shows an image and its Layers palette. The Opacity is set at 62 percent, which allows only part of the fill to show through. Also, I've erased some of the layer mask.

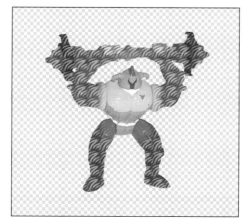

*Figure 7.17: Note the edited mask in the **Pattern Fill 1** layer (left). The final image after selectively applying a pattern fill and setting the layer Opacity to 62 percent (right).*

Note: When you erase by using the Eraser tool on a fill layer, or for that matter, on an adjustment layer, you must make sure the foreground color—found at the bottom of the tool-bar—is set to white. You can also erase from a fill or adjustment layer by using the Brush (▨) found in the toolbar. When using the Brush to erase, make sure the foreground color is set to black.

Adding a Pattern via a Filter

Many filters will create a pattern or texture effect. Especially useful are the ones found on the Filter menu in the Artistic, Noise, Pixelate, Sketch, and Texture submenus. These filters act on the actual pixels of the image, so I suggest you create a duplicate of the layer containing the object you want to alter and apply the filter to the duplicate layer. That way, you can selectively erase or change the layer Mode or Opacity settings, as I did in the preceding example.

Here is an example of using a filter to create a pattern:

1. I duplicated the layer containing the plastic toy and called it **Stained Glass Filter**.

Note: To make a duplicate layer, select the layer you wish to duplicate and either choose Layer ➤ Duplicate Layer from the menu bar or select the layer and then drag it to the Create a New Layer icon (▣) at the top of the Layers palette.

2. I applied the Stained Glass filter to the duplicate layer. (Choose Filter ➤ Texture ➤ Stained Glass from the menu bar, or drag and drop—or double-click—from the Styles and Effects palette.)

3. From the Layers palette, I set the Mode to Color Burn and the Opacity to 46 percent. In Figure 7.18, you can see my Layers palette on the left and the final image on the right.

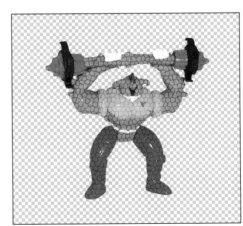

Figure 7.18: Note the duplicate layer called **Stained Glass** *and the Mode and Opacity settings (left). The final image after applying the Stained Glass filter (right).*

And So On...

I think you get the idea. As you can see, there are many ways to add texture and fills to your product shot—or for that matter, to any digital image. Don't forget to experiment with different Opacity and Mode settings in the Layers palette and to use the Eraser tool to erase areas in which the fill or texture isn't needed.

Improving the Background

The background sets the mood, gives a subject context, and helps add depth. Sometimes the simplest background is best. Other times a colorful, flashy background is called for. Regardless of what you use for a background, it should complement and not detract from the main subject.

Simplifying a Complex Background

One of the easiest ways to improve a background is to diminish its effect. Let's apply this to the wine bottles from a previous example (☞ "Separating a Product from Its Background," earlier in this chapter). As noted earlier, the art director basically liked the background but wanted it toned down.

Here's what I did after I selected the wine bottles:

1. I chose Select ➢ Inverse to make the background the active selection. I then slightly feathered this selection 2 pixels to soften the transition between the foreground and background (Select ➢ Feather).

2. The background was too dark, so I adjusted its tonal values and lightened it with the Levels command (shown on the left in Figure 7.19).

Figure 7.19: Just by applying Levels to the background, the image was improved (left). Applying a Gaussian blur made the background less distracting (right).

3. This helped, but to give the picture more depth I applied a Gaussian blur to the background (Filter ➤ Blur ➤ Gaussian Blur). I set the Radius at 13.5 pixels.

4. The label still needs selective burning and dodging, and the reflections at the top of the bottles are too harsh. I'll fix the harsh reflections later in this chapter, but as you can see on the right in Figure 7.19, simplifying the background already has significantly improved this shot.

Creating New Backgrounds

After you have isolated a product from its background, there is no reason why you can't insert any background you want. Backgrounds can come from another photograph or purely from selective Photoshop Elements' effects and a little imagination. Some of the most effective backgrounds are a combination of a real photograph and a Photoshop Elements filter or effect.

In Figure 7.20, you'll see an example of a background created using a combination of a gradient fill adjustment layer and an effect.

Figure 7.20: This green background on the left was quickly replaced using a gradient fill and an effect on the right.

Here's what I did to create the new background:

1. I started by converting the background to a layer, selecting the hideous green with the Color Wand, and deleting it. You may have to do a little more work if your background is not a solid color. Next, I made a new gradient background by clicking the Create Adjustment Layer icon ( ) at the top of the Layers palette and choosing Gradient from the pop-up menu. (You can also select Layer ➤ New Fill Layer ➤ Gradient from the menu bar.)

2. From the various Gradient options, I chose the settings you see on the left in Figure 7.21. To find the Silver gradient, I started by clicking the drop-down arrow adjacent to the word Gradient in the Gradient Fill dialog box. Then, when another palette of options opened, I clicked the arrow pointing to the right. This brought up a drop-down menu with various options. I selected the one called Metals. This loaded several icons into the palette. I chose the one named Silver (the third one from the left—the name appears only when the cursor is placed on top of the icon).

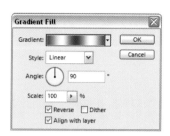 

Figure 7.21: I chose the Silver gradient with the settings you see in the dialog box (left). The Layers palette after step 4 (right).

3. I clicked and dragged the gradient adjustment layer to the bottom of the Layers palette.

4. Making sure that the **Citroen** layer was active, I applied Colorful Center from the Styles and Effects palette (choose Effects and then Image Effects from the pop-up menus). You can see on the right in Figure 7.21 that the Colorful Center effect created a duplicate layer and left the **Citroen** layer intact.

The great thing about creating backgrounds this way is that they are totally changeable. I can go back at any time and adjust the gradient adjustment layer or remove an effect (⌐ "All about Layers" in Chapter 1). My original image remains unchanged.

Figure 7.22 illustrates how easy it is to go back and change a background created this way. I simply selected the first layer in Figure 7.21 called **Gradient Fill**; then in the Styles and Effects palette I selected Layer Styles from the pop-up menu and Complex from the other pop-up menu. Next, I clicked the layer style called **Rainbow**. The Layers palette for this new image is shown on the right in Figure 7.22.

 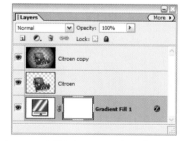

Figure 7.22: It's easy to change or add to a background if it is created with an adjustment layer (left). This is the Layers palette for the image (right).

Modifying an Existing Background

The image shown on the left in Figure 7.23 is a mistake. My digital camera fired unexpectedly. Instead of erasing the blurred image, I kept it and then used it later to create the background shown on the right.

Figure 7.23: This was a mistake (left), but I thought the image might have potential, so I saved it. Later, I used it as the basis for this background (right).

This is what I did to modify the image:

1. I opened the image shown on the left in Figure 7.23 and chose Enhance ➢ Auto Levels.

2. I applied the Add Noise filter (Filters ➢ Noise ➢ Add Noise). I used the following settings: Amount: 57, Distribution: Gaussian.

3. I applied the Radial Blur filter (Filters ➢ Blur ➢ Radial Blur) and used the following settings: Amount: 22, Blur Method: Zoom, Quality: Best. The results are shown in Figure 7.24.

Figure 7.24: The image after applying the Add Noise and Radial Blur filters and with a 1368 × 1676 pixel selection.

4. I opened a new image of a bag and noted its pixel dimensions, 1368 × 1676.

5. Now, with the **Mistake** image, I selected the Rectangular Marquee tool (⬚) from the toolbox and in the options bar I changed Style from Normal to Fixed Size. Then in the Width box I typed 1368, and in the Height box I typed 1676. I then made a selection, placing the constrained Rectangular Marquee over the area that I wanted. I made a copy of this selection (Ctrl+C).

6.   I pasted the **Mistake** selection into the bag image (Ctrl+V). It fit perfectly. I made sure that the **Mistake** image layer was below the one containing the bag. You can easily move layers into different positions (☞ "All about Layers" in Chapter 1).

7.   I added a drop shadow to the bag and I was done (☞ "Adding Depth," next).

Shooting Digital: Are You Sure You Want to Delete?

One of the great features of digital cameras is the capability to erase shots you don't like. A word of caution: As you've seen throughout this book, there are many ways to use a digital photo. Think twice before you erase an accidental shot of the pavement, because it could be used as an interesting background. Think before you erase a picture that is inherently boring but could conceivably be used in a collage. Think before you erase a bad photo of Uncle Jimmy, because the good shot of Aunt Annie next to him could be used for something else. Instead of always erasing, consider investing in more memory for both your camera and computer and building a digital library of those potentially useful "throwaways."

Adding Depth

After you've found a background, you need to give your image a sense of depth. An easy way to do this is to make a clear distinction between the foreground object and the background. Assuming you've isolated your object from the background, you can do this by creating a drop shadow or other layer style.

Drop Shadows

Drop shadows are commonly used to create a sense of depth. Here's what I did to replace the background, rotate, and add a drop shadow to the image shown in Figure 7.25.

Figure 7.25: The original digital camera shot.

1. I selected and removed the background by using the Magic Eraser ()
    (👉 "Separating a Product from Its Background," earlier in this chapter). I
    rotated the image to the right (Image➤ Rotate ➤ 90° Right).

2. I created a new background by clicking the Create Adjustment Layer icon (⬤)
    at the top of the Layers palette and choosing Solid Color from the pop-up menu.
    I chose white. (Alternatively, you can choose Layer ➤ New Fill Layer ➤ Solid
    Color from the menu bar.)

3. With the layer called **Bag** selected, I chose a drop shadow from the Styles and
    Effects palette (Layer Styles from the first pop-up menu and Drop Shadows from
    second pop-up menu). I applied a drop shadow called Soft Edge by simply click-
    ing its icon. After the drop shadow was applied, an f symbol appeared in the
    Bag layer in the Layers palette. I double-clicked the f, which opened the Style
    Settings dialog box. (Choosing Layer ➤ Layer Style ➤ Layer Settings also brings
    up this dialog box.) From this box, I tweaked the drop shadow by using the set-
    tings shown on the left in Figure 7.26. The Layers palette is shown on the right.
    The final image is shown in Figure 7.27 (👉 "Layer Styles" in Chapter 1).

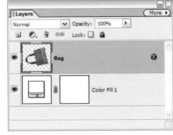

*Figure 7.26: These are the settings I used for my drop shadow (left). The Layers palette
shows the new background and layer with the drop shadow layer style attached (right).*

Figure 7.27: The final image.

Outer Glow

You can use other layer styles such as Outer Glow to also make a distinction between a product and its background, as you can see on the left in Figure 7.28.

Figure 7.28: Use Outer Glow styles to add depth to your image (left). These are the settings I used for my Simple Outer Glow (right).

To add depth with Outer Glow, I started with the previous example and then did the following:

1. I changed the color of the background from white to black by double-clicking the layer thumbnail in the **Color Fill** layer and choosing black from the Color Picker.

2. I deleted the drop shadow effect from the layer called **Bag** by selecting that layer and then choosing Layer ➤ Layer Style ➤ Clear Layer Style from the menu bar.

3. I applied an Outer Glow from the Styles and Effects palette to the layer called **Bag** (choose Layer Styles from the first pop-up menu, then Outer Glows from the second pop-up menu). I chose the Outer Glow called Simple. I used the settings shown on the right in Figure 7.28.

Creating Lighting Effects

Effective lighting can give a product shot dimension and drama. If the interesting lighting isn't there to begin with, you can use Photoshop Elements' Lighting Effects filter to create it. Figure 7.29 shows how lighting effects can alter an original shot.

Figure 7.29: The lighting is even but uninteresting (left). With the help of the Lighting Effects filter, the image is more dramatic (right).

This is what I did to create the effective lighting:

1. I selected the Lighting Effects filter (Filter ➤ Render ➤ Lighting Effects).
2. I applied the settings shown in Figure 7.30 and clicked OK. I dragged the circle in the Preview window on the left to get the desired effect.

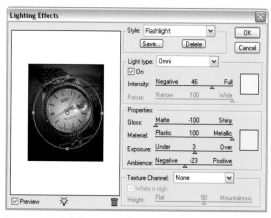

Figure 7.30: These are the settings I used for the Lighting Effects filter.

Making a Product Smile

Will Rutledge is a professional photographer and the manager of the photo studio at QVC, an electronics retailer mostly known for its cable shopping channel. As you can imagine, Will shoots a lot of products. He mostly uses a high-end digital camera, and he often uses Photoshop to fix a photo because something isn't quite right with the product.

Will took the product shot shown on the left in Figure 7.31 for QVC's annual report. He was given creative license to make the image fun, and that is what Will did to make the image shown on the right.

Figure 7.31: A typical shot of an electrical outlet (left). A not-so-typical shot of an electrical outlet, helped along by the 3D filter (right). (Photo by Will Rutledge. Copyright 2000 QVC.)

1. Will used the Lasso tool (🔲) to select one of the rectangular slots.
2. He copied and pasted his selection onto a separate layer. He rotated the slot until it was horizontal by choosing Image ➢ Transform ➢ Free Transform (see Figure 7.32).

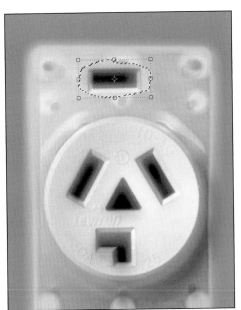 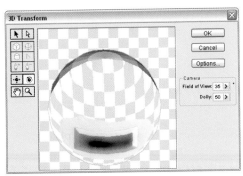

Figure 7.32: After copying and pasting the vertical slot, Will used a Transform command to rotate it to a horizontal position (left). The 3D filter mapped Will's selection to a sphere. When he rotated the sphere, he got a smile (right).

3. With the layer containing the pasted, rotated slot selected, he opened the 3D filter (Filter ➤ Render ➤ 3D Transform).

4. In the 3D Transform filter dialog box, Will selected the Sphere tool (⊕) and drew a circle tightly around the rectangular slot in the preview window. He then clicked the Trackball tool (⬢) and in the preview window, rotated the ball until he got a smile. Then he clicked OK. The result is shown on the right in Figure 7.32.

5. Will used the Move tool (⬆) from the toolbox to position his smile in place. He then used the Eraser tool (⬛) and Clone Stamp tool (⬛) to make the smile completely replace the old slot.

    Who says life always has to be so serious?

Simplifying a Product Shot

Converting a complex product shot into a simple line drawing can be useful for brochures or instructional material. To simplify the shot shown on the left in Figure 7.33, I applied the Photocopy filter with the foreground color set to black (Filter ➤ Sketch ➤ Photocopy). I also set the Detail at 14 and the Darkness at 33. The result is shown on the right.

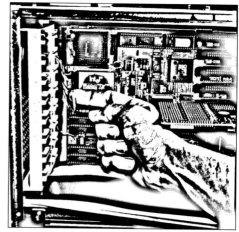

Figure 7.33: The original photo (left). A much simpler image after applying the Photocopy filter (right). (Photo by Maurice Martell)

Shooting Digital: Creating Your Own Mini Photo Studio

It doesn't take a lot of money or equipment to set up a mini photo studio in your office or home. With the following setup, you'll be able to shoot perfect photos of small objects such as books, coins, jewelry, small appliances, or other objects you want to place on an online auction or prepare for a flyer or ad:

- A digital camera
- A white, seamless backdrop and a means to hold it
- Two diffused light sources

Look at the following diagram. The seamless paper is draped over a table. It's important for it to drape smoothly, or it will catch light and create unwanted shadows. Also notice how the object to be photographed is set away from the edge of the paper. This also keeps shadows at a minimum. Two diffused lights are enough for most situations. You can diffuse a light source with a sheet of thick, translucent plastic or a window screen. Move the lights around and try to make the light fall as evenly on the product as possible.

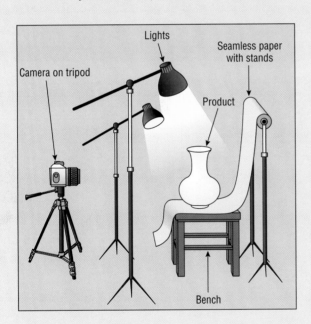

Lights

Seamless paper
with stands

Camera on tripod

Product

Bench

When you shoot, experiment with different angles. But remember to show as much of the product as you can. The shot should be informative as well as interesting.

Where can you find the equipment for this mini studio? Professional photography supply houses all carry the seamless paper, lights, and stands. Go to my website (**www.shooting-digital.com**) for more resources.

Making Photo-Realistic Composites

Composites are like tapestries woven together from the fabric of more than one source. They can be relatively simple to create (adding a missing person to a group shot) or complex (combining many images from many sources). Creating a photo-realistic composite tests nearly all of your Photoshop Elements skills, from selecting to transforming, from cloning to managing multiple layers. But when you're finished, you'll have a single image visually richer than the sum of its individual parts.

Chapter Contents

Adding Yourself (or Anyone) to a Group Shot

I'm not in the shot shown on the left in Figure 8.1, but I wanted to be. It was one of those typical situations when old friends gather and suddenly someone says, "Hey, let's get a group shot of *everyone*!"

Figure 8.1: I wanted to be in this shot (left), but someone had to take the picture. My wife took this second shot with me in it (right).

I had my digital camera but no tripod, and I couldn't find anything high enough to place the camera on for a self-timer shot. Instead, I took a shot of the group and then my wife took a shot with me in it (shown on the right in Figure 8.1).

I left my spot open in the first shot so I could simply copy and paste myself from one image into the other. Here's how I did it:

1. I opened both digital images. Starting with the one that didn't include me (I'll call this Image 1), I adjusted Levels to make the image look lighter using Enhance ➢ Adjust Lighting ➢ Levels.

2. I turned to the second shot, the one with me in it. I'll call this Image 2. I wanted the exact same Levels settings applied to Image 2 so the tonal values of my upper body would match those of the other people in Image 1. I could have noted my Input Levels settings in my Levels controls in Image 1, and with Levels open for Image 2, typed them into the Levels Input boxes.

    Instead, I used a neat shortcut that I learned from Will Rutledge at QVC, Inc. With Image 2 active, I pressed Ctrl+Alt+L. This shortcut automatically applied the same adjusted Levels settings from Image 1 to Image 2, and I got exactly the results I wanted. Cool. I could have continued applying Levels this way to an entire batch of similar images, which would have been a real time-saver.

    Another simple way to do this is to use an adjustment layer for Levels in Image 1 and then drag the adjustment layer over to Image 2 to get the same adjustment (➥ "Adjustment and Fill Layers" in Chapter 1).

3. On Image 2, I used the Lasso tool ( ) to make a loose selection, as shown in Figure 8.2. At this point I wasn't precise, and in fact, I purposely included other areas of the image to help me position my pasted selection.

4. Next, I copied my selection (Ctrl+C).

Figure 8.2: I made a loose selection with the Lasso tool and copied the selection.

5. I pasted my selection (Ctrl+V) into Image 1, and Photoshop Elements placed it automatically into its own layer. From the Layers palette, I set the Opacity to 50 percent so I could see part of the underlying image. I then used the Move tool ( ) to position the selection into place. I used part of my friend Joe's shoulder that I had included in my pasted selection as a reference (see Figure 8.3).

Figure 8.3: I set my layer Opacity to 50 percent so I could see the underlying image.

Note: What is the difference between the Paste and Paste Into Selection commands found on the main menu bar under Edit? Suppose you select an expanse of sky using the Rectangular Marquee selection tool ( ) and then copy the selection. If you Paste this copy into another layer or image, the entire rectangular selection will be pasted into a layer of its own. In contrast, using Paste Into Selection enables you to set different boundaries. Before you paste, suppose you make a selection on the layer or image with, for example, the Elliptical Marquee selection tool ( ). Then when you paste the rectangular selection from before using the Paste Into Selection command, the rectangular selection will appear bounded and defined by the selected circle. No new layer is created. Since the entire copied area is still there beyond the selection boundary, you can place your cursor over it, click and hold, and move it around within the selection. You can use any of the selection tools and create any shape. Paste Into Selection uses that selection as the parameter—or mask, if you will—for your paste.

5. Next came the tricky part. I reset my layer Opacity to 100 percent and used the Eraser tool ( ) with a Hard Round 19 pixels brush to remove the superfluous areas around my head and shoulders. Then I magnified my image from 100 percent to 300 percent and used a Hard Round 9 pixels brush to erase any leftover tidbits. At one point, when I was working on the area to my left, I momentarily changed the layer Opacity back to 50 percent so I could tell where the face of the man in front of me ended and my neck and shoulder started. I finished with a Soft Round 13 pixels brush, brushing the edges of my pasted selection lightly to make them blend into the background.

6. I didn't bring my legs over from Image 1, so I just used the Clone Stamp tool ( ) to clone the shadow that was already there in Image 2. The final image is shown in Figure 8.4.

Figure 8.4: Now the group is complete.

This composite was easy to make because Image 1 and Image 2 were so similar. Creating a realistic composite is more difficult when you are working with shots taken at different times, with different lighting, with different film, or at different pixel resolutions. The next section shows you how to work with images of different resolutions. Later in this chapter you'll learn about keeping composites in mind while taking pictures (☞ "Shooting Digital: Creating Realistic-Looking Composites").

Note: Copying, pasting, and other tasks associated with creating composites can take up a lot of memory, and at some point, the performance of Photoshop Elements could become noticeably compromised. If this happens, you can free up more memory by using the Clear command (Edit ➢ Clear). You'll have a choice of which item type or buffer you want to clear: Undo History, Clipboard Contents, or All. If the item type or buffer is dimmed, it just means it is already empty. You should use the Clear command only as a last resort, because it can't be undone.

Combining Different Resolutions

Look at Figure 8.5. You can't easily tell by looking at the printed page, but the image on the left was taken with a 6 megapixel digital camera that produced an image with a pixel resolution of 2000 × 3008. The image on the right has a pixel resolution of only

1000 × 1504. Figure 8.6 shows what happens when I select the girls from the larger file and paste them into the smaller one. The selection from the larger image "swamps" the smaller target image.

Figure 8.5: The image on the left has a pixel resolution of 2000 × 3008, while the target image on the right has a resolution of only 1000 × 1504.

Figure 8.6: This is what happens when a selection from the larger file is pasted on the smaller one.

How can I scale the selection to fit? Here are two ways:

A. Scale the entire larger image file down *before* selecting and pasting to the smaller image.

B. Use the Resize command (Image ➢ Resize ➢ Scale) *after* selecting and pasting part of the larger image into the smaller one.

I'll get to option B in a minute. If you choose option A, here are the steps:

1. With both images open, select the smaller, target image by clicking anywhere on the image window with your cursor.

2. Determine the pixel dimensions of the smaller, target image. Do this by choosing Image ➢ Resize ➢ Image Size from the menu bar and noting the Width or Height in the dialog box. Figure 8.7 shows the Image Size dialog box. (You need only the width or the height in pixels, not both.) You can also get the image size by right-clicking the title bar of the image window or by going to the Info palette, provided your Ruler Units are set to Pixels (Window ➢ Info). You can set up the ruler dimensions either by clicking the More button on the palette and selecting Palette Options or by selecting Edit ➢ Preferences ➢ Units and Rulers.

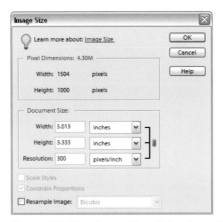

Figure 8.7: The Image Size dialog box. Make note of the Width or Height dimensions. When resizing, make sure the Resample Image check box is selected.

3. Select the larger image. Choose Image ➢ Resize ➢ Image Size from the menu bar. Enter a Width or Height value in pixels as determined by the smaller image. If Constrain Proportions is selected, Photoshop Elements automatically calculates the corresponding width or height. Make sure the Resample Image check box is also selected in the Image Size palette. If you leave the sampling method at its default Bicubic setting, you'll get good results. You might get better results if you select Bicubic Sharper from the pop-up menu. Bicubic Sharper preserves crisp edge transitions and works best when you are resampling *down*. Bicubic Smoother, another option, suppresses image noise and is a good choice when you resample up to a larger pixel resolution.

4. Click OK in the Image Resize dialog.

Note: You can also use the Crop tool to resize one image to match the size of another. With the target image open and selected, simply select the Crop tool from the toolbar ( ). In the Crop tool options bar, use the Aspect Ratio drop-down box to select Use Photo Ratio. Photoshop Elements automatically inserts the dimensions of the selected image in the Width and Height boxes, also located in the options bar. Now click another image. Apply the Crop tool. It automatically applies the values of the previously selected image to the one you are working on. Be sure to set the Aspect Ratio to No Restrictions on the options bar when you are finished. If you don't, the next time you use the Crop tool, it will apply the same settings even if you don't want it to.

After your larger image has been resampled to match the target image, you can use any of the various selection tools to select the part of the image you want to copy and paste. (I used the Lasso tool to select the two girls.) Next, you can copy (Ctrl+C) and paste (Ctrl+V) onto the target image. Alternatively, you can Ctrl+click and hold and drag the copied selection to the target image. Either way, a copy of the selection will appear on a layer of its own. You can use the Move tool (⊹) or arrow keys to precisely position the selection. If you need to tweak the size of the selection to get it just right, use the method described next (Image ➤ Resize ➤ Scale). Just be sure the layer containing the pasted image is selected. Figure 8.8 shows the final composite.

Figure 8.8: The final composite after matching resolutions.

A word of warning: Don't inadvertently close and save the resized image. You'll end up throwing away a lot useful image data.

If you choose option B, take these steps:

1. On the larger image, select and copy (Ctrl+C) the desired element(s).

2. Paste (Ctrl+V) or Ctrl+click, hold, and drag the copied selection to the target image. It's likely, because of the discrepancy in image size, that your pasted selection will block most of or the entire target image, as it did in my example in Figure 8.6.

3. Choose Image ➢ Resize ➢ Scale from the menu bar. Normally you could simply point your cursor to one of the bounding boxes located at the corners of the selection and click, hold, and drag the selection to a desired size. Because the pasted selection is so large relative to the target image, the bounding boxes are often not visible. Instead, go to the options bar (Figure 8.9). Point your cursor to the space between the Width and Height boxes and click on the linked chain. This will lock the width and height together, maintain a fixed aspect ratio, and thereby prevent distortion. Now type in a percentage in either box. Start with 25 percent. Because you've locked the width and height together, you need to type in only one box. You might need to type in a lower percentage, depending on the size of the pasted selection.

Figure 8.9: The Scale options bar. Note the chained link between the Width and Height boxes. Select this link to maintain a fixed aspect ratio and to prevent distortion when you enter percentage values.

4. At some point, with enough reduction, the bounding boxes at the edges of the selection will become visible. You can now point your cursor at one of the boxes and click, hold, and drag the selection to the desired size. Hold the Shift key when you drag to constrain the dimensions. You can also move the selection into place by placing your cursor in the middle of the selection and then clicking, holding, and dragging. After you are finished, select the Commit button in the options bar or press the Enter key.

Swapping Kids

Children will be children. Some children like to be tossed up in the air, and others don't. Photographer Maggie Hallahan couldn't get the kid on the left in Figure 8.10 to be thrown in the air, look at the camera, and smile all at once. What a surprise! But everything else about the picture was fine, so Maggie tried another tack. She shot the other photo shown in Figure 8.10, this time with an older child who smiled but wasn't keen on being thrown in the air. Maggie's client was PJA, an advertising and marketing agency in San Francisco.

Back at the computer, PJA Photoshop pro Bretton Newsom went to work with Photoshop, putting the best parts of Maggie's two shots together. I talked with Bretton before he finished the final composite, and he agreed to walk me through the steps he'd taken so far on a low-resolution file. It should be noted that Bretton, like most pros, works with the full version of Photoshop. However, just about everything he did in this example can be duplicated in Photoshop Elements.

Figure 8.10: Everything about this picture was fine, except for one child (left), who was great but didn't like being thrown in the air. A second picture (right) provides a replacement child for the composite. (Photos by Maggie Hallahan)

Here are the steps Bretton took to create the composite:

1. He used the Clone Stamp tool ( ) to remove the child in the first image (shown on the left side of Figure 8.11).

2. He went to the image of the smiling older child and created a precise selection around the child by using a Quick Mask—a function not available in Photoshop Elements. Fortunately, the program has a roughly equivalent tool: the Selection Brush tool ( ). (For more on using the Selection Brush tool and other selection tools, ↪ see "Selection Tools" in Chapter 1.) After the child was selected, Bretton copied the selection and pasted it into its own layer in the first image, as shown on the right in Figure 8.11. He used the Move tool ( ) to position the pasted selection into the outstretched arms of "mom."

Figure 8.11: Bretton used the Clone Stamp tool to remove the first child (left). After selecting and copying the second child, Bretton pasted the smiling child into the outstretched arms of "mom" (right).

3. As you can see in Figure 8.11, the woman's arm is covered by the pasted image of the child. So Bretton copied and pasted part of the woman's arm and shoulder, as shown on the left in Figure 8.12. He placed the layer containing the arm and shoulder above the layer containing the smiling child, which put the arm and hand in the correct position relative to the child. You can see Bretton's Layers palette in Figure 8.12. (Alternatively, he could have selectively used the Eraser tool on the child to reveal the woman's left arm.)

Figure 8.12: Bretton made a copy of the woman's arm and shoulder and pasted it onto its own layer (left). Bretton's Layers palette is shown to the right. Note that the arm and hand layer is above the layer containing the child.

4. As a final step, Bretton added a very slight shadow on top of the child's dress, as if it came from the outstretched arm. The final image is shown in Figure 8.13.

Figure 8.13: The final composite.

After the client approved this low-resolution "comp," Bretton worked on a high-resolution copy of both images to make a perfect version suitable for print.

Note: Photo-realistic composites make compelling narratives. Mark Ulriksen, a freelance illustrator for *The New Yorker* magazine who is best known for whimsical portraits often derived from photo composites, says that when creating such a composite, you should think of your Photoshop Elements' image window as a stage and all the images you want to use as your props. Let's say you just came back from a family vacation to the Grand Canyon. Your "props" might include shots of the Grand Canyon, the kids, a red-tailed squirrel, and your favorite hamburger stand. You might start by using the Grand Canyon shot as the background. Then pick another image (or prop, if you will) that represents the most memorable part of your vacation. That great meal, the squirrel that ate from your kids' hands, whatever. Place that image in front of the background and make it big so it takes on significance and importance. Now place the other images, or props, in relationship to the dominant image or prop. Use Photoshop Elements' transform tools to play with the size of each image, and use the Move tool to change the relationships between the objects. Experiment, and most importantly, have fun.

Seamlessly Pasting

One of the biggest challenges in composite making is pasting a selection seamlessly into another image so it looks natural without a halo or jagged edges. It's a lot easier when you are pasting a selection into a busy background, as I did in the first example in this chapter, but more difficult when you are pasting to an area of continuous tone, such as a sky.

I use one method with pretty good success. I'll demonstrate by selecting, copying, and pasting the Doggie Diner head from the image on the left in Figure 8.14 to the shot shown on the right.

Figure 8.14: The two components of my composite.

Figure 8.15 shows a close-up of what happens if I simply make a selection, copy it, and paste it into the street shot.

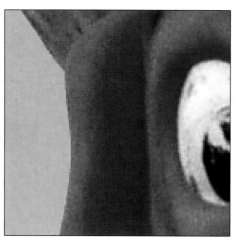

Figure 8.15: By using a simple copy and paste, I get the jagged edges shown here.

Now I'll try something different:

1. I make a selection just as before, using the Magic Wand selection tool (◥). One click on the white background with a Tolerance of 15 pretty much does it, except I'll use the Lasso tool (⟆) to select some of the white areas in the Doggie Diner's hat that were missed by the Magic Wand.

2. I reverse my selection by using Select ➢ Inverse (Ctrl+Shift+I) and shrink it by 2 pixels (Select ➢ Modify ➢ Contract). This tightens up my selection and reduces the chance that I'll copy unwanted background areas.

3. I add a 3-pixel feather (Select ➢ Inverse, then Select ➢ Feather), as shown in Figure 8.16.

Figure 8.16: The Feather Selection dialog box.

4. I copy (Ctrl+C) and paste (Ctrl+V) the selection on top of Telegraph Hill. I use the Move tool (⊕) to position it where I want. Because I slightly shrank my selection and feathered it, the edges of the Doggie Diner head now blend more naturally into the new background.

5. As you can see in Figure 8.17, the paste is almost seamless. Where it is not, I can use the Eraser tool (⬚) with a combination of both hard-edged and soft-edged brushes to make it perfect.

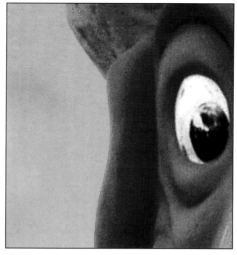

Figure 8.17: Now the Doggie Diner head looks like it's always been on top of Telegraph Hill. Even on closer examination (right), the deception is barely visible.

Cloning Elements from Multiple Images

Up to now, I've shown you mostly select, copy, and paste techniques to combine images. With some images it's just as effective to use the Clone Stamp tool to create photo-realistic composites. For some people, "painting" images with this tool is more intuitive and satisfying than pasting.

Take the screen shot in Figure 8.18. The images were all taken with the same camera, around the same time of day, against a similar background. Using the Clone Stamp tool to combine parts of these images is easy because I don't need to be precise. It would be more difficult if the backgrounds were significantly different. In that case, selecting, copying, and pasting would be the way to go.

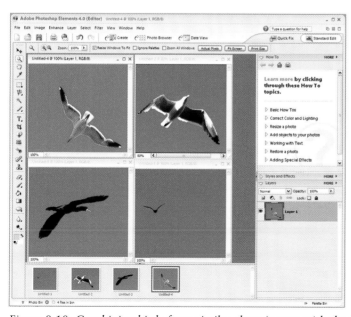

Figure 8.18: Combining birds from similar shots is easy with the Clone Stamp tool.

Note: You can also use the Healing Brush tool to act like the Clone Stamp tool. In the Healing Brush tool option bar, select Replace from the Mode's pop-up window. Select Sampled as your Source. Now the Healing Brush tool replaces pixels from the target with pixels from the source rather than blending them, as it does in the Normal mode.

This is what I did to come up with the composite:

1. I opened the four image files. (To view all your images side by side, choose Window ➤ Images ➤ Tile.)

2. I selected one of the bird photos as a target image. Because I wanted each cloned bird to go on its own layer, I created three new layers: Layer ➤ New ➤ Layer.

3. Next, I selected one of the other three bird images and selected the Clone Stamp tool from the toolbar (![icon]). I picked a Soft Round 100 pixels brush from the options bar and placed my cursor over the bird. Then I held the Alt key and clicked on the bird. This defined my source point.

4. After I had my source point defined, I selected my target image. In the Layers palette, I made sure I was working on one of the new layers. Then I placed my cursor over the target image window, roughly in the area where I wanted to add the new bird. I clicked, held, and painted. After I finished, I selected another image, containing another bird, and repeated the process. On the target image, in the Layers palette, I made sure to select yet another new layer, thereby keeping each bird on its own layer.

5. After I finished cloning the birds, I went back and fine-tuned my composite. I used the Eraser tool to define the edges of some of the birds. I used a Transform command to slightly reduce the size of one of the birds (Image ➤ Resize ➤ Scale). I slightly rotated the orientation of one of the birds (Image ➤ Transform ➤ Free Transform). I could easily do all this because each bird was on its own layer. Figure 8.19 shows the final version.

Figure 8.19: The resulting composite (left); the Layers palette (right). Note that each cloned bird is on its own layer.

Note: If you want to clone within the same image, it's often useful to clone onto a separate layer. To do this, first create a new layer (Layer ➤ New ➤ Layer). Select the layer containing the pixels you want to clone. Select the Clone Stamp tool from the toolbar and—this is very important—go to the options bar and select the box next to Use All Layers. Define your source point by holding the Alt key and clicking. Then, in the Layers palette, select the new layer. Now when you click and hold while painting the image window, the cloned part appears on its own layer. You can move it around separately, or remove it without damaging the original underlying image. This also holds true with the Healing Brush tool. Select Sample All Layers from the Healing Brush tool's option bar to "heal" onto a separate layer.

Pre-visualizing a Scene

Photo-realistic composites are extremely important in the world of architecture. Architects can use a composite not only to show a client what a potential building or remodel will look like, but also to help convince a design review board to approve a project by showing the effect that it will have on a neighborhood.

David Mlodzik is one of those rare architects who is not only versed in design but is also computer-literate and adept with high-end digital imaging. A significant part of his business is providing other architects and the construction community with design visualization and graphic services.

Figure 8.20 shows one of his projects for a Hilton hotel. At the time David started work on the project, the hotel didn't even exist. He took the design done by the San Francisco firm RYS Architects, and used a 3D rendering and animation program to create several views of the hotel. Then he turned to Photoshop. Although he worked in the full version of Photoshop, everything he did is possible using Photoshop Elements.

Here are the steps he took to create an image of the hotel:

1. He scanned the site photograph shown in Figure 8.20.

Figure 8.20: The site photograph. (Photo by David Mlodzik)

2. He copied and pasted the hotel into a layer with the site photograph. The rendering had a black background, which David removed by using the Magic Wand selection tool () and then cutting to transparency.

3. David applied a slight Gaussian blur to the hotel rendering to make it look more realistic (Filters ➤ Blur ➤ Gaussian Blur).

4. As you can see on the left in Figure 8.21, the hotel sits in front of the McDonald's in the site photograph. David created a copy of the background layer containing the site photo. In that layer, he erased the areas shown at the right in Figure 8.21 by using the Eraser tool () and various selection tools to select and delete.

Figure 8.21: When it's pasted in (left), the hotel sits in front. David used various erasing techniques to make room for the hotel (right).

As you can see on the left in Figure 8.22, the hotel looks like it has always been there.

Figure 8.22: The final composite (left). David's Layers palette (right).

Note: If you want to create a composite from several images and are willing to give up some control, try using Photomerge: File ➤ New ➤ Photomerge Panorama. It's fast, it's easy, and it's fun. I'll tell you more about this Photoshop Elements plug-in later in the book (☞ Chapter 9).

Shooting Digital: Creating Realistic-Looking Composites

A while back I got a call from a company in Sweden that wanted a group shot of their board of directors for an annual report. The only problem was that one of the directors, futurist Paul Saffo, lived in California and wasn't about to make the long trip just for a photo opportunity. Would I shoot a picture of Saffo here, and they'd Photoshop him into the group later?

When you attempt to come up with a photo-realistic composite as I did for this one, there are several things to consider. Ideally, all the images should be shot with the same kind of camera and lens and from the same perspective. In my case, I had to rent the same kind of lens they used in Sweden. Unless you want to spend a lot of time trying to match the film grain or the resolution of the digital file, use the same type of film, or if using a digital camera, use the same resolution. As you can see in the following picture, it worked out just fine. And neither Saffo nor, for that matter, I, had to endure a long plane ride.

Creating Panoramics with Photomerge

Until recently, it took an expensive camera or a time-consuming cut-and-paste procedure to produce images that offered a field of view beyond 90 degrees. That's all changed with Photomerge. All you need are two or more sequential, digital images taken with just about any kind of camera, and Photomerge will automatically blend and stitch them together into a panoramic that is both beautiful and informative. This chapter shows you how to use Photomerge to create panoramics and other types of photomontages as well.

9

Chapter Contents

Planning for Photomerge

Photomerge does a very good job of creating panoramics on certain sequenced photographs, especially ones that were shot with the capabilities of Photomerge in mind. To avoid a lot of frustration and to help you manage your expectations about what Photomerge can and cannot do well, keep the following tips in mind:

- Expect mixed results, depending on the content of your image. Expect better results from images that contain a modest amount of edge detail, such as a building with windows.

- Plan to spend time later in Photoshop Elements using the Clone Stamp tool (▧), Healing Brush tool (▨), and the Burn and Dodge tools (▨) (▨) to clean up areas where the merge wasn't perfect.

- Keep an open mind for lucky mistakes that occur when Photomerge doesn't do what you expect it to do.

- Use Photomerge for things other than panoramics—for instance, collages. (I'll show you how to make collages in the last project of this chapter and how to extend latitude with Photomerge in Chapter 11.)

You'll get better results with Photomerge if you follow these suggestions as you shoot:

- Use a tripod and keep the camera level. If you can't use a tripod, plant your feet firmly and keep the camera as level as possible as you turn from your waist. If your camera has one, use the optical viewfinder rather than the LCD. Holding the camera firmly to your eye helps maintain consistency.

- If you are using a zoom lens, don't zoom while you shoot your sequence. Keep a consistent focal length.

- If your camera has an exposure lock, use it to maintain a consistent f-stop and exposure between frames. If you have only an automatic setting, avoid scenes with wide variations in lightness and darkness.

- Don't use a flash in one frame and not in the others.

- Consider rotating your camera 90 degrees into a vertical (or portrait) orientation, which will give you a larger view vertically (up and down) than if you held the camera horizontally.

- Avoid using filters, especially polarizing filters. Filters can cause slight vignetting, or fading, on the edges of the image, which results in noticeable banding when images are merged together.

- Use the camera's viewfinder to pre-visualize the panoramic before shooting. Turn your head slowly and imagine how the panoramic will look. Pay attention to the way the light changes from the start of the panoramic to the end. Avoid extreme fluctuations of light and dark.

- When you shoot, allow a one-third to slightly less than one-half overlap between frames. Use a visual reference to imagine a spot one-third to one-half of the way into the viewfinder, and then rotate the camera so that spot is at the opposite edge of the frame in the next shot. Then, find your next visual reference before rotating again. If you overlap more than one-half of an image between frames, the blending will suffer.

- Use your camera's "stitch assist mode," if it has one, to help you line up the images in the LCD viewfinder. Some digital cameras, such as the Canon PowerShots, have this feature.

Creating a Precious View

To create the panoramic shown in Figure 9.1, I mounted my Nikon D100 digital camera on a tripod and zoomed in on the scene using a long focal length. I chose a long focal length purposely because I wanted to compress the perspective and at the same time create a wider angle of view. If I had used a wider focal length to create the images for my panoramic, it would have required me to shoot fewer frames to cover the same angle of view, but the picture would have been totally different. The buildings would have seemed much farther away, which isn't how they look to the naked eye.

Figure 9.1: This view was created by stitching together several sequenced frames.

To maintain a consistent exposure for each frame, I selected a Nikon function button that locked my auto-exposure. If the exposure doesn't vary from frame to frame, Photomerge creates a smoother stitch. I shot one frame, then rotated the camera and took another, and then rotated the camera and took another, repeating this until I covered the scene. I used visual references to overlap each shot by about a third, but I wasn't particularly precise, and the variations didn't seem to affect the final Photomerge results.

After transferring my digital files to the computer, I did the following:

1. I opened Photomerge from the File menu (File ➤ New ➤ Photomerge Panorama).
2. I chose Browse from the Photomerge dialog box and navigated to my source files. I selected all the image files by Shift+clicking consecutive files. You can also Ctrl+click non-consecutive files. Figure 9.2 shows the Photomerge dialog box after I selected the files. (Photomerge automatically adds any files that are saved and open on the desktop. You can selectively remove them or any other files by using the Remove button.)

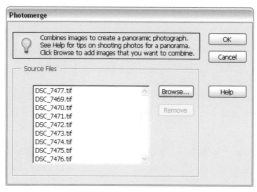

Figure 9.2: The Photomerge dialog box after selecting the sequenced images.

3. In the dialog box, I clicked OK and then waited while Photomerge went through an automatic process of opening, transforming, and stacking images into layers. When the merge was done, the window shown in Figure 9.3 appeared.

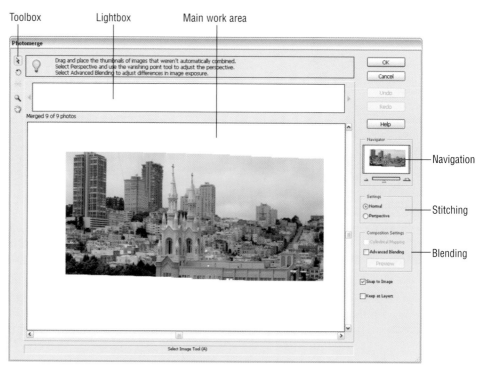

Figure 9.3: The work area in this Photomerge window consists of a toolbox, a lightbox, a main work area, and various navigation, stitching, and perspective options.

At this point, I could click OK and Photomerge would automatically render a perfectly useable, full-resolution version of my panoramic. However, for the sake of this exercise, I'm going to explore some of the Photomerge options available.

Note: You can stop the Photomerge process at any point by simply pressing Esc.

Applying Perspective Control

Look at the Settings box in the Photomerge work area shown in Figure 9.3. You'll see that Normal is selected and Perspective is not. Normal is the default setting, which works fine for most landscape and scenic shots. However, at times, applying a perspective improves a panoramic and makes it look more natural. Often you won't know unless you try.

To apply a perspective to my panoramic, I selected Perspective from the Settings box; Figure 9.4 shows the results. The perspective didn't look right to me, but I tried to fix it by setting a different vanishing point. By default, if Perspective is selected, Photomerge makes the middle image the vanishing point. If you click on the various images with the Select Image tool, the image that is outlined in blue is the vanishing point. Since the images overlap, you have to click carefully.

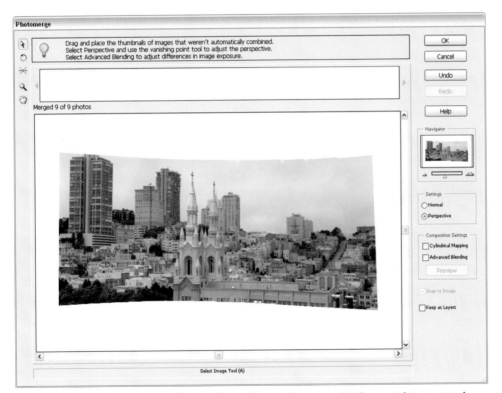

Figure 9.4: Here is the image after applying Perspective control. The vanishing point, by default, is set to the middle image.

What is a vanishing point? It's helpful to think of the *vanishing point* image as a base image, or one that sets the perspective for all the others. For example, if the vanishing point image is in the middle, as it is in this example, the images on either side are transformed so that they lead the eye toward the center. If you look again at Figure 9.4, you'll see the bow-tie configuration that I found objectionable.

To try another vanishing point, I simply selected the Set Vanishing Point tool (✳) and clicked another image in the work area. In Figure 9.5, I made the image on the left the vanishing point. See what happens to the perspective? In an attempt to correct the perspective to the new point of view, the images to the right of the vanishing point are transformed in size and shape. To deselect the vanishing point completely and start over, I simply clicked the Normal radio button. Undo works for this as well.

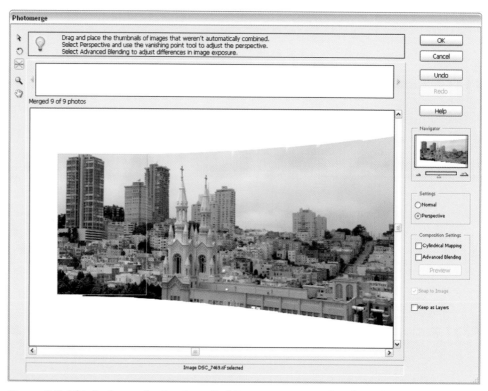

Figure 9.5: This is the result after I applied Perspective control and set the vanishing point to the image on the far left, outlined in blue.

After experimenting with different vanishing points, I decided to turn Perspective off and go with the Normal setting.

Manually Arranging Images

In this example, Photomerge automatically arranged my images. But what happens if your images are shot in such a way that they don't easily match up and Photomerge cannot automatically arrange them? If this happens, you'll see a dialog box like the one shown in Figure 9.6. Then you need to arrange the images yourself.

Figure 9.6: A dialog box appears if Photomerge can't automatically arrange your images. If this happens, you can still try to arrange them manually.

You do this by dragging images from Photomerge's lightbox into the main work area. Figure 9.7 shows how I have started this process by dragging two of the thumbnail representations from the lightbox into the main work area. (I placed my images into the lightbox by holding the Alt key and clicking Reset, but Photomerge automatically places images there if it can't arrange them.) I then dragged the other thumbnail representations from the lightbox to the main work area, placing each one adjacent to the next. Because parts of the underlying image showed through, it made alignment easier.

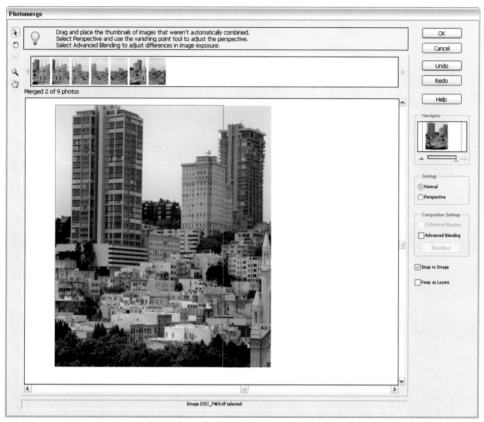

Figure 9.7: When you drag one image so that it overlaps another, you can see part of the underlying image and therefore more easily line up the images.

As similar parts of the adjacent images overlapped, something remarkable occurred. When Photomerge detected similar areas, it automatically snapped them together. The more edge detail it had to work with, the easier it was for Photomerge to line up the adjacent images. (If you have Perspective selected, the program automatically corrects perspective and attempts to compensate for the natural distortion between images. If you have Perspective turned off, Photomerge still looks for similar edges and snaps the images together, albeit without any perspective compensation.)

It's easy to forget where your vanishing point is. To find it, with Perspective checked, simply hold down the Alt key and roll your mouse over the frames. The vanishing point image has a light blue border, and all the other images have red borders.

Note: To move your images from the work area back into the lightbox, you can drag them one by one. To move all the images at once back into the lightbox, hold the Alt key. The Cancel button changes to Reset. Click Reset and start editing your composition again.

Setting Advanced Blending

Next, I tried different blending options. Advanced Blending differentiates between areas of detail and areas of similar tones or colors. When it detects a lot of detail, Advanced Blending applies a sharper blending transition. When it detects similar tones or colors, it applies a more gradual blending transition. In some cases, Advanced Blending can compensate for different exposures in adjacent frames. On these types of images, if you don't use Advanced Blending, you'll see obvious diagonal banding.

In my image, Advanced Blending added several sharp shafts of light shooting down from the top of the image. The shafts of light didn't make any sense, so I attributed the flaw to a bug in the software. I turned Advanced Blending off, and the artifacts disappeared and the blending was just fine. (You can see a preview of the effect of Advanced Blending by selecting the Preview button from the Photomerge window.)

Note: If you select the Keep as Layers check box, Photomerge keeps individual images that make up the panorama on separate layers. (If you select Keep as Layers, Advanced Blending is no longer an option.) Use this option if you are not satisfied with the way Photomerge blends images. With each image on its own layer, you can use a combination of the Eraser with either the Clone Stamp tool or Healing Brush tool to blend the images manually. In Chapter 10, "Extending Dynamic Range with Photomerge," I'll show you a way to use Photomerge and the Keep as Layers option to extend the dynamic range of a digital camera by merging two or more images with different exposures.

Rendering the Final Panoramic

I clicked the OK button and waited while Photomerge merged the higher-resolution versions of my images. Up to this point, Photomerge had worked on and displayed only screen resolution versions of the images. The time it takes for this transformation depends on the size of the final image and the computer's processing speed. With the final panoramic open as a new Photoshop Elements file, I adjusted the Levels controls and used the Healing Brush tool (![icon]) to clean up some of the background. Then I cropped the irregularly shaped image into a rectangle, and I was done.

Creating an Interior Panoramic

How many times have you tried to shoot an interior photo and couldn't get back far enough to fully capture the room? Cutting a hole in the wall behind you might help, but that solution is not practical. Using an expensive super-wide-angle lens might help, but many of these lenses create a fish-eye look.

Professional photographer and panoramic/virtual reality expert Scott Highton encounters logistical problems like this all the time. It's his business and passion to push the boundaries of photography, to take it places it could never go before the advent of the computer. The shot in Figure 9.8 is an example. (The three images that make up this panoramic are not available for download.) Scott created the panoramic of a large satellite control room of a major telecommunications company by stitching together three sequenced images with Photomerge. By doing this, he got a fully corrected shot that would have been virtually impossible otherwise.

Figure 9.8: This interior panoramic is made up of three images stitched together with Photomerge. (Photo by Scott Highton)

Here are the steps Scott took to shoot the images:

1. He set a 35mm camera on a tripod and used an 18mm rectilinear lens. (The *rectilinear lens* is a corrective lens that makes straight lines appear straight in wide-angle images.) He used a medium-speed print film, which gave him a lot of exposure latitude.

2. Using a specially marked tripod head, he shot a sequence of 12 consecutive images at 30-degree intervals, going well beyond the 120-degree view you see in Figure 9.8. Scott used all 12 images and another software program to stitch together a 360-degree panorama for a QuickTime VR presentation, but that's another story. (To see Scott's virtual reality work, go to **www.highton.com**.)

3. He processed the film and had the images digitized onto a Kodak Photo CD.

Scott then took three of the images that covered the field of view he wanted, and in Photoshop Elements he did the following:

1. He selected Photomerge (File ➣ New ➣ Photomerge Panorama).

2. He clicked the Browse button in the dialog box.

3. He selected the three images.

4. Scott started with the central image by dragging and dropping its thumbnail into the main work area. With Perspective selected, this image automatically became his vanishing point image. He then placed the other images on either side of the vanishing point image. As you can see in Figure 9.9, the images came in sideways.

Figure 9.9: When an image comes in like this, use the Rotate Image tool to correct it.

5. Scott used the Rotate Image tool () to turn the images 90 degrees. Holding down the Shift key while turning constrained the move to 45-degree increments. Because the images could be rotated only one at a time, turning them was time-consuming, and Scott wished Photomerge offered some way to turn all the images with one command. The images also came in out of order. That's because the Photomerge Panorama command doesn't follow the sequence of the images in the first Photomerge dialog box but attempts to sequence the images based on their filenames or numbers. Although this may be annoying, you can always rearrange the order of the thumbnails in the lightbox by clicking and dragging.

> **Note:** Photoshop Elements offers several useful Photomerge keyboard shortcuts. You can use the Zoom tool by pressing Z, and holding down the Alt key toggles Zoom In to Zoom Out. You can also nudge your images around with the arrow keys, and you can click and drag your work around the window. Ctrl+Z will step backward, and Ctrl+Shift+Z will step forward in the Undo history.

6. Because the images contained a lot of edge detail, they snapped right into place. The perspective transformation worked well also, and even matched up the lines in the ceiling. Scott used Advanced Blending with good results (see Figure 9.10).

Figure 9.10: Photomerge corrected the perspective and blended the three images together nicely. The light blue box shows the vanishing point image. (Photos by Scott Highton)

7. Scott then clicked OK.

8. The final panoramic was nearly perfect. Scott had to only crop, apply the Levels command, apply a slight Unsharp Mask, and he was done.

Creating an Epic Panoramic

Only a very expensive panoramic camera could have matched the results that Scott Highton got with a conventional camera and Photomerge, shown in Figure 9.11. A fish-eye lens would have covered the same field of view but with a huge perceived distortion. (The five images that make up this panoramic are not available for download.)

Figure 9.11: This is actually five images stitched together. (Photo by Scott Highton)

Scott created this moving panoramic of the Lincoln Memorial in much the same way that he created the interior shot described in the preceding section. His shooting technique was basically the same, and once again, he shot this as a 360-degree panoramic that could be turned into a QuickTime VR. His Photomerge settings were also the same; he kept the Perspective and Advanced Blending settings on. As you can see in Figure 9.12, he set his vanishing point directly in the middle.

Figure 9.12: The vanishing point is in the middle. (Photo by Scott Highton)

Although this image looks great at first, on closer examination it reveals some of the limitations of Photomerge on this type of image. If you look on the left in Figure 9.13, for example, you can see where Photomerge had trouble matching a column. This is because of the lack of edge contrast that Scott had so much of in the previous example. You can also see on the right in Figure 9.13 where Photomerge had trouble correcting the perspective. Still, even with its flaws, it's a dramatic image.

 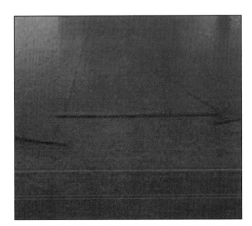

Figure 9.13: Photomerge had trouble aligning the column because of the lack of edge detail. It also had trouble correcting the perspective.

Making a Handheld Vertical Panoramic

I don't want you to get the impression that the only way to use this cool tool is by shooting very carefully in a controlled way. You also don't have to shoot horizontally; you can shoot up and down and create vertical panoramics. Driving past a mountain pass in Norway, I stopped and snapped three quick shots, holding the digital camera by hand. As you can see in Figure 9.14, Photomerge did a fine job stitching the images together. I didn't select Perspective because adding a perspective gave the image a distorted look that I wasn't happy with. I also didn't select Advanced Blending because Photomerge worked fine without applying that option.

Figure 9.14: This is actually three handheld shots, stitched together with Photomerge.

Note: To create 360-degree panoramics, follow these steps: Shoot a 360-degree sequence. Then use those images to make three separate 120-degree panoramics with Photomerge; make sure Cylindrical Mapping is selected and Perspective is deselected. (Photomerge handles only 120 degrees or fewer at a time.) Next, load the three 120-degree panoramics into Photomerge and stitch them together, again with Cylindrical Mapping selected and Perspective deselected.

Photomerging a Collage

There is no reason why your images need to be in sequence to use Photomerge. I brought several images into Photomerge and played with different arrangements until I got the Hockneyesque image you see in Figure 9.15. Sure, I could have created the montage by cutting and pasting the images into their own Photoshop Elements layer. If I had done this, though, the process wouldn't have been nearly as much fun. Every time I wanted to move a particular image, I'd go to its layer, select it, and then move it. Using Photomerge was much faster and more satisfying.

Figure 9.15: This Hockneyesque collage was created in Photomerge.

In this case, I chose Normal instead of Perspective (there was no vanishing point to speak of). To help create a smooth overlap between images, I selected Snap to Image and Advanced Blending.

Using Adobe Camera Raw and Other Advanced Techniques

This chapter includes several examples that require a higher commitment to "getting your hands dirty" and spending a little more time to get an image just right. Ultimately, learning the advanced techniques shown in this chapter will help you take your digital imaging skills to a higher level of expertise.

10

Chapter Contents

Using Adobe's Camera Raw

Many digital cameras offer a choice of file formats. The mostly commonly used file format to save an image in is JPEG. But some of the more advanced digital cameras offer a format that saves the RAW data that comes directly off the sensor. (Check your camera's specs to see whether your camera does. Settings are usually adjusted via the camera's menu.)

Note: When "raw" image data is the product of a digital camera, it's usually called a RAW file to distinguish it from other file formats.

This RAW data is full of potential. It hasn't been touched by on-board camera processing and is therefore full of information that may be very useful. Think of the RAW data as a negative in traditional photography, and the JPEG or TIFF file as a print. If you save the "negative," you can always make a perfect "prints" later. A print from a print is never as good.

To coax the best image from this data, you need special software that interprets the data. You also need to know what you are doing. Some manufacturers include RAW imaging software with their digital cameras, but because you are using Photoshop Elements 4, no worry: It comes with Camera Raw, a powerful plug-in that works with most RAW formats.

Note: RAW data files differ from manufacturer to manufacturer, and even from camera model to camera model. (Here are a few typical file extensions: Nikon **.nef**, Olympus **.orf**, Canon **.crw**, Minolta **.mrw**, and Fuji **.raf**.) RAW formats are constantly being changed, so if you find the plug-in doesn't read your RAW file, go to **www.adobe.com** and download the latest version of the plug-in. You can tell which version you are using by clicking Help in the Editor and selecting the About Plug-In menu and clicking Camera Raw.

Let's start with opening RAW files in Photoshop Elements and then move on to using the powerful Adobe Camera Raw plug-in shown in Figure 10.1.

Shooting Digital: When to Shoot RAW

Assuming your digital camera supports a RAW format, use RAW when quality is critical and you have the time and means to process the results yourself. Consider this musical analogy: When you listen to a symphony, you want the highest possible fidelity to enjoy the nuances and subtleties. Fidelity is less important as the music itself becomes less complex. When you want to see a symphony, think RAW. Conversely, if space on your memory card is an issue, shoot JPEG, because RAW files are generally much larger.

It's also important to remember that with many digital cameras there is no reason why you can't save one image as a JPEG, a subsequent one as a TIFF, and yet another image as RAW, basing your choice on the content of the shot or your needs. Some professional digital cameras can save a single shot in more than one format simultaneously.

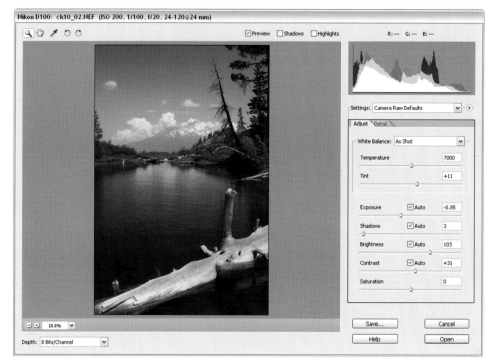

Figure 10.1: The Camera Raw plug-in work area.

Opening RAW Files

To open a RAW file into the Camera Raw plug-in, do *one* of the following:

- Choose File ➢ Open from the Editor menu bar. Navigate to and open your file. The Camera Raw plug-in automatically opens.
- From the Organizer, with one or more images selected, choose Edit ➢ Go to Standard Edit or Go to Quick Fix from the Organizer menu bar, or click the Edit icon at the top of the Organizer to see similar choices. Right-clicking the image reveals the same choices also. After selecting any of these choices, the Camera Raw plug-in automatically opens. An even simpler way to open the Raw plug-in is to select one or more images and then type Ctrl+I.

When the plug-in opens and you finish processing one image, the next one appears in the plug-in if multiple images were selected initially. Selecting Cancel at any time closes the plug-in; the Esc key closes the plug-in also. If you want to skip an image and go on to the next one, pressing the Shift key turns the Open button into a Skip button.

Processing with the Camera Raw Plug-In

As you can see in Figure 10.1, the Camera Raw plug-in offers many options for optimizing your image. Let's go through each component and feature of the plug-in and see how it works. Just keep in mind that in the rapidly evolving world of RAW, the plug-in will be updated—and while the basics of processing a RAW file will remain—you'll likely see additional features in future versions of the plug-in, which can be downloaded for free from the **www.adobe.com** website.

Image Preview Window and Navigation

To the left of the Camera Raw plug-in window is the image preview. Here you'll find familiar navigation and magnification tools. To magnify an image, use the Zoom tool ( ) from the toolbox. To reduce an image, hold down the Alt key while using the Zoom tool. You can also choose a percentage from the zoom level menu. Right-clicking the image brings up the pop-up menu, where you can also change the magnification level.

Note: Right-clicking with the Eyedropper tool active lets you try the various White Balance settings.

You can change the image orientation with the Rotate icons ( ) at the top left of the image preview window. Photoshop Elements saves an image's Camera Raw settings so the rotation will still be applied to the dialog box preview when you reopen the camera RAW file.

Move an image around the image preview window by selecting the Hand tool ( ), and clicking and dragging the image window. You can also press and hold the spacebar at any time to move your image around in the image window.

To the far left of the image area, near the bottom of the plug-in window, is the Depth pop-up menu that enables you to choose between 8 Bits/Channel and 16 Bits/Channel. I suggest you set your Depth to 16 Bits/Channel. I'll explain why later in this chapter.

Histogram and Clipping Tools

At the top right of the Camera Raw window is a histogram, which graphically maps the tonal values of the red, green, and blue colors in your image. The histogram changes accordingly as you apply different color and tonal values. An ideally-exposed image produces a well-distributed histogram, with a range of values spread across the graph. Values clumped to the left or right of the graph often indicate that the image is too dark or too light, respectively. The histogram also indicates color distribution. Red, Green, and Blue values are graphed separately, and dominance of one of these colors signifies a color shift in that direction.

At the top of the image window you'll find other useful indicators for determining proper exposure values. If you select Highlights, any areas containing highlights with no detail (commonly referred to as *highlight blowout*) will appear red. Select Shadows, and shadow areas of your image containing pure black and no details will appear blue. Figure 10.2 shows an image with both blown-out highlights and blocked shadows. You can confirm this by looking at the histogram in the upper right of the Camera Raw plug-in window. The highlight values are shifted to the right and are *clipped* by the edge of the graph, indicating loss of highlight detail. The tonal values are clumped to the far left of the graph and are also clipped.

Figure 10.2: When Highlights is selected, areas of your image that contain blown-out high-lights appear red. Note how the values in the histogram (upper right) are clumped to the left, which confirms highlight *clipping. When Shadows is selected, areas of your image that contain pure black appear blue. Note how the values in the histogram are clumped to the right, which confirms* shadow clipping.

Note: *Clipping* refers to the movement of pixel values to either the highest highlight value (255)—which is represented by the far-right border of the histogram, or the lowest shadow value (0)—which is represented by the far-left border of the histogram. A photo that is *clipped* has areas that are either completely white or completely black and have no image detail. Most people agree that this is not a good thing.

Settings

In the Settings menu of the Camera Raw plug-in, you have the following choices:

Image Settings is relevant only if you have previously updated an image. The first time you open an image, Camera Default is selected. At that moment, Camera Default and Selected Image are the same. However, if you alter the settings from the Camera Default, the next time you open it, the Settings will show Selected Image.

Camera Raw Default applies the exposure, white balance, and sharpness settings of your camera to the image.

Previous Conversion applies the conversions from the previous RAW file.
Custom is automatically selected when you change any of the camera RAW plug-in settings. You can save the Custom setting by choosing Save New Camera Raw Defaults from the pop-up menu that appears when you click the arrow to the right of the Settings menu. The new settings become the new Camera Raw Defaults and will be applied as such to all RAW images you open in the future. You can reset the camera default from this menu as well.

White Balance

In the White Balance menu, you have the following choices: As Shot, Auto, Daylight, Cloudy, Shade, Tungsten, Fluorescent, Flash, and Custom.

If you choose As Shot, the Camera Raw plug-in will apply the white balance setting recorded at the time of exposure. If your settings are correct, there is nothing more to do; just leave the setting to As Shot.

If you are *not* happy with what you see, you can try the other settings. Start with Auto. The Camera Raw plug-in reads the image data and automatically attempts to adjust the white balance. You can also select the other presets and observe the changes in your image. (The presets are available by placing your cursor over the image area and holding Shift and then right-clicking.)

Below the White Balance pop-up menu are two sliders—Temperature and Tint—that can be used to fine-tune the white balance. If you move the Temperature slider to the left, colors appear bluer (or cooler). Move the slider to the right, and the colors appear more yellow (warmer). If you move the Tint slider to the left (negative values), you'll add green to your image. Move it to the right (positive values), and you'll add magenta.

You can also use the White Balance tool in the image window toolbox (✏). (Alternately, you can hold the Shift key, and the cursor becomes the White Balance tool.) Select the tool and click in an area of the image that should be gray, neutral, or white. The White Balance tool then attempts to make the color exactly neutral. The changes are reflected in the Temperature and Tint sliders. You'll also notice a change in the histogram.

Tonal Controls

You have five ways to make tonal adjustments with the Camera Raw plug-in: Exposure, Shadows, Brightness, Contrast, and Saturation.

For many images, leaving the Auto check boxes selected for these settings does the job. The Camera Raw plug-in calculates the correct tonal adjustments automatically.

When Auto doesn't work, as illustrated in the left image of Figure 10.3, you can move the sliders manually to get the correct setting. In this particular case, sliding the Exposure slider to the left and sliding the Shadows slider to the left slightly helped, as shown in the right image in the figure. The histogram confirms the more evenly distributed tonal values.

Figure 10.3: Auto Exposure and Auto Shadows produced an image that was too light (left). Moving the Exposure and Shadows sliders to the left produced a more evenly distributed tonal range, as confirmed by the histogram (right).

In general, start by using the Exposure slider. Sliding this to the right lightens the image, and sliding it to the left darkens it. The values are in increments equivalent to f-stops. For example, a +2 is similar to opening the aperture two stops. Next, try the Shadows slider. Sliding the Shadows slider to the right increases the density of the shadow areas without affecting the highlights. Sliding the slider to the left "opens," or lightens, the shadow areas without affecting the highlights.

For this example, I left the Brightness, Contrast, and Saturation settings alone. Brightness is similar to the Exposure slider; however, it redistributes the midtone values of an image without losing highlights or shadows. Contrast applies an S-curve to the image data and leaves the extremes alone. Saturation increases the strength of the colors.

Sharpness

This control is located in the Details tab. When the Camera Raw plug-in opens a RAW file, it automatically sharpens an image based on camera model, ISO, and exposure compensation. You can increase or decrease sharpening with the Sharpness slider, or leave it alone. A zero value turns sharpening off altogether.

Sharpening, as I explained in Chapter 3, is best saved for last, after you've resized your image to match the needs of your final destination, be it print or screen. With that in mind, I suggest you either leave the default setting or reduce sharpening altogether and do the sharpening later in the editing workspace of Photoshop Elements (☞ "Sharpening" in Chapter 3).

Luminance Smoothing and Color Noise Reduction

These sliders are found on the Details tab. Use the Luminance Smoothing slider to reduce grayscale image noise that makes an image look grainy. Use the Color Noise Reduction slider to reduce chroma (color) noise, which often occurs when you shoot at a high ISO. Moving the Luminance Smoothing or the Color Noise Reduction sliders to the right reduces noise but also "softens" the appearance of the image. It's best to enlarge your image over 100 percent to see the effects. (You can also bring your image into the Photoshop Elements' editing workspace and use the Reduce Noise filter: Filter ➢ Noise ➢ Reduce Noise. This filter, unlike many of the other filters, works in the 16-bit mode.)

Saving RAW Files

Original RAW camera files are never altered. When you make adjustments to them, the adjustment settings are saved in a database so that the next time you open the image in the Camera Raw plug-in, the previous settings are there. This means that if the database gets separated from the images for any reason, the settings are lost.

There is a way to prevent the loss of these settings, however. By clicking the Save button in the plug-in, you can save a copy of the image file in a DNG format. This is Adobe's Digital Negative file format, which stores the plug-in settings within the file rather than in a database.

And, Finally

When you are finished, click the Open button. The altered image opens in the Photoshop Elements editing workspace. Regardless of what you do to the image in the Camera Raw plug-in, the original camera RAW image file remains unaltered for future interpretation.

Example RAW File Workflow

There are a number of possible workflows. This example is intended to help you develop your own workflow based on your particular needs:

1. Transfer RAW files from your digital camera to the Organizer (⊘ Chapter 2, "Importing and Organizing Digital Images").
2. Open a RAW file using one of the methods described previously.
3. Make any adjustments if necessary.
4. Click Save to save the file as a DNG if desired.
5. Click Open to transfer the file to the editing workspace.
6. Make any further adjustments such as cropping or adding text.
7. Save a copy of the file in the PSD format, which is uncompressed and will retain any layers that were created (⊘ Chapter 1, "All About Layers").
8. Save a version in the JPEG format for sharing (⊘ Chapter 11, "Sharing and Auto-Processing Images").

Working in 16-Bit Mode

Photoshop Elements 4 supports 16-bit files, which is especially significant if you're working with RAW files and the Camera Raw plug-in. (Remember, as I mentioned earlier in this chapter, the Camera Raw plug-in gives you an option to work with a RAW image in 8 Bits/Channel or 16 Bits/Channel.) Some flatbed and slide scanners generate 16-bit files, and these files are supported by Photoshop Elements as well.

Why work in 16-bit? 8-bit files can contain up to 16.8 million colors, while 16-bit files can contain up to 281 trillion colors; obviously, working in 16-bit is preferred because you'll greatly increase your color gamut. (One way to see the difference is to perform a Levels adjustment with both 8 and 16 bits. With 16-bit, the resulting histogram is much smoother because of the additional color information.) Working in 16-bit is also desirable when you are using certain filters or downsampling. When data needs to be thrown out, it's always better for the algorithm to have more data than less to work with.

Unfortunately, saving a 16-bit file doubles your file size, so if memory storage is an issue, you might want to convert your images to 8-bit before saving them (I'll show you how to do this shortly). Also, many options and tools available in 8-bit mode—including layering, the Clone Stamp tool, and the Healing Brush tool—aren't available in 16-bit mode.

So what should you do? I suggest the following workflow:

1. Bring in a 16-bit image from the Camera Raw plug-in, or if you are scanning, from the scanning software module.
2. Do any necessary work that's available only in 16-bit:
   - Use the histogram (Window ➤ Histogram), for example, to determine whether tonal or color corrections are necessary (➤ Chapter 3).
   - Use Levels, Quick Fix, Enhance, or whatever commands you are comfortable with to fine-tune tones and color.
3. If you need to resize your image, do it now (Image ➤ Resize ➤ Image Size).
4. Save your file in the PSD or TIFF file format (File ➤ Save As). JPEG doesn't support 16-bit files, so don't even try saving your file in that format. As I said earlier, if storage is an issue, you may choose to avoid this step.
5. After you have saved a 16-bit version of the file, change the mode to 8 Bits/Channel (Image ➤ Convert to 8 Bits/Channel).
6. All Photoshop Elements' tools and commands are now available, so finish preparing and editing your image as necessary with techniques that are available only for 8-bit files, such as the Clone Stamp tool (🔛) and the Healing Brush tool (✏️).
7. After you're finished, save a copy of your image (File ➤ Save As).

Now you may very well have three versions: the unadulterated RAW file (your negative) or the original 16-bit scanned file, a tonally correct and resized 16-bit file, and a final 8-bit image, ready for printing and sharing.

Extending Dynamic Range with Photomerge

Digital cameras notoriously capture a limited dynamic range, certainly when compared with print film. If you look at the left image in Figure 10.4, which was taken with a Nikon D100 digital camera, you'll see what I mean. Although the exposure for the foreground was correct, there was not enough latitude to capture the brighter details. The version on the right shows what happens when the exposure is made for the background. The foreground is now too dark. Professional photographers often use a technique that requires mounting a camera on a tripod and taking a series of images at the same f-stop but different shutter speeds, and then using Photoshop carefully to copy and paste the perfectly aligned images of different exposures into one final image.

Figure 10.4: The exposure for the foreground is correct, but the exposure for the background is not (left). Here, the exposure for the background is correct but not the exposure for the foreground (right).

You can shoot more casually, avoid using a tripod, and still get good results by using the Photomerge feature in Photoshop Elements. Photomerge features a Save As Layers option, which makes the following process—and the results shown in Figure 10.5—possible.

Figure 10.5: After merging the two images with Photomerge, keeping layers intact, and then erasing unwanted parts of one image, you get this perfectly exposed image.

Start by taking at least two shots with your digital camera at different exposures. It's best if you can use the same f-stop and vary the shutter speed to produce the different exposures, but not essential. Frame each shot as close to the next as possible. Refer to your camera manual if you don't know how to set your camera to over- or underexpose. Photomerge doesn't support 16-bit files, but you can still shoot in RAW, and the files will be automatically converted to 8-bit by Photomerge.

Then, in Photoshop Elements, take these steps:

1. Choose File ➢ New ➢ Photomerge.
2. Navigate via the Browse button and select the files containing the different exposures.
3. Click OK. Photomerge automatically attempts to merge the documents. If it fails to do this—and you see a dialog box telling you so—simply drag and drop the images from the photo well on top of each other (➥ Chapter 9 for more on using the Photomerge plug-in).
4. Keep your Photomerge settings at Normal and select Keep as Layers. Keep Snap to Image selected. (Advanced Blending is not an option if you select Keep as Layers.)
5. Click OK. When Photomerge finishes, you're left with one image file and your images perfectly aligned on top of each other in the Layers palette.
6. If it's not already open, open the Layers palette.
7. Erase (🖊) unwanted areas of the top layers to reveal corrected versions of those areas underneath. You might want to move layers around to get the "best" version of your image on top, to minimize the amount of erasing needed.

For this example, I moved the image with the correctly exposed background and dark foreground to the top of the Layers palette, as shown in the shot on the left in Figure 10.6. I then selected the top layer and selected the Magic Eraser (🖊) from the toolbar. In the Magic Eraser options bar I set the Tolerance to 50. (This number will vary depending on the tonal values of the image you are working on.) I left Contiguous selected and Use All Layers deselected. Then I clicked a dark area in the foreground of my image with the Magic Eraser.

Figure 10.6: I moved the layer containing the correctly exposed background to the top of the Layers palette (left). This is what my palette looks like after applying the Magic Eraser to the dark areas of the image in the top layer (right).

The shot on the right of Figure 10.6 shows my Layers palette after applying the Magic Eraser to the top layer. By removing the dark areas in the top layer, the lighter areas of the bottom layer show through. (I used the Eraser tool to fine-tune the results of the Magic Eraser for the final image.) I slightly cropped the image and flattened my layers, and I was finished.

For this example I used the Magic Eraser and Eraser, but you can use other methods to remove the improperly exposed areas of the image in the top layer. For example, you could use the Selection Brush tool () to create a precise selection, and then delete your selection. I've found the Magic Eraser works quickly and often it works well enough.

Note: I got the idea for this Photomerge procedure while talking with Photomerge's creator, John Peterson.

Using Layer Adjustments with Masks

In Chapter 3, I showed you how Photoshop Elements' Smart Fix, Auto Levels, and Levels can be used to correct a poorly exposed image. But these methods don't always work satisfactorily.

Take, for example, the photo of Mt. Shasta in Figure 10.7. When I use the Levels controls to adjust the image, I can either make the foreground trees look good, or the mountain and sky in the background look good. But I can't make both look good at the same time. I need a way to apply a different set of Levels adjustments to each area of the image separately. There are a couple of ways to do this, but I've found a combination of layer adjustments and masks to be the most effective and versatile.

Figure 10.7: The original photo (top). The foreground is okay, but the background is washed out (bottom left). Now the background is okay, but the foreground is too dark (bottom right).

Adjustment layers are layers that apply color and tonal adjustments to an image without permanently modifying the pixels in the image (☞ "All about Layers" in Chapter 1). A *layer mask* can be added to an adjustment layer to protect sections of an adjustment layer and control the effect that the adjustment layer has on the layer beneath it.

This is what I did to improve the digital photo of Mt. Shasta:

1. I created a new adjustment layer by choosing Layer ➢ New Adjustment Layer ➢ Levels from the menu bar (shown on the left in Figure 10.8). I could have created a new adjustment layer by clicking the Create Adjustment Layer button ( ) at the top of the Layers palette and choosing Levels (shown on the right in Figure 10.8). I named this new layer **Trees**.

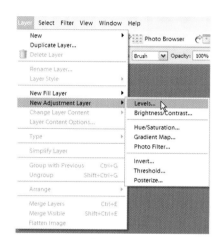

Figure 10.8: Choose an adjustment layer from the Layer menu (left). Or choose an adjustment layer directly from the Layers palette (right).

2. I used the Levels palette to adjust the midtones so my trees looked right. I didn't pay any attention to the sky and the mountain. When I was finished, I turned the layer visibility off by clicking the eye icon in the leftmost column of the Layers palette. I did this so my new adjustment layer wouldn't interfere with the next adjustment in step 3.

3. I created another Levels adjustment layer and called it **Mt./Sky**. I used the Levels controls to adjust the tonal values so Mt. Shasta and the sky looked right, and I didn't worry about my foreground.

4. Next came the tricky part—and if you don't get this part right, this exercise won't work. In the adjustment layer called **Mt./Sky** I created a mask that blocked the effect of the Levels adjustment on the trees. To do this, I clicked the Gradient tool ( ) in the toolbox. In the options bar I selected the following options:

   Gradient: Foreground to Transparent
   Style: Linear Gradient
   Blend mode: Normal
   Opacity: 100 percent

   I made sure that the foreground was set to black by clicking the Default Colors icon ( ) at the bottom of the toolbox and then clicking the Switch arrow ( ). This is necessary on an adjustment layer because the default colors are reversed.

5. With the **Mt./Sky** layer selected, I placed my cursor on the image window. While holding the Shift key, I started at the bottom of the image, and then clicked and dragged about halfway up the image and let go of the mouse. Holding the Shift key and dragging straight up constrained the Gradient tool to a 90-degree angle.

Note: Because the layer mask is represented in tones of gray, what you paint or fill with black will be hidden, what you paint or fill with white will show, and what you paint or fill with gray shades will show in various levels of transparency. Masks can be edited like a grayscale image with any painting or editing tool. Hold down Alt+Shift and click the adjustment layer thumbnail to view the mask in a rubylith masking color. Hold down Alt+Shift and click the thumbnail again to turn off the rubylith display. Shift+click the adjustment layer thumbnail to turn off the masking effects temporarily; click the thumbnail again to turn on the mask. You can also use the Move tool ( ) to move or resize a mask.

6. I selected the adjustment layer called **Trees**, turned on its visibility, which I turned off in step 2, and made another similar mask by using the Gradient tool with the same settings as in step 4. This time I created a mask by holding the Shift key and dragging straight downward from the top of the image. This blocked the effect of the Levels command on the mountain and sky areas of the image.

7. For the most part, the mask created by the Gradient tool was enough. However, I did go back into the adjustment layer called **Mt./Sky** with the paintbrush and mask in a few other areas, including the tree on the right.

As you can see in Figure 10.9, I've managed to get both the foreground and background right. And as long as I keep my adjustment layers, I can go back and tweak the levels at any time.

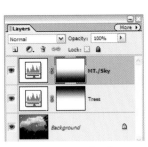

Figure 10.9: Both adjustment layers are selectively masked with gradient fills (left). With just a little work, both the foreground and background look good (right).

Note: You can edit an adjustment layer at any time: double-click the adjustment layer's thumbnail in the Layers palette or choose Layer ➤ Layer Content Options from the menu bar.

Using a Gradient Mask to Combine Multiple Images

In Chapter 9, I showed you an easy way to use Photoshop Elements' Photomerge feature to combine multiple images into a collage. For more control and precise blending, here is a method that uses layers and gradient masks rather than Photomerge. Obviously, this method isn't as straightforward as using Photomerge, and it's a bit time-consuming. But if you master layer adjustments and masking techniques—as you started to do in the previous example—you are on a professional-level track, and a whole new world of options opens up.

As with the previous example, please follow my steps carefully. If you do as I suggest, you'll have no trouble duplicating the effect on images of your own. However, even a slight variation (such as not setting the Gradient tool and the foreground color properly) will produce quite a bit of frustration, and not the results you expect.

Let's begin!

1. Create a new document with the desired dimensions. For this example I created a 10 × 5 inch document at 200 pixels per inch (File ➢ New ➢ Blank File).

2. Open two or more images you wish to combine. I'll use the three images shown in Figure 10.10.

Figure 10.10: I'll start with these three images that I wish to combine.

3. Crop and resize the images to match. I did this by selecting the Crop tool (⌗) in the toolbar and setting my width to 3.3 in., height to 5 in., and resolution to 200 pixels per inch. I applied the fixed crop separately to each image. When you crop, keep in mind you will eventually overlap the images. (When you are finished doing this, click the Clear button in the Crop tool options bar; otherwise, you may inadvertently apply the fixed dimensions later to another image.)

4. Copy and paste the cropped, resized images to the blank document you created in step 1 (Ctrl+A, followed by Ctrl+C and, after selecting the blank file, Ctrl+V). When you are finished, your Layers palette should look like the one in Figure 10.11, with three layers. At this point you can rename the layers if you want.

Figure 10.11: The Layers palette of the blank file after copying and pasting the three images.

5. In the image window, position the images adjacent to each other, with a slight overlap, as shown in Figure 10.12. Do this by selecting the top layer in the Layers palette and the Move tool from the toolbar. In the image window, click and hold while dragging the image to the far left of the image window. Next, select the second layer, and in the image window, move the middle image into the middle position, allowing for a slight overlap with the image to the left. Finally, select the bottom layer (but not the background layer), and in the image window, move that image to the far right.

Figure 10.12: Position the images adjacent to each other with a slight overlap. Place the image contained in the top layer to the far left, the image contained in the middle layer (if you have one) in the middle, and the image in the bottom layer (but not the background layer) to the far right of the image window.

At this point you've finished the "heavy" lifting. Now it's time to finesse the images so the edges blend into one another. You do this by creating a gradient mask that allows only a portion of an image to show through. Because Photoshop Elements doesn't offer gradient "masks" per se, you'll use a clever workaround that turns an adjustment layer and a clipping path into one.

6. In the Layers palette, starting with the top layer, create a Levels adjustment layer for each layer: Click the Create Adjustment Layer button at the top of the palette and select Levels from the pop-up menu, or choose Layer ➢ New Adjustment Layer ➢ Levels. *Don't* change *anything* in the Levels dialog box that appears. Just click the OK button. Apply an adjustment layer to each image layer until your Layers palette looks like the one in Figure 10.13. (By the way, you could create

Brightness/Contrast adjustment layers instead of Levels. It doesn't matter. Just don't touch any setting before clicking OK.)

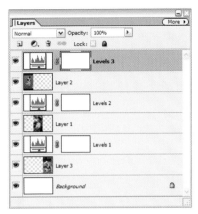

Figure 10.13: After applying a Levels adjustment layer to each layer, your Layers palette will look something like this.

7. Now you need to rearrange the layers in the Layers palette. Move each adjustment layer below its image layer by dragging it into the desired position. Your Layers palette should look like the one in Figure 10.14.

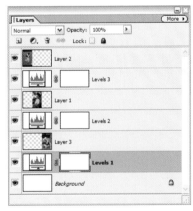

Figure 10.14: Move the adjustment layers below the image layers as shown here.

8. Starting with the top layer, which contains the image located to the far left of the image window, hold the Alt key and (in the Layers palette) click the border between that layer and the adjustment layer located just beneath it. Two intersecting circles, one light and one dark, appear. After you click the top layer, these circles will indent slightly to the right and contain an arrow pointing to the "grouped" layer below. Doing this creates a "clipping" mask, and now the content of the adjustment layer masks the content of the layer above it. You can also create a clipping mask by selecting the top layer, and in the menu bar, selecting Layer ➢ Group with Previous. Now your Layers palette will look something like the one in Figure 10.15. Note that the name of the base layer of the clipping mask is underlined.

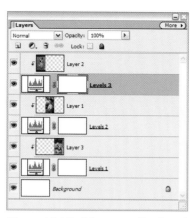

Figure 10.15: After you clip the adjustment layers with the layers containing your images, you'll get something that looks like this.

Now that you have created a "mask" for each image, you need to apply a gradient to the mask that will fade the edges:

9. Select the Gradient tool from the toolbar.

10. In the Gradient options bar, select Foreground to Transparent from the flyout Gradient picker. This is so important I'm going to repeat myself. In the Gradient options bar, select Foreground to Transparent.

11. In the color swatch at the bottom of the toolbar, make sure the foreground color is set to black. Getting the color correct is critical. Again, I repeat: Set the foreground color to black!

12. In the Layers palette, select the second layer. This is the layer containing the adjustment layer, which, remember, is clipped to the topmost image.

13. In the image window, place the cursor on the far right of the leftmost image. Hold the Shift key and drag inward, to the left. Go in about ½ inch and release the mouse. This applies a gradient to the right edge of the image. You should see the results immediately.

14. Highlight the adjustment layer that is below the layer containing the middle image. You may need to turn off the visibility of the top layer to see the leftmost edge of the middle image; do this by clicking the eye icon next to the top layer.

15. On the left edge of the middle image, Shift+drag inward (to the right) about ½ inch and release the mouse. Then Shift+drag from the *right* edge of the middle image about ½ inch inward (to the left).

16. Turn off the visibility of the middle image if necessary to see the image on the right. Highlight the adjustment layer that is below the right-image layer.

17. On the left edge of the right image, Shift+drag inward (to the right) about ½ inch and release the mouse. Turn on all layer visibility, and you will see something like Figure 10.16.

Figure 10.16: With the edges of the three images faded, the images blend together.

To tweak your work, you can move the images in relationship to each other by using the Move tool. However, you must first link the adjustment layer with the layer containing the image, since they have to move together. To do this, hold the Shift key and click both layers to link them. Now when you use the Move tool to move the image, the "linked" adjustment layer moves also. If you just want to move the images horizontally, select the Move tool and use the left and right arrow keys on your keyboard. This ensures that there is no vertical movement.

Converting a Photo to a Painting

The simplest way to convert a photo into a painting is by using one of the Artistic filters such as Watercolor or Rough Pastels (Filter ➢ Artistic from the main menu bar).

However, if you want to convert a photo into a truly unique-looking "painting," follow this slightly more complex procedure. Start with an original photo containing sharply defined lines and shapes, such as the one shown on the left in Figure 10.17.

Figure 10.17: The original image (left); after applying various filters and blending modes (right).

1. Duplicate the background layer twice (Layer ➤ Duplicate Layer from the menu bar, or drag and drop the layer to be duplicated onto the Create a New Layer icon () at the top of the Layers palette). Name one of the duplicate layers **Underpainting** and the second **Find Edges**. The Layers palette is shown in Figure 10.18.

Figure 10.18: The Layers palette so far, with its Background layer and two duplicate layers.

2. Select the layer you named **Underpainting** and apply the Underpainting filter (Filter ➤ Artistic ➤ Underpainting). My settings are shown in Figure 10.19, but you have a lot of discretion with your own settings.

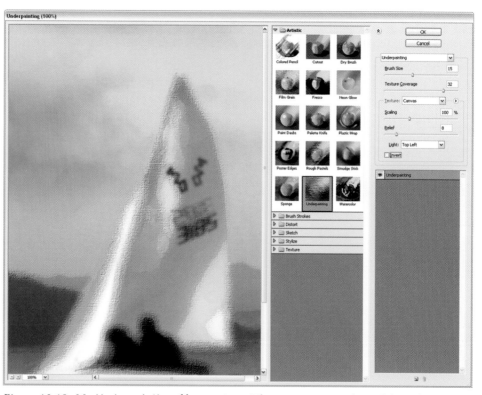

Figure 10.19: My **Underpainting** *filter settings. These are just rough guidelines for you to follow.*

3. Select the layer you named **Find Edges** and apply the Find Edges filter to the layer (Filter ➢ Stylize ➢ Find Edges). No options are available for this filter.

4. Make a duplicate of the layer you just applied the Find Edges filter to and call it **Wave**. You can boost the contrast of the duplicate layer, if you want, by using Levels.

5. On the layer you named **Wave**, apply the Wave filter (Filter ➢ Distort ➢ Wave). My settings are shown in Figure 10.20, but again, you can use other settings.

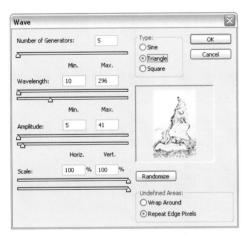

Figure 10.20: My Wave filter settings.

6. Finally, you need to change the blending mode of the **Wave** layer to Soft Light and change the Opacity to 65 percent. Also change the blending mode of the Find Edges layer to Overlay, but keep the mode of the Underpainting layer at Normal. Figure 10.21 shows the final configuration of the Layers palette with the different mode and opacity settings.

Figure 10.21: The final Layers palette.

My finished Layers palette looked like this, in order from top to bottom:

Wave Filter layer: Soft Light mode, 100 percent opacity

Find Edges layer: Overlay mode, 68 percent opacity

Underpainting layer: Normal mode, 100 percent opacity

Background layer

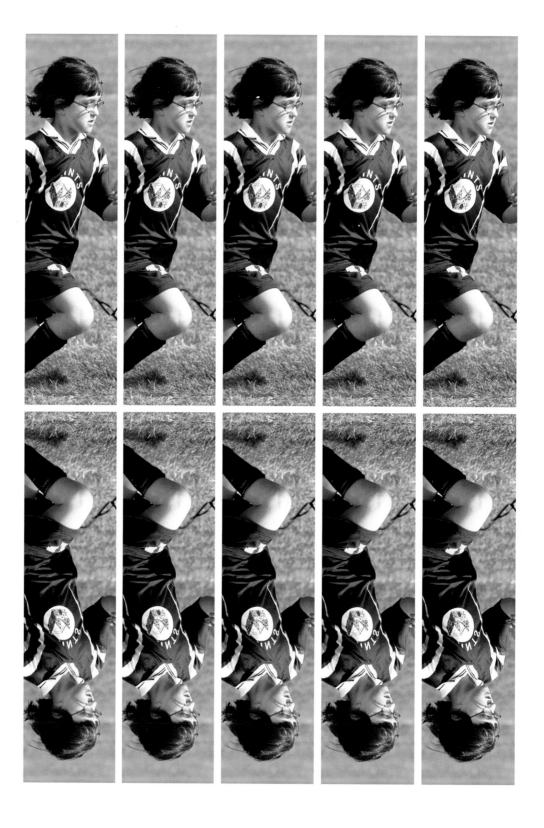

Sharing and Auto-Processing Images

What's the good of having all your hard work available in a digital image if you can't easily share it with friends and colleagues? This chapter focuses on ways to use Photoshop Elements to get the most out of your desktop printer or to access an online photo service. It shows you ways to automatically create picture packages of single pages containing various sizes of the same image and to process folders full of several images to the same file format, size, and resolution. It'll also show you how to make web photo galleries, postcards, slide shows, VCDs, DVDs (with Adobe Premiere Elements), and much more!

11

Chapter Contents

Printing from the Organizer

When you choose Print from the Organizer menu—or if you choose File ≻ Print Multiple Photos from the Editor—you'll get the options shown in Figure 11.1.

Figure 11.1: When you print from the Organizer, you have these options.

This is your gateway to some really useful features. If you look under option 2, for example, you have four choices for printing in the Organizer: Individual Prints, Contact Sheet, Picture Package, and Labels. With these options you'll be able to easily print multiples of the same image on a single page, or a variety of images on a single page.

It's also easy to print individual images on single sheets of paper from the Organizer, but I want to caution you: this isn't the best use of the Organizer's print capabilities, which are mostly about convenience and speed. (When you print from the Organizer, for example, you have only limited control over the print quality.) You can get much better results—with optimal resolution, sharpness, and color fidelity—if you print from the Editor and use its sharpening and resizing controls. I'll get into the details of doing that in a later section, "Printing from the Editor."

Meanwhile, let's see what your print options are from within the Organizer.

Printing Multiple Images

Here's how to print multiple images on a single sheet of paper:

1. Select your images in the Organizer by Ctrl+clicking each one. Do this before choosing File ≻ Print. If you have no images selected, you will be asked whether you want to print all the images in your catalog. (You can amend your selections later, but it's quicker to make your selection up front.)

2. Choose File ≻ Print from the Organizer, or choose File ≻ Print Multiple Photos from the Editor, which takes you to the Organizer.

3. Select the printer from the step 1 drop-down at the top right. (At this point—or at any time in the process before you hit the Print button—you can add more images by clicking the Add button at the bottom left of the dialog box, or remove images by selecting them and then clicking the trash can icon.)

4. Select Individual Prints in step 2.

5. Select a print size in step 3. (In Figure 11.2, I selected two images, which are displayed on the left of the dialog box. As you can see, I chose 5" × 7" for step 3.)

Figure 11.2: For this example I selected two images, set the size to 5" × 7", deselected One Photo Per Page, and selected Crop to Fit. It's easy to preview the results before printing.

6. Deselect the One Photo Per Page check box. If you don't do this, only one image will appear on a page, regardless of size. (If you are printing only one picture per sheet and want optimal quality, I highly recommend you follow the steps I describe later about printing directly from the Editor.)

7. If you want just one copy of each image, leave the Use Each Photo option set to 1. If you want to print two copies of the same image per page, just change Use Each Photo to 2 times.

8. Select Crop to Fit to make your prints exactly the size you chose. Some cropping may occur, because the aspect ratio of digital camera images doesn't always match the aspect ratio of the print. If you don't select Crop to Fit, the printed image will typically be smaller than the chosen dimensions.

9. Click the Print button.

Don't be confused by the Page Setup button, which lets you select Portrait or Landscape for easier previewing. The pictures display differently in the preview window, but they print the same way in either case. However, the filename and caption print in different locations, so be sure to check the preview window before printing.

One point to think about before bringing up the Print dialog box is to enter any information in the Properties dialog box (Window ➤ Properties) that you may want to include with your images. Captions or dates, which you can include by clicking the More Options button in the Print dialog box, must be entered prior to clicking File ➤ Print. You don't want to set everything up, only to have to start over again.

Note: If your image doesn't contain enough pixels to print optimally at the desired size, you'll get a warning message. If you see this message, either select a smaller print size, or go back to the Editor and interpolate more pixels by changing the print dimensions or resolution in the Image Size dialog box. (Keep in mind, when you interpolate pixels, that image quality can suffer depending on the content of the image.) ↩ "Using Image Size to Set Resolution and Print Dimensions" later in this chapter for more information.

Printing a Contact Sheet

The second option in the Print Selected Photos dialog box, under Select Type of Print, is Contact Sheet. In traditional photography, a *contact sheet* is a sheet of negative-sized photographs made by simply placing the printing paper in direct contact with the negatives during exposure. The results allow a viewer to quickly compare smaller versions of each photo side by side.

Digital photos don't have negatives *per se*, but by using the Contact Sheet option, you can control the size of a series of images and group as many as nine images per column. These images can then be printed and the results used for side-by-side comparison and easy reference, as shown in Figure 11.3.

Figure 11.3: Create a contact sheet for side-by-side comparison and easy reference.

To create a Contact Sheet, follow these steps:

1. In the Organizer, select the images you want. There is no limit to the number you select, but the most images you'll fit on a single 8.5" × 11" sheet of paper is 81 very tiny ones.

2. Choose File ➢ Print (Ctrl+P).

3. Select the printer in step 1.

4. Select Contact Sheet in step 2.

5. Select a Layout in step 3. The smaller the number in the Columns box, the fewer (but larger) the number of thumbnails per page. Choose appropriate text labels, and you're done.

6. Click Print.

Remember, as with the previous example using the Individual Prints option, you can click the Add button at any time to add additional images. Also, remember to add any captions prior to bringing up the Contact Sheet dialog box.

Printing a Picture Package

The Picture Package option provides a way to automatically create a variety of layouts with your images that otherwise would be extremely time-consuming. Not only can you produce useful layouts—and customize them to boot—you can automatically add a variety of frames to each image as well. Figure 11.4 shows a Picture Package.

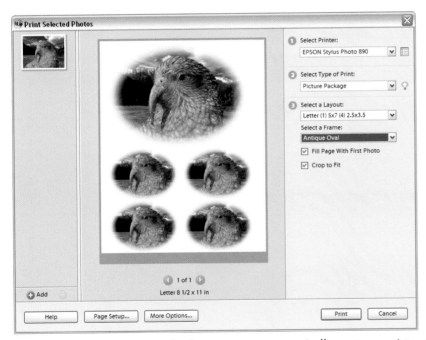

Figure 11.4: By using Picture Package you can automatically create a variety of useful layouts and automatically add frames as well.

Here are the steps for creating the Picture Package shown in Figure 11.4:

1. Select an image or images in the Organizer.

2. Choose File ➢ Print (Ctrl+P).

3. Select the printer in step 1.

4. Select Picture Package in step 2.

5.   Select a Layout in step 3. I selected Letter (2) 4×5 (4) 2.5×3.5. I then selected an Antique Oval frame and selected Fill Page with First Photo. (If I had selected more than one image to begin with, deselecting Fill Page with First Photo would result in Picture Package arranging different photos together on the same page. Fill Page with First Photo would result in multiple picture packages, each containing the same photo on a separate page.)

6.   Preview the results and click Print.

It may not be immediately obvious, but you can create custom layouts with Picture Package as well. Simply place your cursor over an image in the preview box—it'll turn into a hand icon—and then click and drag. You can place the image wherever you want on the page, or place it on top of another image and the two images will exchange places. If you aren't satisfied with your new layout, right-click a thumbnail and select Revert to Original. Now that's cool. (What's not so cool is that Picture Packages are all set for 8.5" × 11" paper. You also can't add captions or credits.)

Printing Labels

This feature is accessed from the Organizer by clicking File ➤ Print and selecting Labels. The process is similar to Picture Package and fairly straightforward:

1.   Select an appropriate layout based on the type of labels you are printing.

2.   If you want, select a frame from the pop-up menu.

3.   If you are printing one image, select Fill Page with First Photo. When printing multiple images, deselect this option to print all the images on a single page.

If you want to add text to your labels, you can't do it from the Organizer Label print control. You'll have to use the Editor's text tool to place the text directly on an image and import the edited image into the Organizer for printing.

As anyone who has printed labels knows, printing small labels can be difficult. Even the slightest misalignment of the paper will result in off-registered images. If you are having difficulty printing, try using the Offset Print Area controls to adjust the labels' print position in increments of 0.1mm, up to plus or minus 50mm.

Printing from the Editor

As I mentioned earlier, if you want to create the best possible print, you'll want to print directly from the Editor and use its resizing and sharpening controls.

Using Image Size to Set Resolution and Print Dimensions

What if you have a photo taken with a 4 megapixel digital camera? How large of a print can you make without loss of quality?

Let's open such an image in Photoshop Elements and take a closer look at it via the Image Size dialog box shown in Figure 11.5 (Image ➤ Resize ➤ Image Size).

As you can see near the top of the Image Size dialog box, the pixel dimensions are 2240 for Width and 1680 for Height. In the Document Size section, you can see the following numbers: 31.111 inches for Width, 23.333 inches for Height, and 72 pixels/inch for Resolution.

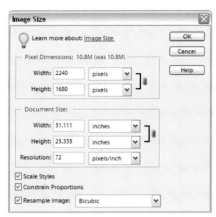

Figure 11.5: The Image Size dialog box for an image taken with a 4 megapixel digital camera.

If you tried to print this image as is, straight out of Photoshop Elements without changing any parameters, you'd create a print approximately 31" × 23" at 72 pixels/inch. (Of course you'd have to have a printer that printed this large.) Most likely the print would appear "grainy" or soft. Technically, there just aren't enough pixels to support this size.

So if 72 pixels/inch isn't enough, how much resolution do you need? Don't be misled by the specifications of your printer. For most desktop inkjet printers, a resolution of 150–250 pixels/inch is plenty, and anything over 250 pixels/inch is a waste. Your print quality won't suffer, nor will it improve with the higher settings. You'll just create a huge file that will take forever to print.

Shooting Digital: Using Metadata to Determine Print Resolution Value

Photoshop Elements uses the metadata created by many digital cameras to determine the print resolution value that appears in the Image Size dialog box. You can see this metadata in the Organizer by clicking the Metadata button in the Properties palette.

Because Photoshop Elements uses the metadata saved with an image, you can open an image taken, say, with a Nikon CoolPix 885, and the numerical value in the Image Size dialog's Resolution field is 300 pixels/inch. You can then open an image taken with an Olympus C-2500L and find Resolution set to 144 pixels/inch. Both cameras produce images that have similar pixel dimensions (Nikon = 2048 × 1536 pixels; Olympus = 1712 × 1368 pixels), but if you were to print the first image with a resolution of 300 pixels/inch, you'd end up with a print size of 6.8" × 5.1". If you printed the second image set at 144 pixels/inch, the print size would be 11.9" × 9.5". If the metadata is absent for some reason, Photoshop Elements defaults to 72 pixels/inch. Remember, you can always change these resolution values by choosing Image ➢ Resize ➢ Image Size and placing a new value in the Resolution box. Make sure that the Resample Image box is not selected.

So what would be an optimal size for this 4 megapixel image? Look at Figure 11.6 and note an important detail: at the bottom of the Image Size dialog box, I deselected the Resample Image check box. By doing this I prevent Photoshop Elements from adding or deleting pixels. It keeps my original pixel count, and only redistributes the existing pixels. I'll explain exactly what that means shortly.

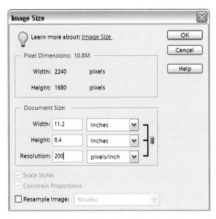

Figure 11.6: By deselecting the Resample Image check box and bumping up the resolution, I arrive at my optimal print size.

Now look at the Resolution input box. I typed in 200 pixels/inch, which is plenty of resolution to produce a high-quality print. Notice the Width and Height numbers have changed. Now, at 200 pixels/inch, I can easily print an 11.2" × 8.4" picture.

Again, because I deselected the Resample Image check box, nothing has been added to or taken away from my image. Instead of using the pixels to produce a large print, albeit at low resolution, the pixels are now distributed so that the resolution is higher and the print dimensions lower.

Okay, up to now I haven't done anything to change the pixel count of my image. I've only realigned my pixels for more depth rather than for size. What happens if I don't have enough pixels? What if I wanted to print at, say 18" × 13.5", but with enough resolution?

If I punch in 18 inches in the Width field, the Height is automatically set to 13.5 inches and my Resolution drops to 124 pixels/inch, which isn't enough for a quality print. Figure 11.7 shows what happens when I select the Resample Image check box and punch in 200 pixels/inch in the Resolution field. You can see at the top of the Image Size dialog box that I have increased my Pixel Dimensions from 10.8MB to 27.8MB. Obviously, a lot of pixels were added, through a process called *interpolation*.

Remember, for this process to work you must make sure that both the Constrain Proportions and Resample Image: Bicubic options at the bottom of the dialog box are selected, which they should be by default. (Use Bicubic Smoother from the pop-up menu if you are resampling up, or use Bicubic Sharper if you are resampling down.)

Note: Allow for at least a 0.25" border because many desktop printers aren't capable of printing, or *bleeding,* an image to the edge of the paper.

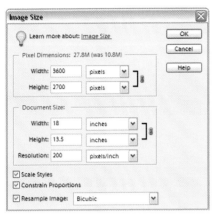

Figure 11.7: Selecting the Resample Image box and typing in 200 pixels/inch at 18" × 13.5" increased my pixel count from 10.8MB to 27.8MB.

After you are finished resizing your image, click OK.

Before printing, I suggest you sharpen your image. The Unsharp Mask filter is best suited for this task (Filter ➢ Sharpen ➢ Unsharp Mask). (For more on using the Unsharp Mask filter, ⟳ "Sharpening" in Chapter 3.)

When you are finished sharpening, choose File ➢ Print from the menu bar or click the printer icon found in the shortcuts bar. The Print Preview dialog box will appear, which I'll now discuss.

Using Print Preview

In the Print Preview dialog box (Figure 11.8), you can set the image dimensions manually, have Photoshop Elements do it for you based on the size of your paper, or print from the dimensions you established earlier in the Image Size dialog box. (You can also click the Print Multiple Images button, which will take you to the Organizer and the options discussed earlier in this chapter.)

Figure 11.8: The Print Preview dialog box (left). After selecting a smaller size (right), my image fits in the preview window, and I'm ready to print.

Here, I've used the 4 megapixel image used in the preceding section and kept the default Print Size settings at Actual Size. As you can see, my image is too big for the preview, and I'm being warned that the resolution will be low ("less than 220dpi"). I can easily fix the fit by choosing a different print size. The second dialog box shows the Print Size changed to Fit on Page; the warning is still there, however, since the print resolution is only 200dpi. But my image fits in the preview window, and now I'm clear to print.

Note: The 220ppi warning is simply a guide. You can obtain good results printing at 200ppi, but I wouldn't recommend going much lower. Several printer manufacturers recommend using 240ppi. If you use the handles to resize the image in the Editor's Print Preview window, you can increase and decrease the image size and watch the 200ppi warning come and go. This is a handy way to tell when your resolution is getting too low for a quality print.

Note: If you select Custom Size from the Print Size pop-up menu, you can type in your own Height and Width values. If you do this and select the Show Bounding Box check box, you can drag a bounding box handle in the preview area to scale the image. Whatever you do, Photoshop Elements won't override the border settings set by your printer.

Keep in mind that you can set the print size in the Print Preview dialog box, but you can't directly set the resolution of your image. It defaults to the setting in the Image Size dialog box. If your image is enlarged in the Print Preview dialog box, either by using a large print size setting or by you manually, the resolution will be automatically reduced proportionally. If you reduce the size of your image, the resolution will automatically increase proportionally. The bottom line is, if you resize by using the Print Preview dialog box, you don't change the overall number of pixels or affect the original image file in any way.

Other options in the Print Preview dialog box include the following:

Change image orientation with the rotate icons located at the bottom right of the preview area.

Add a colored border. To do this, select the Border check box, type in a border thickness, and click the color box to the right to bring up the Color Picker. You can also drag the bounding box to increase the thickness of the border.

Print any caption text typed in the File Info dialog box in 9 point Helvetica, centered just below the image. You have no control over the size, type, or placement. If a caption doesn't show in the preview, it's because you didn't previously add one in the File Info dialog box. Also, if your image fills the page, it's unlikely that the caption or filename will print. For the option to print a caption or filename, click the Show More Options button.

Note: When printing from the Editor, if you choose one of the built-in print sizes such as 4" × 6", switching the orientation only changes where the caption and filename will print. Otherwise, only the paper orientation changes. The filename and caption print on opposite sides of the photo in the Editor, but they print together from the Organizer.

Add corner crop marks to show where a page is to be trimmed by selecting the Print Crop Marks box.

Reposition an image on the paper. In the Position section of the dialog box, either click the Center Image check box to center the image in the printable area, or type values in the Top and Left fields to position the image numerically. You can also select the Show Bounding Box check box and drag the image in the preview area.

Print a selection. Begin by making a selection with the Rectangular Marquee selection tool (▢) in the Editor. This enables the Print Selected Area check box (in the Scaled Print Size section). When you check this box, you only print the selected area. You can enlarge the print by dragging the corner handles prior to clicking the Print button.

Selecting a Paper Size and Orientation

You can select paper size or image orientation through Photoshop Elements' Page Setup dialog box (File ➤ Page Setup, or click the Page Setup button from within the Print Preview dialog box). This dialog will look different depending on the type of printer you are using. However, you can likely access more size/orientation options by using the printer software that comes with your printer.

If the image size you selected in the Image Size dialog box doesn't match the size of the paper set in the Page Setup dialog box (or within your printer software), you'll get a warning message.

Creating and Sharing with the Organizer

Before I get into the details of the many formats you can present your images in, here's a road map of the various ways Photoshop Elements allows you to share your images:

> **Note:** Just a reminder: To create DVDs, Premiere Elements must be installed and you must have a DVD burner.

Sharing one or more images by e-mail from the Editor Choose File ➤ Attach to E-mail. Your choices are Photo Mail (pictures embedded into a message; message size is shown but there are no user choices), Simple PDF Slide Show, or Individual Attachments (many options for file size). (Your choices can vary depending on clients you have installed.)

Sharing one or more images by e-mail from the Organizer Choose File ➤ E-mail or click the Share button and select E-mail. You have the same choices as when e-mailing from the Editor.

Sharing a slide show via e-mail from the Editor Choose File ➤ Create ➤ Slide Show. All images currently open in the Editor will be added to the show. You can add or remove images while in the Slide Show workplace. You can then share the slide show by clicking Output ➤ E-mail Slide Show. You have a choice of sending a video or PDF, each with several different resolutions.

Sharing a slide show via e-mail from the Organizer Choose File ➤ Create ➤ Slide Show. All images currently selected in the Organizer will be added to the show. You can add or remove images while in the Slide Show workplace. You can then share the slide show by clicking Output ➤ E-mail Slide Show. You have a choice of sending a video or PDF, each with several different resolutions.

Sharing an existing single slide show on a VCD or DVD from the Organizer Open a slide show, click Output, and select Burn to Disc. Choose VCD or DVD.

Sharing one or more existing slide shows on a VCD or DVD with menus Click the Create button and choose either VCD with menus or DVD with menus. You can select the slide shows before or after clicking the Create button.

Sharing a combination of images and videos on a DVD Select them in the Organizer and select File ➤ Send to Premiere Elements (right-clicking works also). Menus can be added once you are in Premiere Elements. You can select the slide shows before or after clicking the Create button.

Sharing a combination of images and videos on a VCD Select the files in the Organizer, click the Create button, and select Slide Show. (You can't create a VCD directly from stills or videos.) From the Slide Show, click the Output button and select Burn to Disc.

Sharing any creation from the Organizer If it's a video or PDF, click File ➤ E-mail; otherwise, open the creation and click the Output button.

If you select the Create icon from the Organizer or Editor shortcuts bar, you'll see the window shown in Figure 11.9. There are enough easy-to-use features here to satisfy a variety of creative urges and needs. Most of the features include contextual help and step-by-step procedures. I won't even begin to explain all the details of using these features. Instead, I'll briefly highlight what you can do with them, and point out a few less-than-obvious tips.

Figure 11.9: The Creation Setup window without Premiere Elements installed (left) and the additional option when it's installed (right).

Creating a Slide Show

To create a slide show, start by making a selection of images and/or videos. It's handy if you've already grouped your stills and videos with tags or collections.

Next, click the Create button, select Slide Show on the left, and click OK. The Slide Show Preferences window appears (Figure 11.10). Several options, including Apply Pan & Zoom to All Slides, are not critical since you can change your mind later while creating the slide show. However, once you are in the slide show, you can't change your mind about including captions as text. If you elect to add the captions as text, they will be white in color; they can be changed in the slide show editor, but only one at a time.

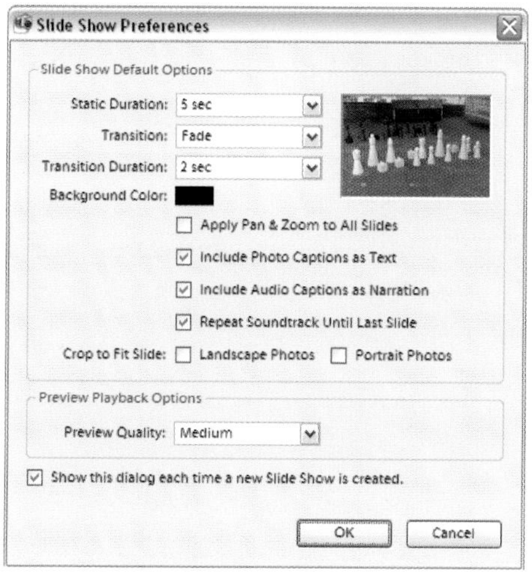

![Slide Show Preferences dialog box showing Slide Show Default Options: Static Duration 5 sec, Transition Fade, Transition Duration 2 sec, Background Color black; checkboxes for Apply Pan & Zoom to All Slides (unchecked), Include Photo Captions as Text (checked), Include Audio Captions as Narration (checked), Repeat Soundtrack Until Last Slide (checked); Crop to Fit Slide: Landscape Photos, Portrait Photos; Preview Playback Options Preview Quality Medium; Show this dialog each time a new Slide Show is created (checked); OK and Cancel buttons.]

Figure 11.10: Slide Show Preferences

To preview the transition while the Preferences window is showing, click the thumbnail on the right. You can do this while trying various transitions.

You can change the duration and transitions at any time while in the slide show. You can also change all of the durations, backgrounds, or transitions at the same time. To change all of the durations, begin by changing the duration of one slide using the black arrow under the thumbnail version of the slide (see Figure 11.11), and then click the black arrow again and select Set All Slides. To apply a transition to all slides, click the transition icon arrow, select a transition, and then select Apply to All from the pop-up menu. For changing all of the backgrounds, select all of the slides in the film strip and then click the Background Color icon.

Click to set transition(s)

Click to set duration(s)

Figure 11.11: You can make one duration or transition apply to all slides in the show.

Note: When a version set is selected, only the top image will be inserted into the slide show (👁 "Version Sets" in Chapter 2).

After clicking OK in the Preferences window, you can now create a slide show complete with transitions, music, and audio annotations.

You can add panning and zooming effects to your images or you can modify them if they already exist. (👁 the following section, "Panning and Zooming.")

With the slide show open, you can save it by clicking the Save Project button on the toolbar, or you can choose any of several output options by clicking the Output button on the toolbar. (👁 "Output Options" later in this chapter.)

The slide show work area is shown in Figure 11.12. If you click a thumbnail in the film strip at the bottom, the work area looks like the image on the left. If you click the slide itself, the work area changes to the image on the right. (Note the differences under Properties to the right of the main image.) When you click the slide, you have various options for editing. For example, to show a zoomed-in portion of a slide during the show, use the Size slider and then reposition the slide as desired by clicking and dragging. This is not to be confused with a pan and zoom effect. To eliminate any black bands (assuming the background is black), click the Crop to Fit button. Be aware that using Crop to Fit may hide some details near the edges including any text you may have added in the Editor.

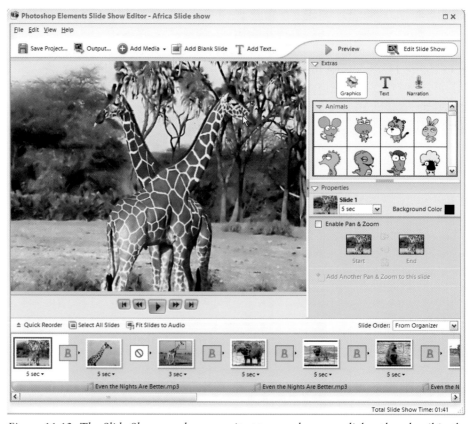

Figure 11.12: The Slide Show work area as it appears when you click a thumbnail in the film strip (above), and as it appears when you click the slide (below).

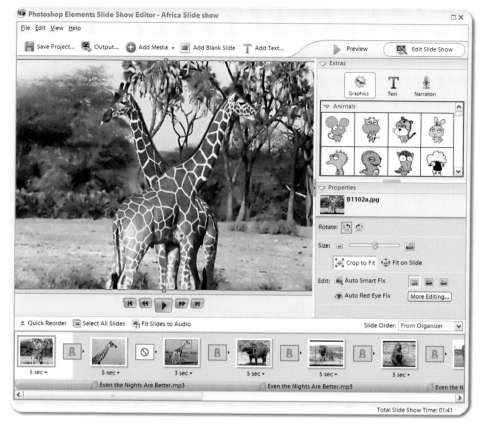

It's extremely easy to rearrange your slides using the Quick Reorder window, as shown in Figure 11.13. To use this feature, select View ➢ Quick Reorder. To return to the Slide Show Editor, use the same menu command or just click the Back button. In the Quick Reorder window, just click and drag any thumbnail or multiple thumbnails to a new location to change the order of your slides. Be sure to save the slide show.

Figure 11.13: The Quick Reorder window.

Panning and Zooming

Elements 4 includes the capability to add a pan and zoom effect to any slide. To enable this feature, select a slide in the film strip and place a check in the box labeled Enable Pan & Zoom. This may be already checked if you chose this option for all slides in the Slide Show Preferences. Once enabled, the Pan and Zoom controls will appear as shown in Figure 11.14.

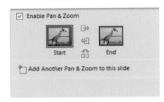

Figure 11.14: Pan and Zoom controls.

There are two icons in the Pan & Zoom properties. The one on the left, with a green rectangle, shows the starting position and zoom amount; the one on the right, with the red rectangle, shows the ending position and zoom amount. These controls are only available when you select an image in the film strip. I wanted to start this slide with a close-up of the giraffe's head and zoom out to the full body; here's what I did:

1. I selected the slide in the film strip.
2. I placed a check in the Enable Pan & Zoom box.
3. I clicked the Start icon, which placed a green rectangle on the slide.
4. I dragged the corners of the rectangle until it just fit the giraffe's head.
5. I clicked the End icon, which was already covering the full body.

The results are shown on the left in Figure 11.15.

Figure 11.5: Pan & Zoom settings for starting with a zoom in to the head and ending with a full body (left), and after swapping the Start and End (right).

I then tested the effect by selecting the Play button in the VCR-like controls. I changed my mind and decided to reverse the effect. I did this with a single click of the last of the three controls located between the Start and End icons. This button reverses the Start and End. The other two icons are for copying the start position to the end and vice versa. The results after swapping the Start and End are shown on the right in Figure 11.15.

Next, I decided to get fancier and have a zoom-in followed by a zoom-out of the same slide. Here's what I did:

1. I placed a check in the Add Another Pan & Zoom to this slide. This added a duplicate of the slide with the End effect of the previous slide copied to both the Start and End of the duplicated slide.

2. I clicked the End icon and dragged the red rectangle to the size I wanted to show at the end. In this case, it was the full image.

3. I selected the first slide in this two-slide effect and clicked the Play button and watched the zoom-in followed by the zoom-out.

If the panning or zooming seems to play too quickly, add a few seconds to the duration. In addition, you can add as many pan and zoom effects to the same slide as you want.

If you want to see one rectangle—the red one for example—while you're adjusting the other one, press the Ctrl key before making the adjustment. This allows you to position one rectangle relative to the other. An example is shown in Figure 11.16.

Figure 11.16: Both of the rectangles showing at the same time by pressing the Ctrl key while clicking the slide.

Creating a Collage Slide

There are times when it would be nice to combine several images into one slide, to create a collage. This technique can be used to reduce the number of slides in your slide show or to tell a story with a single slide. Elements provides no menus for doing this, but there is an easy way to achieve the effect shown in Figure 11.17.

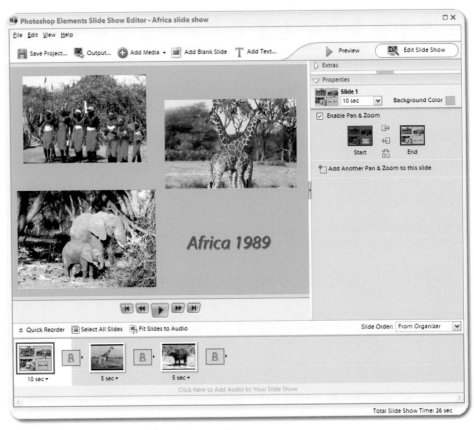

Figure 11.17: Creating a slide with several images.

Here are the steps you take to create a collage:

1. Start with a slide show.
2. Select the slide you want to be a collage.
3. Click the selected slide in the slide show window and drag it until a corner handle is visible.
4. Reduce the size of the image by dragging a corner handle while holding the Shift key to maintain the image's proportionality.
5. Open the folder containing images you want to add. Drag an image from the folder and drop it on the slide show window. Resize and relocate it. You can only drag one image onto the slide show at a time, but you can make several trips to your folder.
6. Change the stacking order by right-clicking an image and sending it forward or backward.
7. If you want, change the slide background color and/or enable Pan & Zoom.
8. Increase the duration to allow more time to view the collage or read any text you may add with the Text button.

Adding Extras to Your Slide Shows

The Extras palette is used to add graphics, text, and audio narrations to individual slides. Both graphics and text can be resized, and the text can be customized. To add text, select the Text icon at the top of the Extras palette and then drag any letter with the desired style and drop it onto the slide. Click Edit Text to modify the text or just double-click the text. To modify the text attributes, select the text by clicking it and then use the various options on the right. Although you can click and drag the text to any location, you cannot resize it by dragging its handles. To delete text, select it with your mouse and press the Delete key. Right-clicking the text also allows you to delete it.

Slide Show Output Options

When you're ready to output your slide show (with a slide show open, click the Output icon), you have several methods to choose from, as shown in Figure 11.18. The following sections cover each of these options:

- Save as a File
- Burn to Disc
- E-mail the Slide Show
- Send to TV

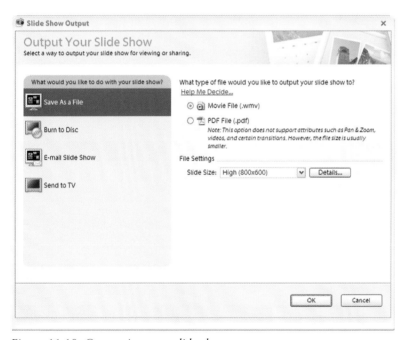

Figure 11.18: Outputting your slide show.

Save as a File

When you output your slide shows to a file, there are two options as follows. Be aware that the resulting file sizes can be quite large:

PDF file (.pdf) These files are in the Portable Document Format, which can be opened by anyone with the Adobe Reader program installed on their computer. (It's available for free from www.adobe.com.) These files can be played back by double-clicking them in the Organizer. After creating the PDF file, Elements will ask if you want it to be imported into the Organizer. Answer Yes to facilitate locating the file in the future and playing it back. Pan and zoom and several of the transitions are not supported by PDF files.

Once a PDF file is in the Organizer, there are several things you can do with it. By right-clicking it and sending it to Standard Edit, you can extract individual images. This may be useful if you've misplaced the originals or wish to extract images from PDFs sent to you by others. The extracted images will be at the size that was selected when the PDF was created. The other thing you can do is e-mail the PDF file if the size is not prohibitive. Just select the PDF and choose File ➢ Email.

Movie File (.wmv) This is the Windows Media Format file type. These videos can be played back with the Windows Media Player application, which is part of the Microsoft Windows operating system. Most DVD playback software—including PowerDVD—can play WMVs also. You can import WMVs into Adobe Premiere Elements or Roxio's Easy Media Creator and burn them to DVDs. The Roxio software has a component called DVD Builder. DVDs created with these applications will play on your computer or on a set-top DVD player. If you plan to do this, use the DVD (NTSC) Slide Size option under File Settings if you live in North America. Europe and many other countries use DVD (PAL).

Here's a comparison of both file types, created with 14 slides, and a resolution of 800 pixels by 600 pixels:

- **PDF:** 3.2 megabytes without audio and 8.6 megabytes with audio added.
- **WMV:** 13.5 megabytes without audio and 14.3 megabytes with audio added. The WMV required six minutes to create, and the PDF required 10 seconds.

Burn to Disc

Slide shows can be burned onto a disk in several ways, as a VCD, or if you have Premiere Elements installed, as a DVD. Premiere Elements integrates well with the Organizer. When you use the Send to Premiere Elements feature, Premiere Elements will launch, if not already open, and all of the images and videos will be added to a Premiere Elements timeline. From there you can add soundtracks, narrations, and pan and zoom effects. You can also add any additional images or videos to your show by switching back to the Organizer and selecting additional images and videos and "sending" them to Premiere Elements or, you can import them directly into Premiere Elements. It's beyond the scope of this book to cover all of the features of Premiere Elements, but the software includes excellent documentation.

To create a VCD (or DVD) with multiple slide shows, take the following steps:

1. Select one or more slide shows in the Organizer.
2. Click the Create button.
3. Select VCD with Menus. (Or if you choose DVD with Menus, Premier Elements will launch.)
4. At the next window, add additional slide shows or delete any you don't want to include on the disk.
5. Place a blank disk into a CD burner.
6. Select the NTSC option if you live in North America and click Burn. (Elements will then proceed to create the WMV files prior to burning the CD.)

7. Next, select an appropriate CD burner drive.

8. Click OK, and the burning process begins.

What's the difference between VCD and DVD? Here's a comparison:

VCD (lower quality) The VCD (Video CD) option creates a CD that can play back on your computer or TV using a set-top DVD player. You can create VCDs with several slide shows, complete with menus that will respond to your DVD player's remote control. During this process, you will have the opportunity to place multiple slide shows on the same VCD. The resolution of a VCD, for NTSC, is 352 × 240 pixels and 352 × 288 pixels for PAL. Compare this to the DVD resolution.

DVD (higher quality) The DVD (Digital Video Disk) option will only work if you have Adobe Premiere Elements installed on your computer. This method is much more flexible than creating a VCD, since you have more control over the menu creation with Premiere Elements. As discussed earlier, there are other options for creating DVDs without Premiere Elements. The resolution of a DVD for NTSC is 720 × 480 pixels and 720 × 576 pixels for PAL. Compare this to the VCD resolution. Compatibility with DVD players is usually higher than that with VCDs.

You should keep these tips in mind regarding VCD and DVD playback:

- VCDs normally play on most DVD players (purchased within the last several years).
- VCDs do not usually start automatically in your computer. To play them, open Windows Media Player, maximize the window to show the menu, and select Play ➤ DVD, VCD or CD Audio ➤ CD Drive (F:). (The drive letter will most likely be different on your computer.) To change the size of the video playback, right-click the video and make your choice there. You can also open Windows Media Player, click File ➤ Open, navigate to the MPGAV folder on the VCD, and select the file with a **.dat** extension. You must first select the Any Type option in the Files Of Type box.
- DVD playback is straightforward on either a TV or computer.

E-mail Slide Show

This option, depending on your choice, will create a PDF or WMV and then open your e-mail application with the file attached. There are six choices of resolution for the slide shows. Prior to sending the e-mail, you will get an opportunity to see the file size.

Send to TV

This choice creates a WMV in a format of your choice for playback on a TV with the Windows XP Media Center Edition. You can examine all seven of the formats by using the Settings drop-down box prior to creating your WMV.

Creating DVDs

If you have Premiere Elements installed, you can create a DVD from the Photoshop Elements Organizer or from a slide show. First, here's how to do it from the Organizer:

1. Select one or more images and/or one or more videos, but no slide shows.

Note: To show only the thumbnails for images in the Organizer, press Alt+1; for videos, press Alt+2. This makes the selection process easier.

2. Right-click any one of the selected items and select Send to Premiere Elements. The videos can be movies that you captured with your digital camera and imported to the Organizer, or movies you created in the Organizer from slide shows (WMVs).
3. Whether or not Premiere Elements is opened, you will get a message that the items you selected will be placed at the end of the timeline. Click OK.
4. You will now be in Premiere Elements, where you can create a DVD or make some modifications to your project first.
5. To add additional stills or videos to your DVD, switch back to the Organizer and select them, right-click one, and select Send to Premiere Elements. They will be added to the end of the timeline, but you can rearrange everything in Premiere Elements.
6. You can add a soundtrack and transitions, and easily create a menu in Premiere Elements before burning the DVD.

You can also create a DVD from within a slide show with the following steps:

1. Open an existing slide show by double-clicking it in the Organizer, or create a new one.
2. Click the Output button at the top of the slide show window.
3. Click Burn to Disc on the left.
4. Select DVD on the right. Place a check in NTSC if you reside in North America.
5. If you want to include additional slide shows on the DVD, place a check in "Include additional slide shows I've made on this disk."
    There is another way to achieve the same result. First, create WMVs from your slide shows, select them in the Organizer, and send them to Premiere Elements.
6. Click OK.
7. You will next be asked to add any additional slide shows if you selected this option in the previous step.
8. Photoshop Elements will then create the appropriate WMV files from your slide shows—even if you previously created WMVs—before launching Premiere Elements. This may take some time, depending on the length and quantity of the slide shows.
9. After the WMVs are created, you will now be in Premiere Elements, where you can create a DVD or make some modifications to your project first.

Finally, if you don't have Premiere Elements, you can create a DVD from Windows using a disk-burning application such as Roxio Easy Media Creator or Nero Ultra. Just generate WMV files from your slide shows and burn them; with Roxio, the DVD builder module can import WMVs and create a DVD. Using Nero, look for the NeroVision Express module.

Creating Specialty Print Layouts: Photo Album Pages, Bound Photo Books, Greeting Cards, and Calendars

You can create printable pages for several specialty purposes by opening the Creation Setup window and clicking a project type in the menu panel at the left. For instance, when you click Album Pages, you'll see the opening window shown in Figure 11.19, with a variety of layouts and styles available. This is step 1 of a five-step procedure. At the end of the process, you can save your creation in a variety of ways. You can save it as PDF, which can be viewed and printed from just about any computer in the world. You can also print the pages directly from the Organizer.

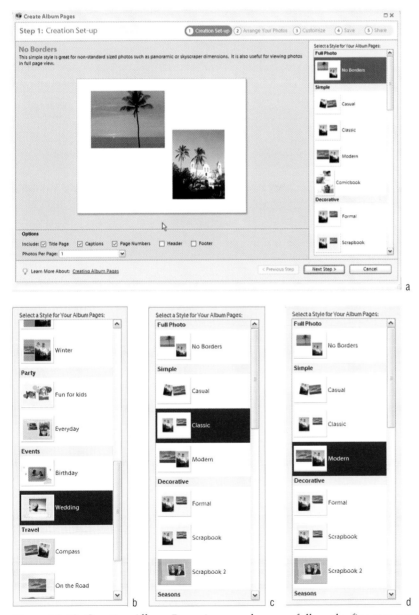

Figure 11.19: Creating Album Pages is easy when you follow the five-step procedure. Shown here is step 1 with layout options on the right (a). Also pictured are some of the layout options for cards (b), postcards (c), and calendars (d).

Other special print projects available in the Creation Setup window include Bound Photo Books, 4-Fold Greeting Cards, Photo Greeting Cards, and Calendars. Photo Greeting Cards can also be used as postcards.

To quickly find all of your creations in the Organizer, select Find ➤ By Media Type ➤ Creations, or use the shortcut Alt+4. When all of the creations are shown, you can't easily distinguish between the various types of creations such as Photo Cards, Album Pages, and Slide Shows. However, when you save them and use descriptive names, they will be listed as shown in Figure 11.20. You must have the Show Filename In Details option enabled in the General Preferences for this to work.

Figure 11.20: Creations with descriptive filenames make it easier to tell the type of creation.

Creating an HTML Photo Gallery

To create an HTML Photo Gallery that can be uploaded to the Web, start by selecting the images you want in the gallery *before* clicking the Create icon. Otherwise, the application will assume you want all the images from the catalog included in the gallery.

Next, open the Creation Setup window and select HTML Photo Gallery from the menu to access the window shown in Figure 11.21.

Figure 11.21: The Organizer's HTML Photo Gallery option window.

You can choose from over 30 gallery styles, add custom banners and colors, and choose the sizes of your images and thumbnails. The default file extension is .html and cannot be changed.

Sharing Images Electronically

If you select the Share icon in the Organizer shortcuts bar, a pop-up menu will give you the following choices:

- E-mail
- Share Online
- E-mail to Mobile Phone
- Send to Palm OS Handheld (This option requires you to have other third-party functionality running on your PC.)

You can access the Attach to E-mail command via the Share icon in the shortcuts bar, or via the Organizer's menu bar: File ➤ E-mail. For those of you who have used Windows XP's Attach to E-mail feature, you'll be pleasantly surprised by all Photoshop Elements offers.

First, open the preferences and select an e-mail client (Edit ➤ Preferences ➤ Sharing). Your choice there will determine your choices later. If, for example, you select Outlook Express as your e-mail client in the Preferences, you'll get the window shown in Figure 11.22 when you select the Share icon in the shortcuts bar and choose Attach to E-mail.

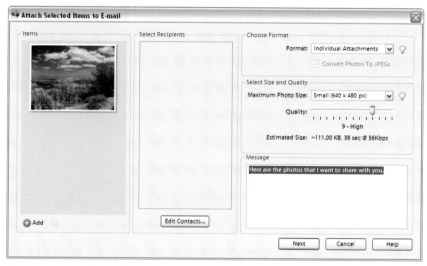

Figure 11.22: If you select Outlook or Outlook Express—or another e-mail client—you'll have the options shown here.

From the Format pop-up menu, you have the following options to choose from:

Photo Mail (HTML) Your images are placed directly into your e-mail body and open automatically upon receipt. With this selection you have no choice for the attachment size; the default set in Preferences is used. However, after clicking Next, the Stationery & Layouts Wizard opens, where you can choose from a huge variety of frames or layouts, as shown in Figure 11.23.

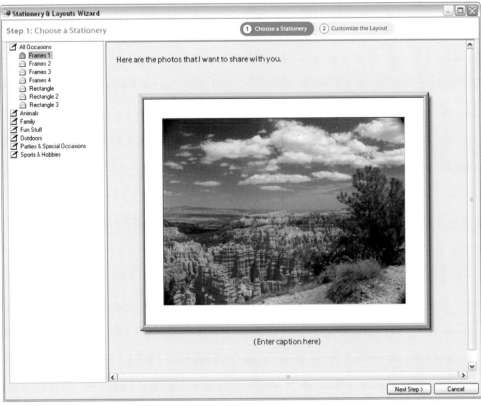

Figure 11.23: Photo Mail Stationery & Layouts Wizard.

Individual attachments You have six choices of image sizes, as you can see in Figure 11.24. Attachments are converted to JPEG files; clicking Next launches your e-mail program with the image(s) attached.

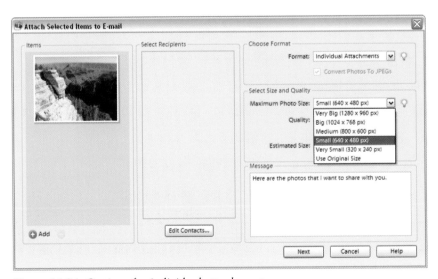

Figure 11.24: Options for individual attachments.

When your e-mail program launches, if you're using Outlook Express, you will get the window shown in Figure 11.25. Notice that there are no recipients yet, since my contacts list in the Organizer was empty. In my case, I prefer to select the recipients from my Outlook Express Address Book. You can also change the subject and message contents before sending. You can see the size of the attached photos, which in this case total up to 619KB for the four photos. The photo size was set at 600 × 800 pixels with a quality of 8. You may only want to send an e-mail this large if you know your recipients have DSL or cable Internet connections.

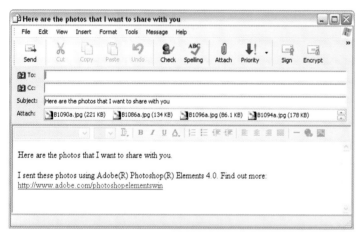

Figure 11.25: Outlook Express's new e-mail window with four photos attached.

Simple Slide Show (PDF) When you select this option, a window pops up telling you the size of the attachment, as shown in Figure 11.26. You can always abort and choose a different Maximum Photo Size. After clicking OK, your e-mail program will launch, and you will have the same choices as discussed earlier. However, your attachment will be a PDF file rather than a JPEG file.

Figure 11.26: A window tells you how large your attachment will be.

For Figure 11.27, I selected four photos in the Organizer, clicked the Share button, and selected Email. Next, I selected the Simple Slide Show (PDF) option and selected the smallest photo size (320 × 240). Then I entered a filename for the attachment and clicked Next. As you can see, the four photos I selected were combined into a single PDF attachment, with a file size of 134KB.

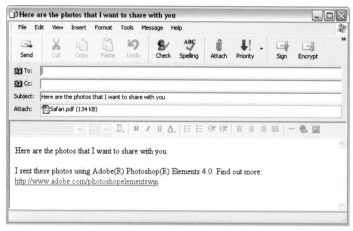

Figure 11.27: An e-mail with a PDF file attached, with a file size of 134KB.

Note: If you use Outlook or Outlook Express, you don't need to select a recipient from the Select Recipients box. Just click OK, and your e-mail program will launch; you can then add a recipient in that program.

On the other hand, if you select Save to Hard Disk and Attach File(s) Yourself from the E-mail Preferences (Edit ➤ Preferences ➤ Sharing) and then use the Attach to E-mail feature, you will get a slightly different window, with fewer options up front. For example, you can no longer select Photo Mail (HTML) as an option in the Format pop-up window, which means you can't add captions or add fancy frames or layout. You'll still be able to change the size for optimal e-mailing. The Save to Hard Disk and Attach File(s) Yourself option is required for Hotmail and Yahoo! users, and might just be preferred by others.

E-mailing Photos While Limiting File Size

Let's assume you have a collection of photos, and you want to send a small thumbnail of each of them in a single e-mail. You also want the total size of the e-mail to be small. Here are the steps you need to follow to generate the e-mail that would look like Figure 11.28. In this example, 10 photos were selected and the file sizes of the attachments added up to just 40KB. We are going to use the E-mail to Mobile Phone option for this, but the recipient can be using a normal e-mail program. Although the file sizes are optimized for viewing on mobile phone screens, this is a handy way to send someone a quick "contact sheet" of your images, so they can select the ones they want to receive later in full size.

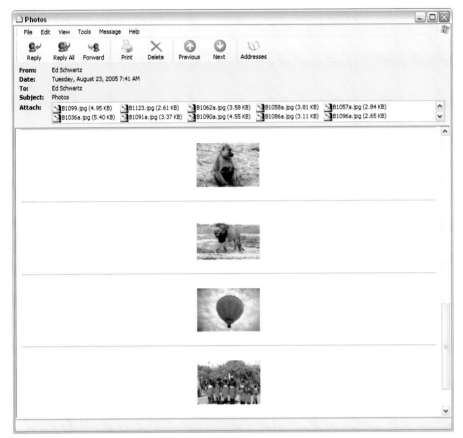

Figure 11.28: A received e-mail containing several thumbnail-sized photos.

1. Select the images in the Organizer.
2. Share ➤ E-mail to Mobile Phone.
3. Choose the size in the upper-right corner. I chose 120 pixels.
4. Click Next. This opens your e-mail program, where you can modify the default subject and message.

Warning: If you continually get an error message that reads, "There was a problem with your Internet connection. Please check that you are connected to the Internet and try again," the problem could originate with your e-mail client preference setting. Try a different setting and see if that helps.

Using Online Photography Services

Online photo services can be easier and cheaper to use than making your own prints: You simply upload your work to their website and order prints produced with real photographic paper and delivered to your doorstep overnight or in a few days. After you place your images online, anyone you designate, anywhere in the world, can go online, view your digital images, and with a single click of the mouse and a few keystrokes, order their own prints in a variety of sizes. Choose File ➤ Order Prints from either the Organizer or the Editor, and follow the prompts. You can also click the Share button and choose Share Online in the Organizer.

Processing Multiple Files

If you have a folder of digital images that you want to print at the same size and resolution, or that you want to convert to a similar file format, or resize, or apply a variety of Quick Fix settings to, you can use the Process Multiple Files processing command to automatically do all of the work for you.

To do so, from the Editor, choose File ➤ Process Multiple Files. You can choose from any or all of the possibilities in the Process Multiple Files dialog box (see Figure 11.29). For example, you can rename the output files, change their resolution, and convert them to a different file type simultaneously.

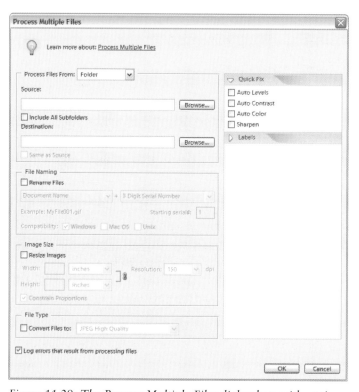

Figure 11.29: The Process Multiple Files dialog box with options.

Here are some of the options available to you:

- Choose a source such as Folder of Files, Import, Opened Files, or File Browser. With the Import option, you can import from any source recognized by your computer, including a digital camera or scanner. If you choose Folder of Files, click the Browse button and select the Include All Subfolders check box if you want subfolders included. Next, choose a destination folder and deselect Same as Source, unless you want to overwrite all the originals.

- In the File Naming section, you can choose different filenames by selecting the Rename Files check box, and you can add different file extension protocols. You are not limited to the choices in the drop-down box; you can enter any name you wish.

- If you select the Resize Images check box, you can specify a resolution for all the images and specify the width and/or height of the processed images. You are limited to one of the resolution choices presented to you. You also have the option to Constrain Proportions. When this option is enabled, you don't have to place a value in both the Width and Height boxes. You can place a value into just one, and Photoshop Elements will calculate the other value based on the proportions of the image.

- You can also use the features shown on the right, either alone or in conjunction with the features on the left. For example, select Auto Contrast, and it will be applied to all of the images selected in the source.

Preparing a JPEG File for E-mail Transmission

Most of the time it's best to send a JPEG file. However, don't just send the JPEG file right out of your camera; for a 5 megapixel digital camera, this is huge. There is no optimal size for an e-mail photo—it depends on the recipient's connection speed. I generally recommend that you try to get your digital photo down to between 40KB and 60KB before sending. (Of course, you can settle for a larger byte size if you know your recipient has a DSL connection or a cable modem.) To shrink your JPEG file, follow these steps:

1. With your digital photo open in the Editor, choose File ➢ Save As.
2. Choose JPEG from the file format options.
3. Select a JPEG value from the JPEG Options dialog box. Start with Medium, make sure the Preview button is selected, and observe the effect on the actual image. If the quality is acceptable, look at the lower-left corner of the dialog box to see the file size. If it is too high, either choose a lower JPEG value or click Cancel and reduce the actual pixel values of the image by using Photoshop Elements' image-resizing features.

To reduce the pixel values, choose Image ➢ Resize ➢ Image Size from the main Photoshop Elements menu. Make sure that the check boxes for Constrained Proportions and Resample Image are selected. Try entering 800 pixels in the Width box under Pixel Dimensions and 72dpi in the Resolution box. When you are finished, click OK. Go back to step 1 and save your image as a JPEG. This time you should be able to get the lower file size that you need.

Index